WOMEN, GUERRILLAS,
AND LOVE

WOMEN, GUERRILLAS, AND LOVE

Understanding War in Central America

ILEANA RODRÍGUEZ

Translated by Ileana Rodríguez with Robert Carr

UNIVERSITY OF MINNESOTA PRESS

Minneapolis / London

Chapter 13 was first published as "Testimonio and Diaries as Narratives of Success or Failure in *They Won't Take Me Alive,* in *Claribel Alegría and Central American Literature: Critical Essays,* ed. Sandra M. Boschetto-Sandoval and Marcia Phillips McGowan (Athens: Ohio University Press, 1994). Reprinted in slightly revised form by permission.

Published by the University of Minnesota Press
111 Third Avenue South, Suite 290, Minneapolis, MN 55401-2520
Printed in the United States of America on acid-free paper

Library of Congress Cataloging-in-Publication Data
Rodríguez, Ileana.
Women, guerrillas, and love : understanding war in Central America
/ Ileana Rodríguez ; translated by Ileana Rodríguez with Robert Carr.
p.   cm.
Includes bibliographical references (p.   ) and index.
ISBN 0-8166-2626-X
ISBN 0-8166-2627-8 (pbk.)
1. Central American fiction—20th century—History and criticism.
2. Revolutions in literature. 3. Guerrillas in literature.
4. Women in literature. I. Title.
PQ7472.N7R63   1996
863—dc20   96-33834

"We lost. Alas, we are free.
We'll never be slaves again."
Sofía Montenegro to Daniel Ortega after the last Congress
of the Sandinista Front, Nicaragua, May 23, 1994

On February 25, 1990, the Sandinista Front was defeated at the polls. In March a group of internationalists coming from all walks of life and nationalities (the United States, Europe, and Latin America) became citizens of a nation for which they had struggled intensively for ten years or more. I dedicate this book to them, to all those who joined their hands to ours in evidence of the strength and conviction of transnational, transcultural, transethnic common-front politics.

To all those whose lovers were separated from them for reasons of state.

To all those women who help women think about women.

Contents

Acknowledgments   xi

Introduction   xiii

Excursus: Eros/Fatherland   xxiii

I: Woman/Nation/States

ONE. The Place of Gender as a Sign of Denationalization   3

TWO. Vanishing Bodies, Woman/Nation:
Deconstructing the Panamanian State   19

THREE. Problems in the Constitution of the
New Individual/Collective Subject as Masculine and Feminine:
Romanticism/"Revolutionary"-ism   30

II: (New) Man

FOUR. Constituting the Narrative "I" as Difference:
The Guerrilla Troop and the Guerrilla Base   41

FIVE. Constituting the Individual Subject "I"
as Difference: Woman   49

SIX. Constructing People/Masses as Subaltern:
"Little Man"/New Man   62

SEVEN. Politico-Military/Poetic Narratives: Who?   77

III: (Wo)man

EIGHT. The Masculine "I" as Other:
The Formation of the Revolutionary Couple   93

NINE. The Body as Excess   105

TEN. Implosions: Narcissus Becomes a "Signifying Monkey"   115

IV: (Subaltern) Nation/(Subaltern) People

ELEVEN. Them   131

TWELVE. "There Is Nothing like a Man Astride . . .
in War, or in Love"   141

V: (Wo)man/Motherland

THIRTEEN. Case B: Of Testimonial and Diaries:
Narratives of Success and Failure   157

FOURTEEN. Solidarity in Affinity: Woman Constitutes Woman   168

Notes   185

Index   193

~

Acknowledgments

As befits a study of revolutionary narratives, this book owes its existence to a deep and enthusiastic belief in and commitment to the possibilities of constructing utopian societies; to the euphoria necessary to endure the hardships of the process; to the relentless sense of community and companionship that inevitably accompanies truly collective endeavors. I owe substantial debts of gratitude to people who taught me by example. Among the many, I can mention only a few, some of them only by pseudonym: Luz Marina Acosta, Claribel Alegría, Daniel Alegría, Javier Amor, María Mercedes Andara, Kristopher Andersson, Alejandro Argüello, Emilio de Armas, Amelia Barahona, Ximena Barreto, Gioconda Belli, Nelba Blandón, Tomás Borge, Alejandro Bravo, Agnes Bushell, Josefina Bustillos, Ernesto Cardenal, Olga Cardenal, Vilma Castillo, Sergio de Castro, Yadira Centeno, Rafaela Cerda, Lizandro, Ramón, and Teresita Chávez, Rita Clark, Fidel Coloma, José Coronel Urtecho, Ana Criquillon, Luisa Cuadra, Marilyn Cuneo, Enrique Díaz Tablada, Cuti Dorta, Tatiana and Niurka Duque, Sonia Duque Estrada, Carlos Eduarte, Mela and Ruth Elizondo, Karen Ellingson, Darwin Flakoll, Manuel García, Sonia García, Silvia Gil, María Mercedes Graham, William Graham, Teresa Granados, Miriam, Roberto, and Robertico Guibernau, Roberto Guibernau Mitat, Galio Guardián, María del Socorro Gutiérrez, Gloria Antonia Henríquez, Elba Hernández, Christina Hoogland, Marisela

Kaufman, Edgar Khül, Lutz Kliche, Roxana Lacayo, Lilian Levy, Margarita López, María Eugenia López-Brun, Rita Martín, Daniel Martínez, Ernesto Martínez, Enrique Meléndez, Theresa Meléndez, Vidaluz Meneses, Adilia Moncada, María Celina Moncada, Sofía Montenegro, Malena de Montis, Mario Roberto Morales, Auxiliadora Moreno, Marta Munguía, Clara Murguialday, Silvia Narváez, Salvadora Navas, Lourdes Oliva, Dolores, Marvin, Roger, and Silvia Ortega, Frutos and Clarisa Paniagua, Ronald Porras, Miriam Radlow, Rogelio and Sergio Ramírez, Gertrudis de Ramírez, Adolfo Rivas, Noel Rivas, Marta Rivas de Torres, Angela Saballos, Christian Santos, Fernando Silva, Pato Silva, Ivonne Siu, Margarita Suzán, Mirta Tablada, Edelberto and Mirna Torres Rivas, Edelberto Torres, Tito Torres, Elena Urrutia, Julio Valle Castillo, Milú and Oscar René Vargas, Ruth Varona, Santiago Vega, Carlos Vilas, Juan Carlos Vilches, Antonina Vivas, Daisy Zamora, and Marc Zimmerman. Aricsa, Arnaldo, Chiquis, Egües, Esmérita, Getulio, Gómez, Humberto, Isolda, José Luis, Josefina, López, María, Marlene, Miche, Olguita, Pilar, Rodolfo, Rosa Amelia. I thank these people for the conversations and the struggles we have shared over the years.

It would be dreadfully remiss of me if I failed to mention my dear friend and colleague, Robert Carr, who has firmly held my hand so that I could continue believing that solidarity and kindness are still possible in this world.

I am grateful for financial support to Stephen Summerhill, chairman of the Department of Spanish and Portuguese, and to Acting Dean David Frantz and Associate Deans Christian Zacher and Isaac Mowoe of the College of Humanities at The Ohio State University. A summer of primary research was made possible by an American Council of Learned Societies grant-in-aid.

I should also like to thank Eugene Friedman and Derek Petrey for their work in editing this manuscript, Ann Knee, who was a patient and painstaking untangler of syntax during the final stages of its composition, and Silvia Chaves, Sylvia Rodríguez, and Lina Méndez for their first drafts. Their hard, assiduous, and imaginative work made this book accessible. I greatly appreciate their help.

I am also in debt to the Cuban and Nicaraguan societies, which gave me the opportunity to experience, in my own flesh and bones, the dilemmas of building a new world, the joys as much as the pains, the elation as well as the terror, the pride in endurance and resiliency as well as the disillusions.

~

Introduction

What is socialism?
The longest road between capitalism and capitalism.

What is the difference between capitalism and socialism?
Capitalism is the exploitation of man by man, and socialism, vice versa.

In the political slogans and jokes about the revolution, one can discern many of the ungrammatical propositions that make us laugh. For instance: in the rhyme *diri-gentes, diplo-gentes, indi-gentes* (people who lead, diplomatic people, indigent people)[1] we can find an amusing commentary on the nature of a purported classless society, and in the jokes about socialism, the tautological turn of phrase makes ideologies appear to mirror one another comically. One of the most disturbing slogans circulating in the United States in the 1960s was "Good grammar is good politics." Since both my English and my Spanish grammar were faltering, I always took the slogan personally and worried excessively about the inevitability of being always politically incorrect. The slogans and jokes heading this introduction enable me to point to the complexities of politics and of political writing.

The following quotation illustrates moments of true bonding, moments of intimacy (erotics), between General Pedro Altamirano and his woman Estela:

I am a general already—she raised her head, only her head, scared, not risk-
ing even a smile.... The general embraced me and gave me this—a piece of
paper folded in four that he took from his shirt pocket. Estela unfolded it,
holding it carefully by the corners. She tilted it toward the light to see the
lines of incomprehensible signs, like traces of a bird she had never seen. This
is the signature—Pedro added, passing his index finger over the skin of the
document. Although the only things he saw were straight and curved lines in
a strange disposition, he knew that what it said there was A. C. Sandino.
(Chávez Alfaro 154)[2]

These protagonists are made equal in love, in class, and in illiteracy. However, he is given the title of general, and she is given nothing. As a general he
transcends his peasant class status, becoming a national hero, an icon in the
political pantheon of the nation (*patriótica*). She is cast against the backdrop
of the land, in the murky area of the cultivation of the soil. He is a nation-
building hero. She is a subsistence farmer. Whereas the title of general makes
the peasant Pedrón a slipping signifier, a discursive shift, she remains just a
redundancy. The scene is somewhat discomfiting, for in it the coupling of
love and faltering grammar, or the grammatically correct representation of
their illiteracy, does not immediately read as discrimination. Equalities are
explicitly intended; inequalities, simply glossed over. Bad politics might then
be located in the good grammar encoding the ironic relationship between
man and woman, politics and culture, the *campesino guerrillero* and the
campesina campesina. But in highlighting the place of woman, Estela, and
her literary representation, I cannot but be puzzled by the following question: Is my grammar really better politics, or is it simply that my politics are
better grammar?

Grammar/Politics

This book is then mostly about political grammar. My aim is to discern
samenesses, distances, differences between the concepts of people, masses,
troops, bases, and vanguard parties within the constitution of revolutionary
states. I am also concerned to pinpoint the relationship between the collective and woman, and then between woman and nation-state. Are women
part of the masses, troops, bases, people, or are we not? If we are, in what
ways? And if we are not, where are we?

In pamphlets and political speeches, in political literature, the vanguard
party's masculine "I" must always adopt a position of authority and self-
sufficiency. The state cannot represent itself as mistaken, erratic, or un-

grounded. The mediation of state power, represented by the absolutism of the narrating subject, or by an I that is always singular and masculine, obstructs democratic representation. State narratives seemingly constitute their subjects from above. It is then from positions of authority, often of commander-in-chief, that political documents are engineered. This is the way revolutionary narratives have constituted people, power, and nation. My hypothesis is that, in these narratives, women, children, and the elderly occupy the same space as people, masses, troops, bases.

On the basis of this hypothesis I argue that vanguard parties, political leaders, and engaged writers neglected, demeaned, and marginalized women, therefore disparaging and omitting all that was synonymous with Woman. Consequently, for all intents and purposes, revolutionary cultures constructed authoritarian narratives about the nature of popular democracies, seizing power and wielding it against Woman and all those holding her subject position. Then, when a political document speaks in the name of the nation, and writes in the name of the people, one is entitled to ask who that narrative persona stands for, whom it represents. The phrase "consultative oligarchy," referring to "revolutionary" governments—or "consultative plutocracies," referring to "democratic" governments—invokes yet another paradoxical way of signaling the relation I am here grappling with. But then, is it truly possible for a narrating subject to give up the position of authority?

I must confess that in writing this book I have been struck by the slippery character of language, and baffled by its circularity. There is always a way of stretching the argument, always a way to make it lapse into its opposite. Phrases like "the fiction of the revolution," although grammatically correct, always struck me as wrong. The same holds true for any and every construction of equivalencies between pronouns. That the masculine I is not the collectivity asserts the self-evident. But in dislodging the first person singular from the first person plural, however, I felt I was trespassing taboos. Disengaging, and revising the relationship between the different narrative persona aroused in me feelings of bad faith, as much as the a-critical persistence of the pronoun "he" made me feel othered—to say the least. But, however grammatically correct all these arguments and positionings might be, I wonder, with John Beverley, if the politics of popular democracy are better served by deconstructive and nitpicking analyses, or whether deconstruction is nothing more than a better convulsive grammar.[3] These questions will forever haunt the margins of this text.

I do not intend here to forget that, to become viable projects, revolutions need money-capital, which is very scarce in poor societies. Neither do I want to gloss over questions relative to wars—questions we cultural critics often neglect but with which the social scientists relentlessly grapple. I simply want to assert that revolutions are also questions of words and wordings. Political leaders often have argued that revolutions are the paramount expressions of culture. Therefore, disengaging pronouns becomes a grammatical issue impinging on representation and power, mainly when, as the 1960s slogan asserted, all power (has not been given) to the people.

This is one of the most important of the many questions feminism wants to take issue with. The malleability of language enables the writer-critic-feminist to reverse the arguments of patriarchy, or to go round and round in circles. I find this particularly true of Catharine MacKinnon, Josefina Ludmer, and Stephanie Jed, whose contributions to the field I discuss later on. By deconstructing the linear logic of masculine power into its circular and tautological components, just by bluntly asking the question of woman's place, feminism contributes to the unraveling of the logic of knowledge. Circularity is the place of women's hermeneutics, and micro-grammar—pronouns, prepositions, possessives—one of the sites of our epistemic struggles. The attempt to prove the relativity of every assertion characterizes the language of the oppressed, and stresses the uncertainty of all ideological positions—including those of women, democrats, and revolutionaries. Occasionally in my writing I had the distinct impression that I was disproving my argument, or that I was proving the opposite of what I wanted to assert. An example of this is my compilation of Che's definition of the *guerrillero*. How can the *guerrillero* become at the same time a member of the group and a nonmember of the group, be simultaneously from the area and foreign to it, national and international? How man can be woman, peasantry be bandits, women be peasantry, autocracy be democracy, fatherland be mother country is what the unraveling of the logic of writing has permitted me, I hope, to demonstrate.

Language is the terrain of the struggle for power; it is in language that the reader interprets the evidence. Language empowers us to moor ourselves fast in the place where signs shift, where, writing the peasantry or women, the revolutionary writer discloses his own unconscious—or positivistic, bourgeois, colonial, elitist thinking. But language is also ambiguous and often serves as a conduit for contradictions. In every text vacant spaces linger. That is the tax affixed to criticism. But grappling with, and proposing alternative meanings for, the text is a way of writing women within the narratives of social change. In this context the relationship between woman and man points, it seems, to the disjunction between the hierarchies, encoding erotics as patriotics.

My aim is first to establish the position of woman within revolutionary narratives and then to see how woman and nation are linked through their literary and political representation. My method consists in examining the congruency between the constitution of self as writer (*guerrillero*, comrade, vanguard, leader), and that of the masses (bases, troops, people as "little man," intellectual urban insurgent, revolutionary couple, Indians, *ladinos*, "nobodies," insurgent women, mistresses, wives, daughters). I am dogged by the question of methodology in making the masses politically viable in writing.

Very clearly, the narrative of the revolution is a narrative of the construction of self first as *guerrillero*, and then as vanguard, party, leader, and government. All those subject positions could then be formulated in a masculine I, aiming at narrating a collective subject that does not include women.

The Masculine "I" Wants to Represent the Collectivity

Women have no interior life comparable to men's. As in Romanticism, we are othered. The literature of the revolution does not record the intention to enfranchise woman, or to make us part of the new republic, the new democracy. The phrasing of the new subject in gendered terms as the "New Man" is then a forthright statement of revolutionary principles. The constitution of self as revolutionary becomes a carbon copy of the constitution of the bourgeois self becoming the "New Man."

The plotting of women now as "repose of the warrior," now as "revolutionary pussy," betrays our exclusion. But since women are located in the same discursive and geographic spaces as people, masses, and bases, the site of woman draws attention to the typology of political ideology that (re)constitutes "democracies" as autocracies. This book thus argues for the feminization of epistemologies as a precondition for the constitution of genuine democracies.

In the first part of the book, I think through feminist paradigms of subject constitution and, from there, through the narratives of the leaders of the revolution—Che, Ramírez, Borge—in search of the democratic constitution of the people. Subsequently, the text shifts to scan the fiction of politically engaged writers—Dalton, Morales, Ramírez, Argueta, Arias—where I entertain the same search: how is the subaltern written and what is its relation to the constitution of women and revolutionary democracies? I also undertake

an analysis of liberal writers—Asturias—and liberal and engaged women—
Guardia, Oreamuno, Alegría/Flakoll, Naranjo—for comparison. I end with
a chapter on testimonials edited by non-Central American women in which
the constitution of a transnational subject, culturally located in Central
America but radiating to the rest of the world, is rendered visible. In that
chapter I highlight the contribution of Margaret Randall to the recording of
Latin American women's views on the process of insurgency, especially in
the Centro-Caribbean area. Her latest book on women in the postrevolutionary period is postscript to her earlier testimonials, and one that sub-
scribes to much of the thesis of this book. The difference between us is that,
while I underscore the constitution of woman as a subject, she emphasizes
the lack of a truly feminist agenda within the revolution, accounting for what
she justifiably calls *Gathering Rage*.[4]

Underlying this text then is the enigma of the constitution of revolutionary nation-states, or simply of liberal Central American "nation-states," and,
therefore, of how to constitute a "post-" or "trans-national" self/culture. Admittedly, the constitution of the revolutionary state was beyond the pale.
The revolutionaries undertook its construction when the formation of the
global paradigm defining the nature of productive capital was already, it
seems, well under way. The forces of entropy straining the social fabric
presided over the State's final collapse. Furthermore, during their brief life
cycle, the revolutionary states discussed the necessity of forming part of
larger marketing structures, capitalist or socialist. The everyday within a
revolutionary process foregrounds certain lacks—of productivity, capital,
training, discipline, willingness. That is why the revolutionary states sought
as their first priority to form a government and to link up with other states.
These lacks governed the balance of forces, making economic and/or political compromise the law of the land, and accounted for the migration effect—first of capital and then of people. Women as transnational laborers
found their place in the informal sector as "higglers"[5] in Nicaragua, as the
so-called apron bourgeoisie or domestic servants, and/or in the productive
sector as workers in *maquiladoras,* a sector of corporate industry wooed by
revolutionary processes. The constitution of the revolutionary subject, then,
came hand in hand with the constitution of a transnational subalternity,
which the large displacement of populations underscores. Within the realities of socialism, defection and desertion are considered two of the twin
principles disorganizing the socius. Defectors and deserters made up local
communities abroad, and later constituted themselves into negotiating teams,

when not armed opposition, with which the revolutionaries, in their twilight, had seriously to contend.

I see the deconstruction of the nation-state inextricably linked to the representation of woman (erotics) as dead. The backdrop is Sommer's thesis on nation-building as a love story, and Franco's metaphor of woman as nation. My argument is that the casting of woman as corpse, and the gradual exclusion of love from literature, signals the nation-state's deconstruction, and the people's de-nationalization—the representation of love for women and love for country operating in tandem.

This is the moment historicized by a large number of studies on Central America, particularly in the social sciences.[6] Studies of Central American literature and culture are not lacking, but the area has not been a favorite subject for explorers of the transnational cultural enterprise. Among the most thorough of those written outside the area is John Beverley and Marc Zimmerman's *Literature and Politics in the Central American Revolutions*,[7] a study of culture arguing for and within the context of the political praxis of revolutionary nation-states. In this sense it is the ideal companion to my book, providing the essential political and historical background. Beverley and Zimmerman's is a very competent study locating its discussion at the height of the revolutionary period, inside revolutionary epistemologies. Had it been in print during the decade of the eighties, the book would have been the definitive statement on Central American literature in the United States. Unfortunately, the electoral defeat of the Sandinistas and the demise of socialism worldwide rendered their discussion historical, the debate no longer framed by their parameters.

My book is located at the end. It is, in a sense, a post-perestroika text: one that reflects on the dilemmas more than on the accomplishments, more on the intricate twisting of the logic of politics and government and less on the scholastic unraveling of the subject, and is determined more by an internal than an external analysis. Their reading is more comprehensive and macro, mine more detailed and micro. But the essential difference is that I aim at linking women to the laborious process of political action and political and poetic writing, and that, in doing so, I am, as the saying goes, "threatening emasculation."

I must in particular acknowledge the contribution of three of my colleagues, María Milagros López, John Beverley, and Patricia Seed, who in reading my manuscript suggested valuable insights I took to heart. Their readings proposed this work as framed within the crisis of Leninism and of socialism, where the patriarchal vanguard subordinated all other social conflicts to that of the "Great Struggle," a strategy which en/gendered the creation of hegemonies. This ordering of things sharpened all other types of subordinations and laid bare the foundational myths, heralding the arrival of new types of societal conflations. In line with this argument several other questions arise, among them those concerning "post-national" identities, new feminized or "de-phallicized" formalizations of the "New Man," the new forms of postcolonial, transnational humanism, and the question of culture after the age of imperialism and deterritorialization.

Admittedly, this text is situated in a series of "posts"—feminism, imperialism, modernism, nationalism—where the decentering of the subject is in order. In fact the text sits on the lap of the new global paradigm, within the chaos of neoliberalism.[8] The question, as Michael Clark once put it in his oral intervention at the Second Latin American Subaltern Studies Conference, at Ohio State University in May 1994, is what the next unit of governance will be, where authority will be located, and how control will be obtained. The cultural paradigm is unraveling, in a state of decomposition, but what is certain, as George Yúdice has demonstrated,[9] is that both "high" culture and "popularly induced electronic" culture constitute some of the terms of the debate.[10] Today's coupling of schooling and industry, intelligence and management, commits the intelligentsia to think of best possible performance scenarios, and to swaying back and forth between input/output, cost/benefit ratios—binding culture to technical and financial criteria. Matching this proposal, a few subsistence cultural economies, like the Jamaican Cultural Yard, will skirt the shoulders of the electronic roads.

Unclear as to what the paradigm to come will be like, the cultural critic is situated within a black hole. The heroic subject has been shattered, class analysis stripped away, the authoritarian and the "popular" authoritarian traditions of the Latin and non-Latin left laid bare, Marxism neutralized by instrumental reason and bureaucracies. The revolutionaries did not show themselves capable of withstanding the implosion of the values of Modernity. Formed within the context of the Cold War, they were detained at the gates of postmodernism. The death of the nation buried their "New Man" side by side with his "revolutionary pussy."

In closing, I want to invoke a revolutionary song by Pablo Milanés that we women particularly liked: "I prefer to have her shared rather than see her lost; she is not perfect, but comes closest to what I always dreamt of." There is no way of guessing what men dreamt, but what we women still dream of is a sincere acceptance of our sexuality and freedom of choice, expressed mainly as our possession of our bodies—womb, vagina, and brains. We want to make the personal political, to write our rights to our own bodies into the legislation. Perhaps we also want to postulate a new postmodern identity, in which women will not be known by their kin, in another present, where we will not have to bear the sadness of Che's sister, commit suicide like Allende's daughter, project the nefarious image of Ortega's wife, or be totally invisible, out of the picture, as Castro's women all have been.

~

Excursus

Eros/Fatherland

"My wife and daughter are adamant about not saying 'love one another,' . . . they think I have to say 'care for.'" It is true that citizenship required a certain intimacy, . . . but "love" carried "so many different inferences" that its meaning could not be controlled. . . . Millions of Americans don't sift the nuances of words . . . and to the "hard-pressed and hard-bitten," the word "love" might hit them as intrusive or offensive. (Branch 36)[1]

Arguing for the distinction between love, care, and intimacy that citizenship requires, President Bill Clinton carefully examines the wording of his inaugural address. Like all other liberal and socialist heads of state, in thinking "nation" he invokes "love." "Care for," he says, while facing a geocultural tableau dominated by war, a landscape heaped with dead bodies. Wherever the eye turns, on land, over water, it stumbles upon dismembered remains. The index finger passing over the page finds the red still wet, the rattle of gunfire unabated. Bloody skirmishes throughout continental Europe, as well as continental Africa, register the mounting dead. In Central America not all the combatants lined up to surrender their weapons. Mouths crying out for succor dissolve into the nothingness of vanguard parties, receding again into impoverished, deterritorialized masses. "Care for," for heroism is gone, and the subaltern peoples, the "hard-pressed, hard-bitten," are much in need of their nation's love.

As their nation-states fold, over 10 million homeless take to the world's oceans, the desolate tossing of the waves silencing their cries. Pacific and Atlantic, Caribbean and Mediterranean, the same waters of the slave trade's famous Middle Passage, carry the boat people to the same promised land. More bodies at the bottom of the ocean—more indentured servants, the "new" migrant workers in search of crops to harvest. On this vast and empty expanse of water there is the universal bedlam of surrender. Lyotard entreats his readers not to misinterpret, not to misjudge. The problem overshadowing all others is not the state, he says, but capital.[2]

While by boat and raft people become the protagonists of the narratives of neoliberalism, by plane, the airborne cultures of the global intelligentsia, already in the service of the corporate world, expedite the closing, not of the narrative of the nation-state, but of nation-building—a masculinist impulse splintering before the sundry aporias of the will of capital as it now prepares the ground for the global rezoning governed by liquidity. The question is what of culture, what of language, what of people?

In other worlds, a picture in the pages of El País brings up the case of the "Poet executed by intolerance." Daniel Ortega, Joaquín Villalobos, and Juan José Dalton, representing a self-critical left, speak of the execution of Roque Dalton, the Salvadoran poet.[3] Many years later the National Directorate of the Salvadoran Insurgency acknowledges, in the voice of Villalobos, a mistake: "I was one of the seven members of the tribunal ordering the execution," Villalobos confesses. "It was a personal, immature, passionate act of ideological radicalization. Dalton was a victim of ignorance, intrigue, dogmatism. It was a grave error."[4] Repentance shreds the last pages of what was once the crucial critical narrative, pushing it out of sight and out of mind.

The story fades into the past, returning to the Romantic narratives of nation-building filled with human debris, periods (con)fusing love with wars, pregnancies, deliveries, and massacres. In tandem with this chaotic transcendence, the deconstitution of the laboring classes as historical forces becomes arguable. Have the working classes ever played a role? Reading revolutionary literatures, one might come to a negative conclusion.

Critics of nationalism and nation-formation, who have argued the fictional character of national narratives and of nations, articulating the processes of their invention, never deny the functionality of these narratives or of the nations they serve to define.[5] More than ten years ago, in his seminal article on power and the state, Edelberto Torres Rivas, in complete agreement with Partha Chatterjee,[6] explained it in the theoretical language of the time. He argued that in dependent societies the genesis of a national form of power could be better explained as a process strictly tied to international capitalist development. He maintained that the international dynamism of the economy generated needs and influences that gave political life "a hyper/sensibility to react by making itself adequate to political international determinations" (245). In peripheral societies, capitalism reproduced pre-capitalist forms of production, which inhibited the social differentiation of classes, conditioning the form of national power as a dependent, subaltern nation-state.[7]

Deconstruction here shows that the articulation of "nation" as an administrative and commercial unit (The Initiative for the Americas, NAFTA) supersedes its definition as an autonomous political territoriality (Torrijos-Carter Canal Treaties). The collegial groups of presidents (The Group of Seven, Esquipulas), as much as the groups formed by ministers and secretaries of state (Contadora), constitute the international and commercial Board of Corporate Directors eroding the articulation of equivalences such as country = nation = state = sovereignty = territory. . . . The Project of the New World Order, practically constituted, comes to situate itself at the center of the periphery. President Clinton's warning to North Korea, in its resistance to atomic inspection—if they don't submit, this is "the last they see of their country as they know it"—unswervingly sets military policy in the New World Order.

Entwining the fates of nations, women, and the people in the process of revolutionary nation-building has been a task of contemporary Central American literature. In what follows I battle with language to engage the politico/libidinal connotations of women, corpses, nations, and wars.

I'm Nobody! Who are you?
Are you—Nobody—Too?
Then there's a pair of us?
Don't tell! they'd advertise—you know!

How dreary—to be—Somebody!
How public—like a Frog—
To tell one's name—the livelong June—
To an admiring Bog!

Emily Dickinson

PART I

Woman/Nation/States

The Place of Gender as a
Sign of Denationalization

For more than seven years the Sandinistas had refused to talk to the contra leaders. To engage in dialogue with them was considered madness. Invoking a biblical figure, Tomás Borge asserted that before negotiating, the contras first had "to count all the stars in the sky, all the grains of sand on the shore." However, at the end of the decade of the 1980s, the Sandinistas came to admit that unless they wanted to give up their project they had to sit down with the contras and talk. A meeting was agreed upon and the two groups assembled at Zapoa, a small town in the middle of the Nicaraguan hinterland. Although even to speak of such a meeting or agreement was at the very least odd, and largely incongruent with the Sandinistas' earlier assertions, by that time, the two groups had come to realize they were demanding the impossible. The contras' ranks were on the brink of splitting, and the Sandinistas on the verge of taking issue with their own programs. The national geography had been thoroughly bled, and corpses lined up patriotically in support of each of the contending forces. Having learned from scratch the bare essentials of politics, each within their respective modest abodes, they sat down and conducted themselves at the behest of insurmountable mandates.

It was at Zapoa, then, that the two groups claiming to represent the true nation met. As a point of conversion, Zapoa became a point of inversion, the space of negation, the realization of the unimaginable. This small town, lost in the wilderness, was the spot where the unacceptable had to be accepted, political reality becoming a sign, "not truly in conformity with the things themselves" (Foucault xix).[1]

In Zapoa, what had been bloody opposition became quasi-amicable dialogue, demarcating the frontiers dividing future notions of revolutionary states and nations. The *guerrillero* became a suited politician, and his new garb came to reinforce the image of the fading agendas of the revolutionary state. The boundary once dividing the state from its opposition blurred. The constituting notion of the opposition itself, invoking the presence of alternative notions of state and nation, fogged. Paradoxically, this confusion became Central America's own form of glasnost.

Masculine narratives reporting this moment plotted denials and closures. The most representative metaphor invoking open spaces, the Mountain, as that "something more than," shut, giving way to the negotiating table, constituting that "something less than" that cannot achieve itself. Any serious political discussion was barely discernible in this dim light. Analysts had to make do with hearsay and suspicions. Party militants could not suspect their leaders of deceit, but they could never remember which set of explanations made sense. The inconceivable was the order of the day. Any and everything defied designation in words, for words always led to their opposites, making understanding impossible. It was a moment of skepticism, a moment of confusion ensuing from a paradigm shift, the rise of global market dynamics that restructured geographies according to the unblushing principles of neoliberalism. The construction of the Nicaraguan revolutionary state had come to a halt.

This recomposition of the ideological universe, or that which Foucault termed "the order of things," licenses us to reread Nicaraguan testimonial literature and fiction at their most ironic, particularly Sergio Ramírez's novel *Castigo Divino* (1989) and Tomás Borge's *The Patient Impatience* (1989), both of which appeared in print just at that juncture when the revolutionary *guerrilleros* rolled up their sleeves and sat down at the negotiating table.[2] Tinged with deceptive erotic delight, the two texts speak of the perverse "de-eroticization" of woman, centered around the clinical investigation of her body. Woman's clinical discernment occurs symmetrically with the process of dissolution of the revolutionary state. Death of the state and death—murder, or disappearance—of woman occur simultaneously. Jean Franco points out, along these lines, that the loss of traditional topophilias, such as church and home, arises at the same time as the threatened state manifests its terror and disregards "the power of the family as a place of refuge and shelter."[3] Dead women, therefore, are available metaphors for the deconstruction of nation-states.

Erotica as Rape: Readings and Writings

> During adolescence we'd go out in mixed groups without ever knowing what
> was going to happen; that is, nothing did happen except for Leonore's loss
> of her virginity at the hands, so-to-speak, of Consuelo Baldizón's brother,
> Rodolfo, and Auxiliadora's loss of hers through the resources, likewise a figure
> of speech, of Jaime Varga's brother, whose name was also Rodolfo. Both were
> experts in voice modulation, placement of the right hand and eye avoidance.
> Some of us collected stamps, shooting stars and Wu Li drawings cut from old
> oriental magazines; others collected sea-shells, gonorrhea and round stones.
> The two Rodolfos collected girlfriends, which was precisely what the rest of
> us wanted to do. Not until now have I given vent to the envy I felt towards
> them back then. (Borge 51)

It took Tomás Borge, interior minister and only survivor of the original founding members of the group named the Sandinista National Liberation Front, more than a decade to write his autobiography; and when he did it, his testimony, *The Patient Impatience*, purported to be more a personal autobiography than a narrative of his political commitment, although it is that too.

In contrast to other testimonials (for example, those of Omar Cabezas and Comandante Francisco Rivera, alias El Zorro) that narrate the construction of self as *guerrillero*, Borge's text narrates formative events in his life—his childhood, his adolescence, his education, his militancy in the Sandinista National Liberation Front, some of his political actions in both the city and the Mountain, his love for his friends/comrades. Borge's narrative reconstructs his adolescence; the youthful years in the company of Carlos Fonseca, who was later to become the leader of the Sandinista Revolution; what Matagalpa, as an uneventful small town, meant to them; and how they made use of their time. In this respect, the text falls squarely within the category of the bildungsroman. Carlos is an overwhelming presence in his memory.

> Carlos Fonseca, on the verge of adolescence, and ensconced in that small
> town—compact inferno and obvious paradise—remained a spectator of
> those initial skirmishes. . . . Victim of each winter's mud, Carlos walked all
> the streets of Matagalpa. . . . On moonless nights, we suffered a city subject to
> fusillades of fireflies and besieged by columns of crickets, frogs, rabbits and
> deer. Unemployed bricklayers and students, spitting and laughing, hung out
> at Pedro Culito's billiard parlor. . . . Carlos confined himself to playing
> pool. . . . (73)

Carlos gained his first notions of revolutionary consciousness at the end of his secondary school year, around 1954. At about that time, a Student Committee was formed at the Institute in response to the Guatemalan experience, with links to the feeble workers' movement in Matagalpa. (80)

In fact, his book is here more personal than political, more the autobiography of an intellectual than the testimonial of a *guerrillero*: it begs us to read it as a narrative about narratives; as more than a biography, as a particular kind of self-representation by means of the author's cultural critical education. That is, Borge urges the reader to privilege Borge's construction of himself as a literary man, as an intellectual, rather than as a political leader. In it we must read Borge as a citizen of the Republic of letters, as Angel Rama would have it, rather than as the leader of the Nicaraguan Revolution and founder of the new nation-state. He tirelessly informs the reader of what he reads, and the list of books is a bibliography of genres. Tomás Borge wants us to know he is a cultivated, well-read man:

> On the banks of the Matagalpa River, in view of the heights that looked down on us, I read *Azul*. It was written by Rubén Darío, known even to generals. I read it when they were building the bridge that connects the city with the hospital across the river at the foot of El Calvario. I read it with amazement. . . . Realism is better. Let's read "El Fardo," said Douglas. The Naturalist school, brother, in Zola's style. It's like a page from Gorki, reiterates Stuart, who's also read Gogol. (12–13)

His unrelenting enacting of himself as an avid consumer of books would seem to support this hypothesis, and the interpretation the text proffers is convenient to my argument of the adjoining functions of politics and culture in the representation of women and nation-states, for Borge's reading of texts focuses on affect and eroticism. His narrative strategies regarding gender are very open. Here I want to explain how, in telling the his/tory of his life, Borge's discursive strategy is to produce a narrative of his readings and writings, in which the topos of erotica/patriotica as rape is paramount.

Reading Women and Indians

I have selected two particular instances of his reading of two of his literary favorites, the North American saga of the Native American Winnetou and the French realist novel of the white woman Emma Bovary. Both offer a reflection on dead bodies. The implication of textualizing Amerindians next to white women far from his mind, he begins his testimonial by announcing an Amerindian death and confessing his love for a white woman:

Shortly before midnight one summer evening in Matagalpa, anesthetized by the twilight while my mother thought I was studying ratio and proportion problems and verbal declensions, Winnetou died. Old Shatterhand, with whom the Indian had explored all geographies and emotions, provided they were difficult, refused to believe he was dead. (10)

In those days I was hopelessly in love with Emma Rouault, who would become Madame Bovary. I felt such compassion for her that I wound up loving her, amazed by her ability to immortalize herself. How easy it was for that woman to transform herself into a fountain or a tongue with which to lap up her summers! (40)

The first sample is an epic involving Winnetou's perfect body, all muscle and nerve—signs of manliness; the second, a romance involving Emma Bovary's languorous corpse—signs of *tendresse*. In both cases, a disappearance by death and the effect of an absence are enacted, but in the first instance the author ponders whether Winnetou's beautiful body is "disintegrating, being eaten by worms," while in the second he celebrates the female body's beauty in death. Emma Bovary lies "wearing the rose of her tempest," "languishing on a quilt of foam, expired, unhinged, with a trickle of blood that I wanted to drink, her neck motionless" (Borge 40).

Winnetou's physical disappearance is later lamented and denied, and the affirmation of his being slips into the symbolic: "Loyalty, rectitude, defense of the humble were not buried with Winnetou" (10). Emma's physical disappearance, on the contrary, is celebrated and glorified, and the reader/witness slips into a passive role as voyeur, inviting other readers to enjoy, with him, the full sight of Emma's (dead) body—a sight previously concealed behind closed curtains, as Emma unbuttoned her brassiere and opened her legs.

Winnetou's death and Emma Bovary's "languishing," however, demarcate two types of erotica. The first follows a system codified by testimony, as we will see later, in which the eroticization of the text constitutes a homonym within a hom(m)osexual or homosocial relationship (Borge–Winnetou): the erotic-patriotic. As one character merges into the other, the two exemplify the family-nation as brotherhood, solidarity, mastery.

The second instance, a typical heterosexual relationship in a work of fiction, belongs to the heteronymic system—where the erotic-nonpatriotic (Borge–Madame Bovary) is an (illegal) relationship within the practices of the nuclear family (Charles Bovary–Emma). Emma, a woman, belongs to a collective subject, women, which is not part of, or included in, the collective, heroic subject. This heterosexual, nuclear relationship lies at the center of a social imaginary that contains numerous types of eroticisms, including those outside the law, and in which the necrophiliac finds its place as an expression of Thanatos.

The examples of how Borge reads the saga of Winnetou and the story of Emma Bovary presume the referential function of language, belief in the mimetic fallacy. In both, the avid reader takes the place of protagonist, or of author, (an) "other" with whom he exchanges identities. Borge takes the place of, or becomes, the heroic Native American Winnetou or the European bourgeois Charles Bovary. From those positions he reconstructs his own space and Matagalpa becomes the Great Plains of North America or Tostes and Yonville L'Abbaye. Yet the two readings are very different: in one this identification with the character is epic-symbolic, whereas in the other it reproduces precisely the distancing alienation/identification of a gothic horror movie.

True erotica is true patriotica—what Borge expresses for Winnetou. True erotica is also self-love or self-aggrandizement fusing Borge, the protagonist of the autobiography, with Winnetou, the protagonist of fiction. The identification introduces a disclaimer on the text's plea to read self as literary and not as political. By the same token, Emma's example nourishes our belief that false erotica is, as most women have always suspected, just fucking—in this case, Emma's corpse.

In *The Patient Impatience,* both readings, however, are treated as ironic attempts to distance life (activity, politics, History) from literature (writing, poetics, story)—Borge's own *desideratum.* The solemnity and drama of Winnetou become farce and irony in Emma, and Borge's autobiography, as testimonial, falls squarely within the divisions between the two, that is, halfway between saga and romance. Now if we return to the first example and look at it closely, we see the lyrical subjects of both the testimonial (Borge) and the work of fiction (Winnetou) fuse themselves in the patriotic heroism of Winnetou. Winnetou-Borge becomes a legendary figure, in many ways portending the coming of Che Guevara—paradigmatic hero of the Latin American guerrillas. Just as the subjects of other testimonials ultimately identify themselves with the heroic subject epitomized by the eponymous figure of this *guerrillero,* in Borge's model of heroism, the fictional Winnetou serves to underscore Che. Che is the man who "absorbed light like parched earth absorbs water" (123); the man who looks gently upon other men, then embraces them. It also underscores the other eponymous figure of the guerrilla pantheon, Fidel, "the author of a veritable metamorphosis," a man of "intransigent devotion to the truth, [and] never-ending search for an answer to hieroglyphics," but a man who also manifests clearly "the delicacy [*tendresse*] with which he treats his comrades in struggle" (124). In this manner, Winnetou in fiction and Che, Fidel, and Borge in reality—a most resonant Christian trinity—merge, making the copula, the narrative I that stands for the male collective us, come to fruition. Furthermore, by invoking Winnetou, Borge politicizes his childhood formation. His reading of and into Winnetou is an indelible trace of his political sensibility constituted *ab initio* as presumably innately masculine.

In two distinct registers, then, the eroticization of the text (Borge's fondness for Winnetou and lust for Emma) comes to constitute itself in instances of readings, readings of a divided subject, subject to a theory of signification that, as Kristeva holds, formulates the signified as "the act of a *transcendental ego* cut off from his body, its unconscious, and also its history." This is the theory of "the speaking subject as a divided subject (conscious/unconscious)."[4] What, she asks, are the "types of operation characteristic of the two sides of this split," operations yet to be unraveled, and "the two different kinds of logic regulating the bio-physical processes" (214)? In both registers, the symbolic functions of language are called into question in these processes of interpretation—for example, how the French and the North American texts are used to qualify the Nicaraguan revolutionary sensibility in the process of constituting itself.

In these instances of readings, moreover, Borge parodies and mimics feminist readings such as those discussed by Cora Kaplan in "The Thorn Birds: Fiction, Fantasy, Femininity" (43).[5] His narrative contracts are transparent. He merely transfers gender relations from politics to literature, the realm of the political to the poetic, that of writing to rewriting, reducing questions of eroticism/patriotism to gender relations. The representation of the erotic—as the rape of corpses—seems to correspond, I argue, to the depatriotization of writing.

But now we can come full circle and argue the opposite, maintaining that Borge's text is more than a discussion of his readings of literature, and suggest that his rewriting of literary works is, in fact, a way of averting politics or of writing politics into life and making the personal political; that is, a transliteration of novel into testimonial, and of literature into politics. Consequently, his literary readings retrace the lines of the patriotic body of his political practice. As autobiography, the events of which he writes are life, a life overwhelmed by his love for dead bodies (Emma Bovary's, as well as Carlos Fonseca's) and for all fallen patriots, dear friends, and comrades, who are lovingly repossessed in death through his writing.

Despite its attempts to be different, then, this register remains the same.

Emma/Winnetou/Literature (or the illusion of homeosemanticism, that is, the naive belief in the identity between sign and referent, in this case of reading and reality) and Carlos/Che/Politics (or the pretended homeosemanticism of reality as writing) are the two faces of a single narrative. In its asymmetries, or what Kristeva would read as the trace of the "speaking subject as a divided subject," this narrative leaves space for the irony that blankets Borge's literary reading. In his literary readings, the narrator/subject (Borge) defends himself from that Other (the other dead bodies sublimated in Winnetou—not in Emma). In them he also distances himself from that "something more than," which the testimonial pursues in its "reality effect," and from that "something less than," which the politics of the nation-state displays in its effects of the real. Personal defense (hiding) and political defense (protecting), Kristeva's two sides of the conscious/unconscious split, merge in the writing of the ex-minister of the interior of the Nicaraguan Revolutionary Government (58).

Mock Writings of State Writings

From Borge's example we can move to another case of de-eroticization of women, by Sergio Ramírez. In his novel *Castigo Divino* Ramírez recounts the story of an ill-fated, provincial Central American playboy, the Guatemalan Oliverio Castañeda, accused, prosecuted, and condemned for the killing of several women, among them his mother, his wife, and another "beautiful señorita." Oliverio is portrayed as a very handsome man,

> of regular height, white, clean-shaven; oval face with a protruding lower jaw; straight, black hair; a gaze peaceful and vague behind the glasses; small mouth and thin lips, sunken temples, medium-size forehead, the base of the nose also sunken, straight nose. A physiognomical ensemble accusing him of determination, cunning, and calculation and in which criminologists could test, on the basis of the size of the skull and correct determination of morphological traits and proportions, their famous thesis on heredity and the predetermination to crime. But beyond all those scientific considerations, we could not negate ourselves to recognize that this was an attractive masculine specimen, whom the fair sex of the society of León came to consider, more or less unanimously, as irresistible. Irresistible and cruel? Does one thing hide the other? (32)

With a mock criminal profile in mind, the novelist rewrites the legal case history of the real Oliverio Castañeda, a man who in fact poisoned several women, creating a scandal in the provincial city of León, Nicaragua. The text could be read as narrating the vicissitudes of a Don Juan who carries seduction to the extreme of murder. But the text is richer than that, for the novel is an experimental text written over other texts, particularly the written depositions, arraignments, indictments, newspaper articles, and, ultimately, all the conversations elicited by the legal case of the accused protagonist. Ramírez writes over the depositions to deride them:

> The witness states that once the poison was obtained at the Argüello Drugstore they no longer dedicated themselves to the study of the degree exam . . . but that they returned to his home address in the Barrio San Juan, to the end of preparing the poisoned portions; Castañeda absenting himself for long enough to go all the way to the house of the Contreras family looking for the meat promised by Don Carmen. (28)

Sex, knowledge, and power (from Foucault) constitute the subject of conversation among the all-male groups of doctors and lawyers who carry on discussions in every masculine stronghold—prison, city hall, morgue, autopsy room, bar. Men discuss the act of seduction and determine whether it is necessarily complete possession—absolute seizure—of the eroticized body of woman:

> At the table of the damned, they examine and certify the authenticity of all kinds of titillating stories (adulteries, jiltings, forced abortions, pregnancies fixed at gunpoint, and people living secretly in sin); there is a punctual accounting of children born of tragic couplings, of the widows who open their doors at the stroke of midnight, and the feats in the sacristies of priests who frequent brothels; there are also meticulously registered scandals involving the most important families of the city, and among them, inheritors stripped, deceptions, debts unpaid, falsifications, liens on property, and fraudulent bankruptcies. (18)

At the end of the novel, to prove the veracity of judgment and provide evidence of the crime the excavation of viscera is imperative. At this moment, the accompanying stench of decay first underscores the absurdity of the case and, second, points to the metonymy of woman as organ (sexual reproducer). The fact that women are putrid, or the ideology that holds that women stink, is invoked in that fetid rankness, stressing the distaste for a relationship between men and women problematized by the gender division. The oral world and the written documents, the entire process of signification, is impregnated by farce within a necrophilia that—unlike the individual readings of Borge—involves the spectrum of society:

> The rumor was hanging in the air like a stench, and the stench remains. It is palpable, can be cut with a knife. If while walking down the street one spots,

from a distance, two people talking on a street corner, in a door, it's a fore-
gone conclusion that they're embroiled in conversation over the possible
cause of this last death, as well as the causes of the others to which it is linked.
(222)

We are therefore again faced with a case of writing literature by rewriting
literature, in this instance nonfiction, the legal documents constituting the
records of the state. Coming from different perspectives both Borge and
Ramírez start out mocking mimesis: first Ramírez reads Oliverio's legal case
and rewrites it as a novel. He then operates a genre shift, from an instance of
legality to an instance of fiction. He first reads the writings and then rewrites.
Reader and author (Ramírez the vice-president writer) put themselves in
each other's position, from which they reconstruct the narrative spaces, here
of legal case history, as farce.

If, through his text, Borge the politician becomes Borge the writer, in
Castigo Divino Ramírez the writer/politician effects a symbiosis of knowledge, power, and sexuality on the order of Foucault's when he reinscribes a
text of legal case histories as fiction. He processes a real-life event through
the multiple filters of literary representations—legal, medical, journalistic,
and novelistic.

With his fiction, based on the record of the murder of several women,
Ramírez constructs a mock framework of desire and seduction (de Certeau's
play on *mort et petit mort* as orgasm), at the same time underlining the farce
of the narrative of the state's exercise of power through its legal writings. Through legal writing, the state apparatus establishes justice, applies
knowledge, and demonstrates the logic of its power. For example, in a state-
performed autopsy:

> The legal autopsy having been performed in the manner described, the fol-
> lowing conclusion can be arrived at regarding the state of the organs: wide-
> spread congestion of the spleen . . . and bloody foam in both lungs, all of
> which point to likely death by acute intoxication. . . . Having performed the
> histological examination of the organs: marked congestion of the spleen,
> cloudy inflammation of the kidneys and widespread congestion of the white
> tissues of the spleen. . . . The presence of poison should be determined once
> the appropriate chemical procedures are performed. (304)

> The organs having been subjected to a preliminary examination under the
> microscope . . . there was found no crystallization that would indicate the
> presence of strychnine, nor any other alkaloid. (260)

Ramírez's style carefully affixes both obverse and reverse of the state-
family—two of the murdered victims are relatives—, his seams and edges

showing the de-eroticization of literature (official documents as well as fiction) and introducing, in its place, the mysterious vanishing of the body and the investigation of its disappearance. The merit of the book is that it places two mirrors face to face, erotica (love affairs) and patriotica (legality), to see how they reproduce each other infinitely.

The bodies of women, sites of eroticism and of affections, are not present. They are buried. Their mysterious deaths and the inefficiencies of the state underscore the fading of the epic of the formation and transformation of nation-states. Even though the absurdity of the crimes committed fascinates the reader, it is the presentation of legality that makes for truly stirring reading. The provincial style of the writing, the oral and forensic arguments that accompany the legal maneuverings—all of these transform the law into an epic of the absurd:

> At this point the defense requests an end to the cross-examination, it being obvious that the witness' will has been bought . . . as her mere presence indicates, given that she is wearing both new shoes and a new dress, all of fine quality, luxuries which had never been made available to her in the home where she works as a domestic; and, furthermore, because the judge has excluded key questions which were the main purpose of this line of questioning. . . . The judge accepts the end of the cross examination, as requested by the defense, who prepared the line of questioning, but admits the prosecution's objection and resolves not to draw conclusions regarding the will of the witness. As regards the damage done to the line of questioning by the suppression of certain questions therein contained, the defense is reminded that under Article 225, the judge is empowered to do precisely that, and is not required to explain his motives. (418)

The pleasure of the text in its absurd referentiality (the legal code and its interpretation) blossoms. The conversion of case histories into literature, and of medical knowledge into legal argumentation, and of both into an object of supposition, gossip, and barroom chatter—that is, into orality—deconstructs the coherence of linear history in which knowledge, science, sexuality, and power constitute a single system.

Reconstruction—of an "anomalous" subjectivity (killer/seducer), of seduction as anomaly and deviation—invokes that which de Certeau calls the unconscious of "le remords qui re-mord," remorse that bites back. In rewriting the legal case history of anomaly/deviation, man's supposed eroticization by woman and her death converge in a single plot. In other words, death (mort) is evoked as the supreme erotic act, and appears united with climax, with orgasm, *petit mort*. *Re-mord* lends itself to a play on words—*re-mord* and *re-mort*, remorse, and a dying again.

This remorse persists as traces of that which is hidden or absent—that is, true *tendresse*. Remorse is the trace of an anomalous subjectivity that is continually made present and absent in a plea invoking the spirit of the law. Consequently it re-inscribes, in or through literature, the order of the nation-state in its supreme codification to settle disputes at the level of the most intimate social relationships—erotic ones—which have become ironic in the incessant cannibalism of the man devouring woman's body, and whose acts are subsequently analyzed—incessantly—throughout the city.

Naturally, like Borge, Sergio Ramírez is in a subject position similar to that which de Certeau attributes to Freud's writing of his analyses as novels. In them poetics and institution are invoked simultaneously—that is, literature and authority. In both cases, it is the very state institution that they represent that authorizes us to inquire (as de Certeau does in the case of Freud) about the cases of intradiscursive constructions and transferences as processes simultaneous with poeticization and legitimation. How are we to distinguish literary authority (the rhetorical process that permits us to posit the relationship between the erotic and the patriotic) from the historic authority that, from its political offices, allows the authors to postulate the decodification of gender relationships as the imagination and absurdity of the state? How to distinguish when their discourse is literature, and when politics? Could it be, perhaps, that their relationship with the text separates, in writing, the writer-analyst (the vice president, the minister of the interior) from the analyzed (the absurdity of official documentation)? Should their relationship with the text separate, in the writing, the analyst/writer (or the vice president, the minister of the interior) from that which is being analyzed (the absurdity of official documentation)?

Duplicated Representations

In our attempts to establish not total presences but partial ones, by searching for the trace of that which is grafted onto the text, we may find that the juxtaposition of rhetoric from the past (sign/text/state 1) re-narrated in the present (sign/text/state 2) places us in two terrains simultaneously: allegory and paradox.

Sign/text/state 1 pretends to register a reality, a historic fact, a legal fact (the violation of the order) and sign/text/state 2, to re-narrate the first. The first instance is a recording of a legal case, the second, literature; in the first, "truth," in the second, "fiction." In the first, the state, with its order and legality, seeks to constitute itself as a serious presence, and in the second, literature merely seeks its representation. Or perhaps, in the first, the "realistic" narration postulates the identity of the sign with its referent, whereas the second presumes its essential difference.

Narrative of the narrative (allegory), fiction of the legality (literature), Ramírez's text, like Borge's, as it accumulates textual layers, distances itself from the primary object (the state, the "real" event) and from "the serious placement" of its veracity. The same fictitious reconstruction of the event, the act of re-writing it, questions the validity of the first as referential sign, questions its claim to representation or sameness.

The exercise of writing about writing (hermeneutics, philology), of writing as the shadow of writing (humanistic practices), brings to mind, on the one hand, Stephanie Jed's work on chaste thinking as chaste text and its interpretation as chastising (hermeneutics as rape and rape as the foundation of republics), and, on the other, Louis Marin's study of the paradox of Pascal's shipwreck, or Akira Kurosawa's *Kagemusha* (1980), in which the resemblance between two men enables one to take the place of the other. The (con)fusion between one and the other, or the interchangeability of their subject positions, is one of the many possible illustrations of the problem of the duplicity of representation, duplicity in which each term is, at the same time, one and the other, one man reciprocally the alter ego of the other. Ramírez's decoding of the first by the second reproduces this ambiguous and dialogic condition of representation, a representation whose rhetorical form is allegory, and whose logical form is paradox, ironically a "representation that proposes to represent itself to itself" (Foucault 16).

Thus, as we will later see in the fiction of Salvadoran poet Roque Dalton, the real/serious and the mocking/fictive, or the discourse of law and the discourse of literature, link up in a relationship of power where production and reproduction are identical. *Castigo Divino* is produced in perpetual reproduction of Oliverio Castañeda's legal case. The author keeps re-impressing one signified upon the other, re-impressing one through the mockery of the other. (Re)writing is then a discursive strategy, and the author's other (in analogy to the state),

> a function by which certain discourses in a given society are characterized . . . a certain mode . . . of the functioning of the discourse . . . a function which is added to or grafted onto discourse . . . , [by which] one limits, excludes, and chooses, in short, by which one impedes the free circulation, the free manipulation, the free composition, decomposition, and recomposition of fiction. (Harari 42)[6]

In this game of "duplicated representation" (the phrase is, of course, Foucault's), I am hoping to show that, as he says, discourse is the object of the struggle for power. Given that *Castigo Divino* is a mock (re)production of a legal case, what is in question is a representation of previous incarnations of the state by the state itself. The novel then, first mocks legality, and, thereafter, displays the possibilities of an infinite process of representation. *Castigo Divino* is a very reiterative text, a narrative (re)examining Oliverio's case from many angles, and opening a space for many voices and multiple interpretations. "And representation, freed finally from the relation that was impeding it, can offer itself as representation in its pure form" (16).

Nevertheless, the logic of these propositions does not end in this rewriting of writing. It does not end with *Castigo Divino*. Neither does it begin with it. For what is the first writing (the first state, the referent), about which the rewritings are postulated? And what is that which is proposed as the last rewriting? Ramírez is playing with precisely the endless nature of the processes of representation, side by side with the possibilities of mocking the referent, whatever this might be. In his case, I am interested in establishing that his referent is a previous form of state representation being farcically introduced through its legal proceedings. And since its legal proceedings are shown to be faulty, the state itself is proved flawed. However, since the name of the game is playing with mirrors, the logic of that other, mocked state, or that which is grafted onto the stylistic, can, by means of the same mechanism, be applicable to the state not judging Oliverio Castañeda, that is, the Sandinista administration, for processes of infinite allegorization could well be understood. The word *state* can be freed of its textual concretions, presenting itself as divided. Or, in Marin's words, "Decoding of the narrative (which is presented as an image) is at work in the narrative itself, and it is this code and its rules that quite naturally the text presents" (Harari 242).

Thus, from his position as vice president (or, in the case of Borge, minister of the interior), Sergio Ramírez writes what might well be read as an allegory of the very state he represents. Paradox, as a central figure of his discourse, exercises that function of reciprocal textual referentiality. Paradox does not exhaust itself in the two supposed referential instances it contains, but rather, is represented as hermeneutics, a theory of reflection, mirroring and shadowing the other. The two men, in the case of Marin's and Kurosawa's examples, and the two states, in the case of Ramírez, prolong each other and (re)produce each other ad infinitum. With their asymmetries of subject, this is the same dilemma Foucault studied in his essay on Velázquez, where

the relation of language to painting is an infinite relation. It is not that words
are imperfect, or that, when confronted by the visible, they prove insuperably
inadequate. Neither can be reduced to the other's terms: it is in vain that we
say what we see; what we see never resides in what we say. (1973, 9)[7]

Literary discourse as discourse of knowledge and power, however, at the
same time suggests in perpetual hallucination a state of order and legality
different from that which is represented, a state of order and legality that can
be inferred as the absent, the other. In these two narrators, that other/absent
may be their own state that they co-command but that, as the unconscious,
is never mentioned. To speak of repetition as a dynamic between tragedy
and farce might seem at this point perverse. Therefore, it is not that the Sandinista State, in particular, is a farce, but that the weakness of dependent
states, of which both these writers have inside knowledge at the moment of
writing, comes out in its logic as paradox or allegory. Nevertheless, farce is
the manner in which self-involvement is narrated. In line with my opening
scenario, the duplicity of representation (Sandinistas/contra) is a concern of
the state's authority, power, and knowledge of itself.

In the case of Ramírez (as in the case of Borge), writing about the exercise
of the law over the domain of seduction, of the practices of the art of seduction exercised over the body of (dead) women, impinges upon their own
selves as representatives of a state. Woman is, in that instance, simultaneously the erotic subject of both law and writing, an absolute possession, a
total denial of (her) self.

Litigation, at once production and reproduction of legal prose, is, as such,
therefore, also an act of writing, of ownership and possession of woman.
Woman belongs to man in private and to society in public; to the individual
man in life, and to the state in death. Perhaps the state is concerned with legislating over women's bodies only as dead bodies? At the end of the novel, in
order to unravel the crime, the evisceration of the corpse and the exhuma-
tion of its parts is mandated. Curiously, both stand for slips of the episteme
in its struggle to establish the truth of the case. The investigation of who
raped whom, who killed whom, who caused whose body to disappear, affirms, in its truth, the relationship of power of some men over others.

> There is ample conjecture regarding the passionate plotting which is, or could
> have been, behind these violent and mysterious deaths: repressed flirtations,
> untimely and emotional jealousies . . . and it is there where the rumor is
> raised, with a thousand fingers, pointing to names and misfortunes of the
> heart which until now had remained hidden beneath a veil, albeit a diapha-
> nous one, of secrecy. (222)

The possibility of interpreting takes us, in this case, to the affirmation of absences situated in the style itself, in the constant reiteration of nonsense (that of legal prose, of deviant eroticism, of the murder of women?) that provokes laughter. In the irony of the treatment of the serious (the reproduction of another text, the erotic heterosexual relationship, the murder of women), in that absence, the author(ity) laughs at and mocks first the type of eroticism represented and, consequently, the statehood represented in that case history and the killing of women. The putrefied body of the victim proves the culpability of the man Oliverio Castañeda, and affirms the death of woman. Her body disappears twice, first as murdered subject and second as subject of mediation of an episteme.

The irreducible plurality, or the incomprehensibility of the metonymic character of the text Barthes spoke of, permits us to postulate a second moment of analysis. In this second moment, the representation of the state's absurdity paradoxically accredits the same narrative of the state institutions that it denies. The narrative of *Castigo Divino* could also be reconstructed as doubt, as the writing of the unconscious of the revolutionary state itself, as the institution in relation to its opposite and to itself.

We can conclude, then, by invoking the opening statement, the dialogue between two contending factions, the Sandinistas and the Contra, two different nation-building projects mirroring each other. The polarity of representation, and their alternative outlooks, are concurrent with my reading of the paramount stylistic devices of two texts written by two members of the revolutionary government. Allegory and paradox seem then to be two modes mirroring the impossible. I now must conclude by reinvoking the third term in discord, woman. I have been arguing that the death or disappearance of woman, the de-eroticization of the text, corresponds to the denationalization processes. In the case of Nicaraguan literature, this is taken to an extreme, where the massacred nation and the massacred woman pair in the male imaginary of its revolutionary leaders at the twilight of the Sandinista nation-state.

CHAPTER TWO

Vanishing Bodies, Woman/Nation

Deconstructing the Panamanian State

It was Doris Sommer's provocative essay "Irresistible Romance: Foundational Fictions of Latin America" that persuaded me to rethink the relationship between literature and nation, and between literature and the state. She brought to my attention the intricacies of plotting love and nations in narratives, the construction as well as the destruction of states, writing novels and writing history; of writing novels about history, about nations, and about legislation in pre- and postrevolutionary Central America.[1] Most of the Central American texts I study here are written by politically engaged men and women, people who call themselves revolutionaries—guerrilla fighters, combatants, and well-meaning ministers of revolutionary governments. Most of them link the fate of insurgency and the revolution to that of the nation, the masses, and women, that is, to that of the subaltern.

Their literature establishes a relationship between erotic love (the heterosexual love of men for women), and patriotic love (the homosocial love of men for men and of men for their country). This is the tenor of Jean Franco's metaphors of house and blood, centered around woman as mother, the image of Aureliano Buendía's blood streaming through the city until it stops at his mother's feet. This metaphor invokes the not-so-obvious symbiosis of motherly love and patriotic love (the house-home and the family-nation), as well as suggesting new perspectives for retracing questions of history and narrative,[2] illuminating the feminist dictum, that since men need both their women (mothers) and their nations (country), they tend to collapse one into the other.[3]

Unraveling patriotic love into erotic love, however, made revolutionary epistemologies vulnerable and accountable to women and to feminist criticism. For in the conjunction of these two types of love, two dissimilar and separate logics merged. I am arguing here that the hermeneutics of such conflations perhaps make it possible to understand some of the reasons for the collapse of revolutionary states, feminist agendas and feminism securely fastening the terms of the discussion to women in the assessment of revolutionary nation-states, revolutionary nation building, and nationhood.

Erotic (Il)legality/Patriotic (Il)legality

Gloria Guardia's novel *El último juego* (1977) brings all these strands together.[4] In the novel, the love Tito Garrido feels for Mariana becomes evident precisely at the moment a revolutionary group, Commando Urraca, seizes Tito's house, taking its occupants hostage during a social gathering. During the takeover, Mariana is shot, and her death, coupled with the seizure of the house, is the pretext for Tito to tell the story of both his love (eros) and the holding of the house—a symbolic fatherland:

> Joaquín was holding the *guerrillera* by the arm, cross-examining her, last night, when we were besieged; a bullet escaped the *cholo* when she was coming out of the bathroom, it was an accident, a mistake followed by a loud scream, "Fucking whitey!" and the pain overcoming me, bending me over, the pain prolonging itself, running from the lips to the legs, saying, saying your name, repeating it on the radio, in the mouths of the hostages and *guerrilleros* at the same time, your name. . . . Mariana, you? you, extended over the hard stretcher? your smooth body? your long and warm thighs? I close my eyes. (197)

Long after the house has been delivered and the woman's body removed, Tito begins to recapitulate the event:

> Yesterday, I saw you, Mariana, for the last time, and I would have liked to look at you deeply and attentively because you had a visage to be watched thus; I mean, look at you unblushingly, openly, and with enough malice in the recording gaze: the full lips, the high forehead, the brown high cheek bones, I came close to you, "Good evening, Mariana," with a quick gesture, crossing, barely smile, and you walked across the living room in the direction of a group of guests talking. (9)

It is evident that the death of woman and the politics of Commando Urraca are braided together. The Garrido family history, in turn, entwines woman, revolutionary politics, and the political and economic history of Panama, for the Garrido family is part of the governing elite. The narrative of genealogy entwines erotics, history, houses, families, politics, and country. "Roberto Augusto Garrido III, the Son of the Man, an acceptable face, respectable, pleasant, a passable face" (159). In the clandestine erotic relationship between Mariana and Tito there is a pact that in many ways resembles the desire for the construction of the nation/fatherland.

Guardia's paramount rhetorical device to ensnare nation in woman is metonymy. Through metonymy, the history of the country, Panama, and the history of woman, Mariana, are plotted as a symmetry displaying the same possessive anxiety. Anxiety and inapprehension seem to be, then, the twin principles structuring this novel. Guardia makes up lists of items, masculine and feminine. The longest feminine lists are all composed of items relating to the women's sphere—embroideries, goldsmithing, food platters, lineages. The longest masculine ones relate to banking and commerce. These lists come to constitute that which Riffaterre calls a hypogram, a "system of signs that comprise at least one predication."[5] I want to argue here that, in so far as country and woman are interchangeable signifiers, this predication is of country, and of woman as vacant space:

> Petticoats . . . the one mended in red, certainly inherited from some great-grandmother, another embroidered in blue or yellow, one marked in cross-stitch, another with drawn thread embroidery, appliqué, suns, little doll's eyes, jasmine . . . gold chains and headpieces and the other jewels from our traditional dress: the Bismarck, the witch . . . the solitary, the half-orange, the dog's tail, the salomonical, the *guachapalí* . . . the rosary, the mosque rope, the herringbone, the plain combs . . . the earrings, the sleepers, . . . the filigree buttons, the pearl rosette, the cufflinks. . . . (74, 76)

This inventory makes evident Guardia's effort to signify by adding, but the series denotes unreachable wholes, coitus interruptus, and, as in Jakobson's metonymic aphasia, what is highlighted is the anxiety to define the unnameable referent (nation/woman), pointing to the slippery character of that sign.[6] When one looks at the listings closely, they seemingly collapse national cultural symbols with feminine accoutrements and occupations—for example, the national dress, the national cuisine. But the series listing women's affairs constitutes metaphors of nation (not of state) and of the feminized political space. They rather represent country, Panama, through the culture of the everyday. Absences—such as national sovereignty (jurisdiction over territoriality), or consummated love—are thus narrated through them.

However, the invocation of genealogies, mothers, fathers, and birth stands for the poetics of oligarchic state politics, based on family alliances and nepotism representing rather the inverse, that is, nonpatriotic feelings of territoriality: Panama as imaginary community en-gendered through rape. The Canal (vagina) provides the metaphor for pregnancies and genesis, or rather for rape adumbrating the nation. The Canal (vagina) taken (raped) by the U.S. military bases and the house (motherland) taken (raped) by Commando Urraca underscore the territorial traits as blank spaces, as lacks, for instance of sovereignty:

> Roberto Augusto Garrido III, I am the Son of the Man who came to seal his lineage for posterity and to disengage him from the others, the unhappy, the embittered, the mediocre, the retarded, the strong and weak, and that is why from the moment I was born he engraved my name in silver spoons, plates and glasses . . . school desk . . . Parker [pen] . . . and later, later on, everything was reduced to anagrams, and I had clips and cufflinks, and gold buckles with that rag, . . . which he had carried encrusted in the forehead, in the heart . . . and he had carried it through the corridors of the National Assembly while reassuring Mr. Gibbens of the contract protecting him against taxes. (39)

The smooth unfolding of metonymy creates an order and establishes a symmetry, snarling the destiny and logic of one (woman) in the destiny and logic of the other (nation). Negation and absence are thus attributes of both fatherland and woman. The presence of the feminine only as absence (death) is the synecdoche representing the absence of nation. Their writing as a series, expressed through a distressing metonymic aphasia, suggests the Panamanian's stammering jurisdiction. The narrator's subject position is, consequently, one of impotence.

The string of signifiers denoting nation and woman, however, does not signify state (= territory + jurisdiction). It signifies only a geography, or a country (Panama), a single institution (military bases), and one woman (Mariana):

> The 1903 Treaty is a leonine document, a fraud that has left us with a mediated sovereignty in the Canal Zone and the Government of the United States, broadly enjoying our privileged geographic position and placing this at the service of their own interest and economy, and you and I, love, that night, the two of us on the National Theater terrace and I holding your face between my hands discovering the immense magic of your eyes, and "That shit is over, gentlemen!", your eyes looking at me and I looking at them and feeling

the flood of tenderness, your velvet softness, "Now the entire world knows it and the Panamanian people are not ready to surrender anymore to any master!" (49–50)

But if woman is, as Franco holds, a representation of nation, then in Guardia's narrative, the plotting of woman's death, the abduction of her body, her reduction to an evoked and invoked referent, comes to constitute the loose rhetoric of nation as fiction (Sommer passim).

In this sense, as Michel de Certeau argues, the literary space is a playing field where social strategies protect themselves. It is the "terrain where the logic of the other is exercised" (30).[7] Nation as rhetoric and as fiction is feminized, and, insofar as it is an inapprehensible signifying chain, nation (as woman) remains codified as body. That is, it remains "in process" in the semiotic, "the primary organization (in Freudian Terms) of drives by rhythms, intonations and primary processes (displacement, slippage, condensation)" (Kristeva 216).[8]

Perhaps it is in this same sense that for de Certeau the stylistic process of discourse is "in the text the trace of the place of its production," or nothing: "a fiction which deprives itself of experimental referentiality . . . the act of writing consists here, in effect, in throwing oneself into the nothingness [rien]" (de Certeau 29, 30).

Francine Masiello could well be tracing the void and nothingness when she says that "putting the feminine in the vanguard of political action leads us into a utopian vision. In this, woman means the non-codifiable, the blank space which introduces a mystery in the literary text" (1989; 157, 158).[9]

As vanishing bodies, both woman and nation are put into question by Guardia in the dynamics of seizing (raping) a house (national family) and its deliverance. The dispossession (of a nation/of the body of woman) and the occupation (of the house by a guerrilla group and of the nation by the U.S. military) enable Guardia to expose the bond between the family's ache for the evacuation of the house and Commando Urraca's ache for the evacuation of the Bases, as well as the distinction between the two groups. It is on the deliverance of both, as (re)possession of both—the physical body of the house and the geographic body of the nation—that this narrative predicates (il)legitimacies or (il)legalities.

Both the residents of the house and the citizens of the (house) nation desire to have their home (family/love/woman) delivered. It is from this perspective that Tito Garrido begins his dialogue with the absent (dead) woman. This dialogue (re)turns reiteratively to the same point, the seizure of the house. The occupation of the house is a liminal point defining simultaneously the limits of this fiction and the limits (of the history) of nation as fiction. The narrative situates Tito Garrido and Mariana's (illegal) love affair—sexual possession, coitus, sensuality, and pleasure—over against the needs and attributes of the nation-state-canal. Ironically, in this plotted drama of possessions and deliverances, the revolutionary Commando Urraca and the nonrevolutionary owners of the house seem to be temporarily in accord. That is, there is a convergence between the insurgent group and the group representing the administrative sector of the nation, negotiators of political treaties—the nonbourgeoisie. The (illegal) presence in the house/residence and in the house/nation violates a basic sense of jurisdiction and independence. In fact, the metaphor of occupancy works for both. But if metonymy is the main narrative articulating device, melancholy is the tone defining the narrator as protagonist's monologue:

> Garrido takes a few steps around the room, his chin trembling, and he takes his hands to his temples. The pain is there, now, static, and he feels it hit him, and his body is covered by a cold sweat . . . and again he walks, always with his head bent, toward the window and hears the pitter-patter of the rain and the noise of the passing cars . . . his hands shaking, he places his head against the cold glass of the window. . . . It has been a while, Garrido has stayed quiet on the sofa, immobile, with his head bent. Everything returns; each scene projects itself as it is: a technicolor reality. The script, Garrido knows it, and he comes to close his eyes again and he already knows that there is nothing, that is, nothing, that will make him forget. (51–52, 59)

Sadness then suggests multiple losses, the loss of sovereignty, the loss of independence, the loss of love. Garrido's closed, internal, clandestine, and repressed discourse expresses, in a different dimension, the solitude of the administrative class caught between two fires, and condemned to murmur to itself its discontent.

But his memory is thematically selective, generating two complementary, symmetrical narratives: the erotic (as purification of unfulfilled love) and the patriotic (as dispossession and unfulfilled power). In this account, the His/tory of the micro-his/tory (of Panama) is catalogued only as maelstrom. History is confrontation and not transition, as Spivak has it.[10] This is the His/tory of illegalities told and retold by the inner voice of the male protagonist, which in turn is the his/tory of his erotic love as an (il)legal affair—a parallelism between one incident in the life of a nation and one incident in the life of a man. For that reason, the homonyms of Mariana as much as those of the country-canal are represented in Commando Urraca's slogans as negation: "Bases no, a thousand times no." "Neither joint defense, nor unilateral defense." "Joint defense = joint repression" (91).

> Today, the words of the illustrious Panamanian thinker Justo Arosamena hold a painful historical currency. "There is no doubt we have committed great mistakes. We have forgotten the character and propensity of our neighbors, we have turned over to them, so to speak, the universal commercial post that the genius of Isabel and Colón had gained for our race." These words were uttered with a profound vision of what was transpiring, but we did not want to learn the story. These words are directed today, like yesterday, to the ambitious ones who see in the fatherland markets to fill their purses. (93)

"No Bases" is Commando Urraca's edict to the group gathered at the house. "No love" is Tito Garrido's prohibition to Mariana. This interdiction of the couple is postulated as a duality mother/not mother–virgin; not virgin/not mother–whore (the semiotic diagram is Franco's).[11] In this diagram the two women (wife/lover) like the two nations (Panama/United States), like the two groups (revolutionaries/administrators), sunder. The history of the (il)legal, heterosexual sexual relations (Mariana/Tito) is an idyllic plot linking virgin/whore, that is, what cannot be attained. The history of the (il)legal seizure of the house is also a political plot linking national/international, Panama/United States, that is, what cannot be attained.

Repeatedly, the subject of obsession is transgression—political transgression and erotic transgression. Transgression entwines the history of the pathology of social and personal histories. To acquiesce to the Bases is to acquiesce to clandestine eroticism, the two unspoken opposing symmetries within Garrido's sexual ethos. In (il)legal erotic relations the male enjoys but does not possess and the female enjoys but is not possessed. The same holds true for the nation. And this nonpossession features a compromise. The compromise is phrased as "No to the Bases," which was, for a while, the political position of a belatedly "enlightened" nonbourgeoisie expressed in the Torrijos/Carter Treaties.

The metonymic decomposition of eroticism (and patriotism) into codifiable fragmentary parts (for example in the body of woman as long legs, breasts) indicts the woman-gender-country-canal. In as remote a manner as possible, the discourse of gender stitches the erotic and the patriotic of lovemaking, political treaties, concessions, oppositions, joint military maneuvers, unraveling what Foucault calls the asymmetry of power.[12]

The crux of gender and nation is that they seem to fold over onto each other in processes of assimilation and symbiosis from which the family scenes and the urban scenes are fleshed out. The two systems constituting a

nonpatriotic patriotism are petticoats, embroidery, laces, cuisine (the feminine) and stores, banking, architecture (the masculine):

> Mariana, I look for you, Mariana-love, in the syllables of your name . . . I
> raised my eyes, "Welcome to Panama's House of Liquors, Johnny Walker's
> Swing—Old Parr—Canicas—Chivas Regal—Royal Salute, and the Arch-
> bishop with Zero," on the threshold of the door that interminable Saturday
> morning, and the *guerrillero* calling the musicians. . . . I advance a few steps,
> "Boutique Lulu for the elegant woman" . . . "The Peninsular Life Insurance
> Company insures you against everything." (127)

At the end of the text all comes back to normality, and all the negotiating
groups obtain what they wanted: Commando Urraca gets hold of its prison-
ers, the house is evacuated, the colonel identifies his negotiator and secures
his negotiating proposal. The administrating "bourgeoisie" is pleased. But
the agreement has left one casualty: woman. Over her dead body, then, all
counts are tallied. Garrido's discourse juxtaposes Mariana's moans of orgasm and her moans of death. The spasms of a lovemaking body becoming
flaccid in orgasm and the flaccid living flesh becoming rigid in death finish
the seams of love, desire, possession, woman, and fatherland in death.

The desire to expropriate/appropriate—the Bases or the woman—transforms the male enunciation in a reversible speech that joins, at its borders,
patriotism (military symmetry in both contending groups, revolutionaries/
administrators) and eroticism (symmetry of virgin/whore in "the other").
Within eroticism, woman, metaphor of nation, marks the limits of the
(independent) nation. Within patriotism, nation, as hampered eroticism,
leaves its borders basted. This is the uncodifiable zone of the anxious search,
blank space and empty sign. On the patriotic body and on the human
body the seams are stitched: the politico-administrative discourse is eroticized and the erotic discourse is politicized. Coitus as love, transgression/
transformation, slips from one enunciation to the other in a closed, privatized, clandestine, and politicized discourse within the man's mind:

> Mariana, I already know what you have meant to me, I know it very well, for
> me, you have been the eclipse, love, noon. . . . And I, Mariana? What have I
> been for you? A surrender, perhaps? I bend my head and I only know that my
> hands tremble. (159–60)

The interrelation and dialogue between man and woman, like national
autonomy, is located beyond signification, degree zero/option zero of
"national" sovereignty. What is codifiable, that is, the listings, are reproduced in the hushed world of woman; what is not codifiable radiates in the

forcefulness of silence. Mariamor's discourse is meager. Like Commando Urraca, she speaks in negations: "Don't turn that into a project" (159), don't put up a struggle, don't think about it, which is the zero point of national options.

In "The Freudian Novel," de Certeau proposed the literary space as a place for the theoretical discourse of the historical process, as a non-topos and logic that enables contemplation. Literature thus throws itself upon a void and a trace, while history looks for referentiality and realism, that is, "the realization of a gliding toward poetics, [which produces] alterations, inversions, equivocations, or deformations inherent when playing on circumstances (chance) and with the locus defining identifications (the masks) in one's relationship to the other (relating to chances and masks)" (23). The novelistic mode comes to be, as in Freud, the theoretical writing of the historical process.

For the sake of comparison, we can make brief reference to a classic Mexican text, *The Death of Artemio Cruz* by Carlos Fuentes. Like Artemio Cruz, Tito rethinks the patriotic incidents, and, like him, he addresses absent interlocutors, equally silent voices, and the Other with whom he pretends to traverse the signifying chain of "national" his/tory. It is with woman (which later on, in political revolutionary writing will become masses—masses, nation, and woman occupying the same discursive space) and with themselves that both Tito Garrido and Artemio Cruz pretend to share and/or argue the cultural and political discursive contract. It is with woman and with themselves that they seem to want to prove their own hypothesis. But it is with them (woman and masses) that they seemingly disagree in their skeptical, nihilistic, pragmatic, and ultimately denationalized stance. Tito Garrido, Gloria Guardia's character, is a simulacrum of Artemio Cruz by Fuentes, and Panamanian "independence" a simulacrum of Mexican independence.

In Guardia's novel, however, woman's hegemony is present in her authorship. In her writing I have aimed first to deconstruct the copula of woman/fatherland, and, second, to deconstruct fatherland. This is one of the consequences of reading into the logics of gender. The modern Panamanian novel renders a postmodern reading of nation as fiction, and of woman as its metaphor. Guardia borrows a style from Fuentes and (re)plays it in a minor key, the revolution reduced to a trivial incident, a flirtation with a guerrilla assault. General Artemio Cruz has regressed to an attorney-manager, and woman has been physically removed from plot.

Patriotism/Eroticism

In another Panamanian text, one laying out, accentuating, and propagating nation-building designs and aspirations, *Mi general Torrijos* (1987), José de Jesús Martínez also interlaces eroticism and patriotism (at liminal moments as much textual/sexual as historical) with the narrative of the Canal treaty negotiations.[13]

Although written from a very different perspective, his work also immediately brings to mind Sommer's thesis on nation building in fiction—as fiction?—based, in her opinion, on the "relentless attraction" of a romantic plot. Novels like Guardia's and Martínez's, I believe, show the opposite trajectory, the inverse of the works Sommer studies.

The rhetoric of other Central American writers—Ramírez and Borge, the quintessential Romantic symbioses of a man of letters and a man of government reproduced on the contemporary stage—utilizes, in even more sophisticated ways, similar stylistic devices. In contrast to Sommer's studies of nineteenth-century nation-building novels, the literature of revolutionary nation building in the twentieth century shows a process of invagination. *Invagination* is a word that accurately describes the constructive process of such novels, for it not only implies a natural reversal of directions, but it also is gender related, referring both to death—of women in textuality, and of nations in reality—and to the birth of something new.

Here eros is directly related to the fatherland. The fatherland is always oxymoronically female—something to possess, to conquer, to penetrate, to control, to govern. That something is what is being lost, and that something is that which is being written and metaphorized through the representation of the dead bodies of women in literature and of the dead bodies of people in war. Here the "relentless attraction" is no longer to love, but to death.

A nation obviously disintegrating in Guardia, as in Martínez, as in that "reality" textualized by the mass media in words and images after the U.S. occupation of Panama, displays a textuality indiscernible from the terms encoding heterosexual love. The tensions between heterosexual love (eroticism) and love of country (patriotism) are indistinguishable. In the plotting and articulation of this kind of love as mistress/wife, displacing eroticism from the legal to what I will call the "(il)legal," lie the very dynamics of Commando Urraca, and of international relations between Panama and the United States.

The play of legitimizations and violations—national/sexual/international—is defined as a limit, that is, a final bout. There is nothing easier than demonstrating this thesis in the "national" literature of a country whose political status has been in question since its artificial inception in 1903. Panama, an imagined community split by a canal that constitutes its only source of revenue. Panama, a country that does not have a national currency, except for a coin, named significantly after Balboa, the Spanish explorer. Panama, an intervened country whose leader was seized by the United States, and tried, condemned, and imprisoned by a U.S. court.

Farther south, Argentinean women are, in Masiello's article, inscribed as alive. For Masiello the presence of women in the public arena, in the public space of Plaza de Mayo, is a sign of women's empowerment. Both Masiello's and Franco's essays stress the feminization of public spaces and the politicization of private spaces as a means of empowering women within current epistemic agendas. However, the presence of live bodies in Argentinean narratives is predicated on the absence of dead bodies; and on those vanished dead bodies, the bodies of the disappeared, the same thesis of denationalization, and hence of Argentina's becoming a "Banana Republic," could very well be predicated.

CHAPTER THREE

Problems in the Constitution of the New Individual/Collective Subject as Masculine and Feminine

Romanticism/"Revolutionary"-ism

In raising the questions of eros and fatherland in revolutionary and non-revolutionary writings, in terms of a process of gender inversion, I want to move now to distinguish the difference between the construction of a revolutionary gendered subject by "bourgeois" women, on one hand, and the construction of a traditionally gendered subject by revolutionary men on the other. In her incisive study *Las Románticas: Women Writers and Subjectivity in Spain, 1835–1850*, Susan Kirkpatrick analyzes the logic inherent in the constitution of the Romantic self as a writing subject.[1] Liberal subjectivity, she argues, constructs gender as difference (man—analytical, creative, intellectual; woman—loving, tender, sentimental), administering gender relations as economies of difference (production/reproduction). Thus, she reads subjectivity/difference through a materialist take on the history of the formation of difference and its attributes.[2]

Kirkpatrick demonstrates the constitution of difference serving the formation of "bourgeois" masculinity, which comes to reflect the formation of the bourgeois nation-state. Difference, she says, feminizes society by "domesticating heroism" and by opening up a new space of authority for the feminine:

> The power of the new domestic woman . . . was psychological: it was the power
> to regulate her own and others' desire, producing within the household a
> space free of conflict, competition . . . a necessary subjective complement to

> the marketplace of labor created by the new economic forms of capitalism. . . .
> The new gender scheme allowed women the power of subjectivity only at the
> cost of curtailing their desire. (26)

In its descending curve, in both Romanticism and revolutionary-ism, "difference" comes to occupy the site of conflict between the individual subject and his social milieu.

Kirkpatrick, as much as Sommer, assimilates love's nature into the restorative character love possesses, presenting both as equally necessary attributes for the construction of bourgeois nation-states. Sommer, for instance, maintains that the quality that makes those narratives of foundation so "relentlessly attractive . . . owes much to the erotic and romantic rhetoric that organizes apparently historical novels" (76).[3] Kirkpatrick's ideas on the constitution of the Romantic Subject, the "I," which is masculine, elucidate the persistence of Romanticism or, what is more important, the bearing of Romanticism on the constitution of the new revolutionary subjectivities, for what she states of the former applies equally to the latter. Consequently, the counterposition/identity between the subject of contemporary revolutionary literature and revolutionary Romantic literature, the I that speaks in the name of a group, as us, must be explained. All evidence seems to indicate that at the foundation of revolutionary republics, the new leadership recycles the problems of the earlier ontologies and epistemologies. In order to firmly ground their identities, the revolutionaries turn to the stable, liberal, republican iconographies of the past (Bolivar = El Che = Cabezas = *el guerrillero*). Ludmer's book on the *gauchesco* genre and fatherland is, in these matters, very enlightening. Answers to this question will lead us to address the constitution of the gendered subject, but also matters considered far weightier, such as the merging of concepts of people, masses, woman, nation, and democracy.

At the intersection of eros and fatherland at the moment of destruction (disarming) of the constituted revolutionary nation-states, I locate the dilemma of what political theorists and economists call the new globalism. In reading Borge, Ramírez, and Guardia, we have seen the place of woman at the liminal moments of (de)constitution. Now we can go back to the beginning of revolutionary Central American literature and plot the discursive fate of woman from there. In the rest of this study, Sommer's thesis of an uncontested heterosexual eroticization of nation-building narratives stands in contrast to the de-eroticization of contemporary revolutionary nation-building narratives. The feminization of contemporary revolutionary epis-temes then engenders, at best, an oxymoronic proposition of androgyny, bisexuality, and hom(m)osexuality/homosociality in constituting the state as national and revolutionary—an I that is collective and speaks for women.

Bringing into focus the essential attributes of that *new* poetic and politi-cal subject, that I that pretends to speak in the name of the collectivity, we can read the variations on the theme experienced, above all, in Nicaraguan testimonials. In both Cabezas and Borge, the new subject is characterized in terms of endurance and tenderness, a man resilient to the adverse surround-ings of a political geography—the Mountain—and tender to other men, his comrades in struggle. Here is an example that illustrates the point. Two dear friends meet in the Mountain:

> It was about three in the morning when I came to El Gato's hammock. . . . He was asleep. There was a moon, and moonlight filtered through the straggly trees that grew in that area. Then I saw El Gato's rifle, an AR-15. El Gato's weapon was a better weapon than my M-1 carbine, which made sense, since he was better than me, and older. I knelt beside El Gato and breathed in the same odor I had myself, the same odor my pack had, and my hammock and my blanket . . . And let me tell you, I was nervous. I didn't know if El Gato would be happy to see me. I didn't know if he would feel what I was feeling. I was nervous, because I didn't know how he would react. What if El Gato only said, "Hey, how's it going?" . . . So, after staring at him in the hammock . . . I nudged him and said, "Ventura . . . Ventura . . . Ventura," and El Gato woke up. . . . "Ventura, it's me, Eugenio." When I said "Eugenio," El Gato sat straight up with a jerk . . . He must have thought he was dreaming. He was soaked with sweat. Then, "Gato," I said, "it's me, Eugenio," and I took his head in the moonlight. "Skinny!" he cried, and took me in his arms, and I hugged him, and El Gato slipped down out of the hammock and the two of us fell onto the ground embracing. And we stayed like that, the two of us there on the ground. (Cabezas 136)[4]

The constitution of the New and revolutionary subject as difference (in the sense in which feminism uses the term), and as differend (in the sense in which Lyotard uses the term, as sets of statements circulating in compart-mentalized logical spaces) becomes evident. In reading this subject against the grain, the dispute between philology and politics explores the conse-quences involved, then, in the theme of the New as difference, a collective subject that does not include women. In this respect, Gioconda Belli's argu-ment against the New Man makes the point clear:

> In her opinion [the protagonist's], men involved with the business of being revolutionaries shouldn't act that way. Would Che Guevara have acted that

way? Flor said that Che had written that women were ideal for being cooks and couriers for the guerrilla forces, although later, when he was in Bolivia, he was with a guerrilla named Tania. He changed, Flor said. Who had Tania been? Had Che loved her? she wondered. . . .

Who cared about Che's love life? History paid no attention to those details. It wasn't interested in the private lives of heroes. It was "feminine" to always wonder about love. (150)[5]

The shift signaled by difference and differend is the key to understanding the aborted epistemic change. All evidence seems to indicate that what this new subject was separating or distinguishing himself from in order to be New was not maleness itself. The revolutionaries deluded themselves in believing that by proposing an "alternative maleness," one incorporating "female" traits such as *tendresse*, they would deliver the New Man.

Inscribing himself in writing as t/he agent of change, this New Subject posits that his agency is love. Here love is the famous feminine *tendresse* of the displaced bourgeois revolutionary horizon Terry Eagleton analyzes.[6] The first incidence of revolutionary feminization emerges in the transition of this *tendresse* from a feminine attribute of the "real" woman to the masculine subject, to the "real" man, and from the family to the State. *Tendresse* is a revolving concept turning from a homosociality to a homosexuality, androgyny, and the third sex. Franco and Masiello have demonstrated in their writings that in this transitional moment the social spaces for the empowerment of women crack wide open.

As a result, the gendered subject constructed by revolutionary men is not very different from that of bourgeois Romanticism. In his texts, the guerrilla writer recycles ideas of woman as "the angel of hearth and home," or "the resting-place of the guerrilla," the apotheosis of his desire. They believe that what the old male needs to become a New Man is *tendresse*. As such, *tendresse* is proposed as an instrumental term mending a rift. It is then on feminine bourgeois *tendresse* that, unwittingly, the guerrilla rests the metamorphosis that delivers his being as the "new" heroic:

> The most impressive thing about Fidel Castro is his intransigent devotion to the truth, his never-ending search for an answer to hieroglyphics, his personal courage and the singular delicacy with which he treats his comrades in struggle. . . . Carlos resembles him in his purity. (Borge 124)[7]

But, examined closely, the logical asymmetries of Lyotard's differend chart the dynamics of *tendresse*. In proving their love to the fatherland, men practice *tendresse* on their companions-in-arms—Fidel on his comrades; Carlos

Fonseca on the members of the FSLN; Che on the *Guerrilleros*. And while men practice *tendresse* on other men, they withdraw it from women. A homosocial tendency signified by a proclivity for the New Man, and a heterosexual tendency signified by women being transformed into "revolutionary pussy," vie in an effort to unravel the en-gendered perplexity. In dovetailing both logics, I argue, a displacement occurs. In reconstructing his society, the testimonial subject reveals asymmetries that, regarding women, display a double standard, abandoning the aspirations of equality, collectivity, and democracy that his pamphlets, speeches, and slogans so vociferously proclaim.

Kirkpatrick's study enables us to understand where the concept of a New revolutionary subject, in transition from individual to collective ontologies, went astray. Across the arc of history, "man" moves from revolutionary Romanticism to the New Man of Marxist revolutions tied to the development of "democratic" nation-states. It is perhaps utopian to expect this New revolutionary collective subject to position himself in an antinomic relationship to the textual subject of the liberal Romantic horizon, that subject of the "heroic bourgeoisie . . . of the French Enlightenment" constituted by Romanticism (Jameson 18).[8] And, in fact, he does not. Instead, he incorporates feminine *tendresse* into self to justify male bonding in male insurgencies and governments, what I call homosociality. Tenderness is the glue keeping the insurgents together under the harsh conditions of guerrilla warfare, clandestinity, and, later on, a besieged, embargoed revolutionary nation-state. Violating the principles of male bonding and secrecy, in her novel *Days of the Dead,* Agnes Barr Bushell dramatizes this principle by plotting homosexuality into the revolutionary insurgencies and making her heroes hold true to their sexual preferences.[9] The shift from homosociality to homosexuality and the epistemes of androgyny and the "third sex" are the two horns of a dilemma, acknowledging tenderness as the crossroad, a sign indicating the intersection between affection (political or sexual) and sexual preferences in the making of guerrilla military bodies.

This is the reason women writers and theoreticians question the newness of this New revolutionary subject using the logic of domestic life. The use of this logic enables women to trace the constitution of the bourgeois subject back to Romanticism, and to examine the epistemological propositions of this genre. When we contrast the bourgeois subject constructed by Romanticism with the new subject invented by revolutionary literatures, what is at stake is the sexual/textual identity of the New. In the literature of Central

America, these problems come back with a renewed force.[10] Three moments can be discerned in this process.

Counter-position/Identity between the Subject of Contemporary Literature and the Romantic Revolutionary

As producers of literature, although as politicians as well, the revolutionaries saw themselves obliged to resolve the problem of representing the attributes proper to their own ontologies. They represented their difference as bifrontal heroic subjects, as protagonists of revolutionary narratives (political, social, historical), and as individual protagonists of their own autobiographies written as testimonials. But political narrative practices, like any literary practice, could not escape the tensions and strife inherent in the struggle for signification.

Thus, revolutionary writers were caught up in the dilemma of literature, registering their desire for a sign shift from the primary descriptive unit of the self, the masculine "I" (= Romanticism), toward the social group in the constitution of the collective New: the "masses," "people," "troop," "bases," (= revolutionary-ism). The revolutionary intended to excise and dislodge the unique individual subject of Romanticism, the autonomous, monadic I, governed more by the laws of psychology than of sociology, as Jameson puts it. The revolutionary wanted to speak, not in the name of, but as, a collective subject. In that act of excision, when the New Man could speak from the spaces of the collectivity (masses, people, troops, bases, woman), representing it, incarnating that collectivity as a true Us, revolutionary literature hoped to engender its concept of democracy. The revolutionary's struggle consisted of attempting to expunge from psychology the (de)formations of pre-revolutionary ontologies.

But the tensions within the revolutionary-subject-not-yet-wholly-constituted, evidenced in testimonials, seem to be located in the conflation of the two narrative subjects, the lyrical masculine I of Romanticism and the collective subject of revolutionary-ism. To try the coincidence of opposing forces in this New revolutionary social subject, was the task of the entire revolutionary literary corpus—testimonials, proclamations, pamphlets, and political speeches. In struggling to represent the New revolutionary subjectivity (the I that is masculine becoming a collective subject representing the totality, understood as male and female in all their political spaces), the revolutionary texts mark a series of tensions to which I will return in the beginning of Part Three, entitled (Wo)man.

The Intersection of Eroticism and Patriotism at the Moment of Destruction of the Constituted Nation-State

In revolutionary writings, mediation between the lyrical masculine I representing the collectivity, and the social subject, are superseded only illusorily in poetic structuration, narratives of the revolution as the fictions of the revolution (Sommer passim). Granted, the revolutionary writes his personal autobiography (I, Tomás Borge) as a group testimonial, as a socio-biography of a political party, in this case, the FSLN. Nevertheless, he does preclude the distinction between the masculine I and the collective when attempting to elucidate similar questions in political narratives. Here the collective, the Party, is confused with the people.

Tomás Borge's writings serve as an example of the poetic resolution of political desiderata. In Borge, the collective subject is as structuring as the individual I. The opening sentence of his testimonial—"Shortly before midnight one summer evening in Matagalpa, anesthetized by the twilight while my mother thought I was studying ratio and proportion problems and verbal declensions, Winnetou died" (10)[11]—sets up an intersubjectivity between himself and his friend, and between the two and the literary characters as real people, that foretells the ensuing group formation. The newly born Sandinista Front ties political activism to friendship with Carlos Fonseca. Situating Fonseca as a hero in this text, Borge establishes the parallelism between himself as the real political hero and himself as Winnetou, the poetic fictive hero. Friendship is here predicated as a transcendence of the difference between the individual being (Fonseca or Winnetou) and the community established *ab initio* (Sandinista National Liberation Front). However, this series of conflations refers to a collective subject, us, which stands for the group of people composing the vanguard party called FSLN. But the distances originating in the Party membership's expropriation of the place of the people-masses assumed by the lyrical masculine I speaking for, or in the name of, the people, are not obviated. Nor, as I will argue later, does this conflation between myself, my friend, and the Party, as one, account for the differences between the three of them and other group entities, for example, other political parties, other people. Nor, for that matter, does it explain the difference between the subject position in autobiographies and the other narratives engendered by the Party, the government, or the mass organizations, even though the primordial function of the Party is homogenization. In other words, the difference between Party members and masses was always outstanding in political parties defining themselves either as mass parties or as parties of cadres. In both there was a rift, a caesura dividing the militancy from the nonmilitancy, the militancy from the rest of the people they proclaimed to represent.

The Feminization of Contemporary Revolutionary Epistemes and the Constitution of the State as National and Revolutionary

In the constitution of the revolutionary subject, then, revolutionary epistemes propose several simultaneously unfulfilled conflations. The hegemonic one is that between the individual and the collective subject—locus of their concept of democracy; then, situated in a different hierarchical order, that of psychology and sociology—two disciplines vying for the hegemonic construction of ontologies; at a poetic level, that of autobiography and social history, advocating testimonial as group narrative; that of sexuality and textuality constructing gender difference as gender neutrality. In the convergence of reality and fiction they envisaged political ideology as a "real" relation with reality, and reality as materiality. Present and future, or the transmutation of dystopias into utopias, was also embedded in their program. Such an ambitious agenda is severely questioned by feminist deconstruction forged in the smithy of Woman.

Jardine, for example, points out that materialism incorporates "mater" in its etymology, suggesting the (mater)ial world functions like Woman, though (mater)ialism as productivity is male, marking within the concept a critical androgyny. And Hélène Cixous wonders if the logical functions of all these opposing "couples" defining borders are not, in fact, couples, and if it does not evidence that symbolic processes are based on gender construction, that "logocentrism forces all thought—all concepts, all codes, all values to submit to a system of 2 terms, might that not be in relationship to 'the' couple: man/woman?" (116).[12] Epistemological couples as double subjects— masculine/feminine, individual/collective—are both very much in question here.

Regardless of how that tension of logical coupling is formulated, I have been formulating it as intercodification between the masses, and the masculine I. The fact that revolutionary writing uses the first person plural, we, obscures the relationship between the masses as people, the members of the party as a group, and the singular narrating subject I, which is masculine, and individual, impersonating them all. The essential caveat of these revolutionary ontologies is to present the categorical concept of "social transformation" as "self-transformation," as resolution: the textual/sexual/individual/

collective subject is predicated as t/he agent of change. And in the transition initiated from the individual I to the collective subject resides the construction of the socio-textual utopia.

In this manner, the relation between the textual subject of Romanticism and his social universe (the dystopic present and the utopic future) is erased in revolutionary literature when the lyrical sexual/textual I assumes the (mater)iality of the social universe as a possibility and the necessity for change. The state (as people), still "unreal," "imaginary," nonexistent (fiction), exists, however, in the minds of the people (as leaders) as a project to be realized—the idea is Marx's.[13] Therefore, this narrative subject, as the agent of history, embodies Lukács's concept of true consciousness.[14]

PART II

(New) Man

CHAPTER FOUR

Constituting the Narrative
"I" as Difference
The Guerrilla Troop and the Guerrilla Base

The "we" of reflection and modesty would, in *The Critique of Arms*,
come to be preferred over the odious "I" and "Me," except when impossible.
In the political sphere . . . the singular signifies majesty. As much as
with techniques of action as with theoretical discourses, the individual
is object prior to being subject, an interchangeable "element" in
which no one is irreplaceable. The militants have a right to a soul, but
only the adventurous are permitted to speak about it. Psychological
analysis or the autobiographical story may require the use of the "I," and
we reserve the right to such an impertinence in other circumstances as
well. Regardless, the mixture of genre and voice is worse than a
confusion of the spirit, or a sign of fatuousness: it is a political error.
Regis Debray, *Che's Guerrilla War*

The problem of the construction of the revolutionary subject as that masculine "I," which is not the collectivity, is evident also in pamphlets, proclamations, and political speeches, and in the *guerrilleros'* revisions of national
history.[1] In all these documents, writing itself betrays the presence of the
desire for the collective, that unreachable that stands for the people-masses-
troops-base. The *guerrilleros* aspire to represent, both in the literary and the
political spaces, all of these groups, or at least to speak in their name. The
being as ventriloquist—characteristic of women's literature, according to

Franco—is another strategy of articulation of guerrilla texts, as, for example, in the writings of Che.

In *Guerrilla Warfare* he postulates the idea of the revolutionary subject as a warrior/guerrilla-*guerrillero,* paradigm of the New Man.[2] After Che, revolutionary literature arrived at this idea of the "man-warrior/guerrilla" as a construction of a "different" subjectivity, but not as a construction of subjectivity as difference (Other)—which might, perhaps, have been a fruitful revolutionary path to follow. As I stated before, the first proposition of this New subject is that of constituting a revolutionary masculine alterity, debunking "bourgeois" masculinity. Yet, at this very moment, a lacuna between "the warrior/guerrilla" and the masses-people-troops-base is revealed. In Che's text, for example, he writes the warrior/guerrilla as "one who shares the longing of the people for liberation" (32). In this "sharing" the warrior/guerrilla denotes a moving toward, a positioning, but also marks a difference between himself and the people. For Che the warrior/guerrilla is "a guiding angel, who has fallen into the zone, helping the poor" (32); he is a "standard-bearer in the cause of the people." In "fallen," and in "the cause of the people" whose standard the warrior/guerrilla bears, there is a differentiated, distinct, and separate subjectivity. In the process of trying to define the warrior/guerrilla as "the people," the warrior/guerrilla paradoxically becomes "the other."

In Bolivia the theoretical question of "fallen into the zone" acquires its concrete importance. El Che was not linked to the class by ancestral ties, ancestral ties constituting sources of the elemental human acquaintance and knowledge of the terrain, without which in a remote and backward region a person can be fatally treated as a stranger and a suspicious alien. Debray puts this knowledge at the level of instincts:

> In the manner of sociologists or of *compadres,* only that kind of intimate knowledge of the *specific, local* nature of class exploitation would have made it possible to discover the immediate and concrete, though perhaps unrecognized, needs of the really poor—including the "regionalist" demands of concern to the population as a whole, which are of overwhelming importance in Bolivia at present (tax exemptions, the reinvestment of petroleum royalties, building roads, municipal credits, election of local authorities, and so on). (90–91)

In Bolivia the guerrilla lacked the means and the instruments to approach the masses. Difference signals two different epistemic spaces constituting Lyotard's *differend.* This alterity, however, passes unremarked within the text, even though, Che explains, the warrior/guerrillas are not men who have bent their backs day after day over the furrow. They are men who understand the necessity for changes in the social treatment accorded peasants, without having suffered in the usual case this bitter treatment in their own persons. (34–35)

But the difference between "bending backs," and "understanding" is established. What is certain is that he, *el guerrillero,* Che, is not a *campesino,* the paradigmatic social subject of agrarian societies whom revolutionaries seek to transform. However, his "understanding" (intellect) and his "standard bearing" are qualifications enabling him to lead, to be the vanguard; that is, the text marks the warrior/guerrilla's epistemological place as power. When Che describes the *guerrilleros* as "men who understand," we can interpret "men" to stand for the I of Che himself. Although the vague territorial localization of the warrior/guerrilla is not identical to his own subject position, the maleness of the warrior/guerrilla and the I of Che seem to merge. He says that the guerrilla

> should preferably be an inhabitant of the zone. If this is the case, he will have friends who will help him . . . he will know it . . . ; and since he will be habituated to local peculiarities he will be able to do better work, not to mention that he will add to all this the enthusiasm that arises from defending his own people and fighting to change a social regime that hurts his own world. (35)

Being local within the idea of "proletarian internationalism" is the site of another tension in Che's construction of the warrior/guerrilla-*guerrillero.* Between the masculine I (director-intellectual-international "proletariat," Che) and the collective (masses-troops-base-"men who have bent their backs"), there is a logical linguistic distancing. In Bolivia it includes differentiation by languages: "They were plenty of Aymara or Quechua-speaking Bolivians, but unfortunately neither of those languages were spoken here; in this region near Paraguay many of the *peones* spoke Guaraní, which no one in the guerilla group knew" (Debray 129). Here the acritical character of Che's writings (and the other guerrillas' readings) surfaces once again. The *guerrilleros* have no reason to be philologists, but are obliged by their ideology to be clear, for, as Franco says, the syntagm "is perforce a battlefield where women [people, the subjugated] confront the exclusions and the marginalities of the past" (41). On the basis of Che's predications of the warrior/guerrilla, the distancing of the leaders from the masses (bases) could be argued. In the written distancing between him and the people, the silent separation between the individual and the collective could be located.

Distance and silence are but two of the problems detectable in this construction, however. For the reformulation of this New, lyrical I is merely an attempt to erase the borders between the individual subject and the social subject. Dedication is just one of the identifiable sites of the struggle between sociology and psychology over the ontological definitions of the warrior/guerrilla-subject. The question of who defines whom as a subject is also plagued by contradictions: how the New is constituted in the textual/social subject, and how the dynamics of change proposed in any and all signifying chains are defined.

Che struggles with these questions. For example, in attempting to approximate his warrior/guerrilla-subject he writes three different types of predication. The warrior/guerrilla is "anchorite," "ascetic," "mystic," "priest," "angel"—a series befitting the religious patristic. Second, the warrior/guerrilla is signified as possessing self-control, "rigidity," "austerity," "intransigence," utilizing the terminology of Protestant personal repression. Third, the adjectives "slippery," "nocturnal," "stealthy," "surprising," applied to the guerrilla-warrior identifies in him the ideal traits of insurgents, that is, those needed for war (Guevara 34).

These three sign series, however, constitute authority, the first in the moral terrain, the other two in the psychic-emotional terrain, and all three in the terrain of war. The first and last correspond to Jameson's "genuine philosophies of history" (18), and the second to the history of bourgeois heroism in its vision of capitalist progress. The constitution of that lyrical individual/collective subject from these three series of attributes is clearly outlined in the poetics of the testimonials by Cabezas, Ramírez, Borge, Payeras, and Alegría.

But we can synthesize those attributes in two words: discipline (masculine) and love (feminine). The guerrilla-subject moves from one series to the other in a paradoxical way, for instance, in discipline disguised as love, and in love expressed as intransigence—love toward himself, like the ascetic's, and toward others, like "intransigence." Failure to fulfill the exigent demands of discipline can trigger this dynamic:

> Tello was always rough; he always wanted more from us, more and more. It got to the point where we couldn't stand him, it was as if he was a member of the Guard. . . . We started back carrying about seventy-five to eighty-five pounds a piece. . . . I remember that when I tried to hoist the pack onto my back I couldn't lift it. . . . I saw that Tello was really busting his balls to get his pack on. . . . When we saw all the weight we were supposed to carry it didn't seem right to us. . . . Tello said something then that hurt us all: "Can't you sons of bitches learn to carry the food you stuff in your mouths?" . . . Tello

stomped back, furious. . . . We had a long way to go, but we didn't know whether Tello kept beating us over the head so we would keep on growing, or if he was just a damn bully who didn't understand. (Cabezas 90, 91–92)[3]

Tello's behavior elicits rebellion. The guerrillas disobey the leader, and then the leader must be persuasive, coupling discipline and *tendresse*. A bit later, Tello begins addressing them in the gentle tone leaders use when they want to coax their troops.

In Cabezas, fatigue, hunger, and discomfort can be translated into lack of discipline, failure to comply with orders. A man who cannot overcome, who cannot endure, fails to embody the criteria established by Che for the New Man. When somebody falls short, the leader then harangues the men to ask them to keep pushing themselves. To keep pushing oneself, to be resilient and strong, giving more than the body's physical strength and endurance allow, always giving a little bit more, making an extra effort is what proves one worthy of the title *guerrillero*. For those lacking that drive, there is no place in the future (utopia)—the leader, Tello, says. Overexertion, overcoming the body's needs, is a virtue. It means being endowed, having that mystique, what it takes to belong in the here and now of the heterotopias. And the Mountain is that "something more than," the ideal "beyond," utopia:

> The new man is in the future, the man we want to create with the new society, when the revolution triumphs. . . . The new man has gone beyond his tired legs. The new man has gone beyond hunger, beyond rain, beyond mosquitos, beyond loneliness. The new man is there, in that supereffort. There where the average man starts to give more than the average man. To give more than the typical man. (93–94)

To continually give more, to keep pushing oneself in the here and now engenders the New Man. The New Man is "the man who gives everything for others" (87). To keep on pushing oneself is discipline, and discipline comes to be an exercise in giving, and giving, a synonym of *tendresse* (love). When they don't continue struggling, Tello, the instructor, the "man who understands," becomes intransigent, and his intransigence signals his love for the troop. He harangues them because he loves them, and because he loves them, he humiliates them, insults them: you are "a bunch of little women . . . a bunch of faggots" (105; translation modified). Then he cries. With tears in his eyes he explains the meaning of the New Man:

> In a little while Tello came back and in a gentle, persuasive tone that he used sometimes when he wanted to, "Compañeros," he said, "you've heard talk of the new man." We just looked at each other. "You know where to find the new

man? The new man is in the future, the man we want to create with the new society, when the revolution triumphs." (93)

Paradox forms the center of the dilemma revolutionary definitions struggle with in finding the New. Disciplining the troops is defined as *tendresse,* love. But in this instance love is an exercise of power, authority, violence. Love is violation. It takes the form of that tyranny they love to hate. The New Man is born with an injunction, that he is not to be a "little woman," he is not to be a "faggot." The figure of the Mountain as the symbiosis of the feminine-masculine is very useful at this point: for it is through this violence that the fatherland is engendered, and it is engendered in the Mountain. Over the feminine-masculine body of the Mountain, men deliver men. Thus, it is in the Mountain that tyranny as patriarchy is recast as tyranny. Over the feminine body of the Mountain men engender the fatherland. In the Mountain, love/tenderness is violence, violence is discipline. In this instance the nation is inseminated through rape, and aborted.

The New Man is to be neither woman nor faggot. Tello's analogy between women and homosexuals—disposable people—attacks women on two counts, and serves to institutionalize a rather tyrannical and authoritarian idea of the New Man. Sacrifice and punishment, discipline and repression, love and intransigence, grow increasingly oxymoronic. These coupling concepts are positioned as either supporting the you-plural collective (troop as feminine), or the I-individual (Tello, the leader, the vanguard, as the masculine). In trying to neutralize this contradiction the narrator opts for a lyrical resolution:

> The new man began to be born with fungus, infections, and with his feet oozing worms . . . with loneliness . . . and eaten alive by mosquitoes; he began to be born stinking . . . the new man was being born with the freshness of the mountains. A man—it might seem incredible—but an open, an unegotistical man, no longer petty—a tender man who sacrifices himself for others, a man who gives everything for others, who suffers when others suffer and who also laughs when others laugh. (87)

In short, a woman. Although most certainly that "man" described to exhaustion leaves no doubt that "he" really is a man, that is, a sexuality. But this New Man newly born is not Tello. Just as in the case of "that *guerrillero*" impersonating "Che," "a man" is not "the troop," a collectivity, but rather Omar Cabezas disguised as "a man." This is the simulacrum of orality.

In the caesura left by the tension established within this simulacrum of orality, the text is the emotive discourse of the leader impersonating the collectivity. It is the lyrical word of the subject-guerrilla as troop(s) impersonating the I. This is how literature sublimates; this is how it becomes a laboratory in which, according to de Certeau, the epistemological conflicts of alterity are resolved. The tension is created by wanting to present an attractive image of the New textual/social guerrilla-subject and contradicting the very attributes of the New Man. Intransigence remains an authoritative exercise of power. Here again we face the same anxiety and disorientation distancing leader from troops in Che's political texts, and between the vanguard and the masses. Uneasiness, then, is a key to the narratologies of power, in autocracies disguised as democracies.

It is no coincidence that the most lyrical moments of the testimonials are found in this masculine representation of the authority of the New Man and in the virile sensibility that he displays. The New Man, priest and tyrant, to himself and the rest, becomes his opposite, not he who understands but rather he who does (not) understand. Writing here is obviously the predication of virility. Man as a sexuality assumes interlocution is masculine: the number of times the word man appears in Cabezas's testimonial is its sign. There are no contradictions between the ascetic, the austere man, the anchorite and the sly man, the nocturnal man, the rigid, repressed man, the priest, Che's definition of the New Man-*guerrillero*. But if, indeed, there are, and serious ones at that, they linger between those series and the feminine signs Cabezas attributes to the New Man, though it may seem impossible: freshness, candor, surrender, sacrifice, suffering.

By comparison, Borge's testimonial does not frame its self-image in the sublime discourse of the religious patristic. Although in Borge the relation of the masculine-collective is also lyrical, he frames his self-image in the grotesque, the absurd terrain in which the New Men gestate. In Borge the Mountain is a sterile "mother," no-man's-land. This image is surprising, for he belongs to the group that believed in the Protracted Popular War, for whom the fatherland was engendered in the Mountain. In Belli the New Man gestating the nation tells woman what follows:

> She recalled how Felipe had listened to her in silence, nodding, agreeing with her.
> "I know that we can't swim together. . . . You are the shore of my river. . . ."
> It was obvious that Felipe didn't want her involved at all, and she had, unsuspectingly, paved the way for him. . . . She was with a man whose goals were nothing at all like hers, a man who obviously considered her just a "pleasant refuge" in his life. (109–10)

Finally, in order to effect the shift from the psychological to the social, it is necessary to re-edit the symbolic system, and not only that New subject, in terms of repression and endurance. The revolutionary should have been critical of that which de Lauretis calls the systems of signs and habitual codes, for "it is this work or activity which constitutes and/or transforms the codes at the same time as it constitutes and transforms the individuals using the codes, performing the work" (167).[4]

Constructing the New social subject with religious attributes, repressing the emotive components of the psyche, leads to the denial of that which represents the intervention of the subjective element in the revolutionary lexicon's social revolutionary formations. Language plays logical tricks, and makes $A = -A$: in proposing the conjunction of the individual/collective, they projected those same attributes of the masculine I onto the collective. In making the emotive personal-social expressions clandestine, they favored the economies of false consciousness and made a simulacrum of daily political life. It is this characterization of resistance as repression, and of strength as endurance, that stymied the New in the New Man.

CHAPTER FIVE

Constituting the Individual
Subject "I" as Difference

Woman

A most unusual man insofar as his ability to bring together in one
personality not only the characteristics of a man of action but those of
a man of thought as well, of a man of immaculate revolutionary
virtues and extraordinary human sensitivity, all united in a character
of iron and a will of steel, in an indomitable tenacity.
Fidel Castro, *La guerra de guerillas*

We can now move to consider that disturbing quality, unfamiliar to masculinity, that "most unusual" characteristic in Che's personality to which
men consistently refer, a trait men admire in other men, a femininity, perhaps.[1] Yet, here is a way of acting, a behavior that seems as surprising to him
who possesses it as to him who beholds it. Certainly, it is surprising to speak
of qualities that are attractive to the masculine yet do nothing to accommo-
date masculine epistemes. "Most unusual" is the domain of the individual, a
space in which the masculine "I" may, perhaps, become a collective subject,
or else dissociate from it completely. Where does this element reside within
the personality of Che, a man destined to become the model of manliness
for the Latin American guerrilla?

Fidel Castro gives as an answer a combination of factors, presented in an
unusual masculine formation—action secured with thought; sensitivity with

a character of iron. It is as if Che were at least four different men at the same time: one of action and another of thought; one revolutionary and another sensitive.

Raul Roa finds Che's irresistible attraction lies in the combination of "dry wit . . . a serene demeanor, an inquisitive look, trenchant thought, gentle words, vibrant senses, a clear laugh and a halo of lofty dreams surrounding his personality" (Guevara 20).[2]

Che's power, that is, results from the combined effect of disparate aspects; for example, he is inquisitive, yet gentle; dry, yet vibrant; trenchant, yet serene. Beyond this, however, is a kind of canonization, an aura of the lay saint men see in him, a figure in whom they can deposit and safeguard the image of the Romantic revolutionary hero, bearer of the aureole. The extraordinary aspect of this New being, the guerrilla-man, lies within the halo that envelops his figure.

In Guevara, these two leaders and thinkers find the gifts (among which we must include sensitivity, *tendresse,* generally a feminine attribute) necessary for the exercise of leadership and power, the characterization of themselves or of that which they demand of men who would be "real" men. Hence Castro's prescription: "What do we hope that *our* revolutionary combatants, *our* militants, *our* men should be? We should say without hesitation: May they be like Che!" (Castro 16; emphasis mine). Regis Debray, who was for a while his *compañero* in Bolivia, says:

> What is odd is that Ñancahuazú seems ever further away, while Che comes closer. Gradually, as that piece of history is buried in the past and time moves on, as life continues and the struggle is renewed, faithful to itself, the figure of Che stands out more and more clearly; with his quiet step, his gaze, and his clear voice, he seems to remind us of the reality of war, and to awaken us from the false dream of peace we find so tempting. Che seems to survive his last venture better every day, seeming somehow bigger than his own frustrated plans even though it was the whole of himself that he put into them. (146)[3]

Che becomes the model of the masculine desire for manliness, the narcissism of the image, Lacan's Oedipal triangle, which expresses, at least, a sense of solidarity among kin—the locus of our quotation.

From a position of power, Che is enunciated and consecrated institutionally as the paradigmatic aspiration of the revolutionary man, and as the constitution of that ontology par excellence, which, being ideally that of the masses, will be that of the new revolutionary nation; and which, as such, will bring about the convergence of the masculine, individual I with the collective subject representing the people.

In reading *The Diary of Che Guevara,* I want to track the moments constituting those three subjectivities, realized by Che himself, by the guerrilla, and by the peasantry, in order to ascertain, from the feminist point of view, wherein resides that attraction men encounter in Che—that "most unusual" quality appearing only in him—and, above all, the meaning of the "human sensitivity" they attribute to him. The contrasts in the narratives by and about Che also attract my attention as attributes of the New Man, model for the society of the future, discursive contracts signed by the revolutionary and the guerrilla.

In his diary, Che moves away from the mode of his earlier texts, in which he describes how a guerrilla should be; here we instead discover the difference between "guerrilla" and guerrilla—Che, it seems, occupying the role of the first, and all others the second. In the process of guerrilla formation, the narrative traces, first, the path of the constitution of a geography (the Mountain), the map, the topography of an insurgence, and beyond this, on that material terrain, atop the obstacles resulting from that enterprise, we find the formation of the guerrilla. According to the theoretical writings of this author/guerrilla, the subject achieves himself in guerrilla combat. Or rather, in the diary, Guevara the narrator works at constituting disparate subjects at the same time: that of the leader (guerrilla), that of the guerrilla (troops/base) and that of the peasantry (people/masses), where the first is both the least focused, and the place in which he positions himself as the sweet object of desire. In Bolivia all these distinctions become clear in his assessment of the Bolivian *campesinado,* in whom, Debray states, difference was politically decisive, because in Bolivia it was noticed as the absence of a

> fuse, to carry the flame along to the explosives: if the guerrilla operation is not in direct contact with a socially favorable medium, if the really powerful social charge that is ready to explode is somewhere else.... In Bolivia in 1967 no such technical system had been established by the time military operations began, and the embryonic system which should have supplied for it was not in evidence at all.... The two characteristics I have mentioned—the sterility of the immediate area around the guerrilla headquarters, and the lack of any system of communication between the guerrilla and the social forces of the revolution—combined to make the small motor working at full capacity (the guerrilla war) out of phase with the large motor which was at that time barely ticking over (the national mass movement). (Debray 17, 18)

A warning is in order, however, that Che's diary, despite all its simplicity and candor, is a (de)classified narrative in which a large portion of the information is missing, and there are blank spaces indicated by the narrator himself, blank spaces that would explain certain instances of the formation of the guerrilla, and of himself as leader, to which we have no access. For example, the specific role of the Cubans, their selection and classification, their incorporation, the components since and toward Cuba, are left blank.

Nonetheless, these leaps do not obscure the desire for a topography that covers the entire Latin American continent as the aspiration of guerrilla struggle, and as such they include the formation of the Latin American as a guerrilla. Despite attempts to transcend nationality, at that moment, subjects are identified as Peruvians, Bolivians, Venezuelans, Argentineans:

> There are no ranks for anybody, there is no political organization yet, we need to avoid polemics about national or international discrepancies. . . . I forestalled a tendency observed in the vanguard to put down the Cubans, which had crystallized yesterday in the form of Camba, who trusts the Cubans less every time. . . . I made a new call for integration as the only possibility of developing our army. (Guevara 69, 149)

> Now, the guerrilla doesn't have at his disposal a complicity of this kind, since prior to the launching of military operations in the region no clandestine or semilegal political work had taken place. (109)

In both Che's *Diary* and Debray's *Che's Guerrilla War,* we can trace the obsession to

> establish roots in the area, be it only on a single acre, in a single family, a single hamlet, an isolated household. (. . .) "Give me but one firm spot among the peasants, wholehearted and sincere, [says Che,] however small, and I shall destroy the whole imperialist pack of hounds unleashed against me." (Debray 125)

In a narrative rife with smokescreens and omissions, in which no one knows or inquires about the discussions, the information, what to do with the dispatches, the classified documents that arrive from Havana; in a narrative in which one senses an improvisation *in toto*—one has no sense of direction, nor can one know why one is doing what one is doing, what the design is—the mission becomes the formation of an international guerrilla corps and of its guerrillas.

"El Che" by El Che: Stabat Mater: A Self-Portrait in Steel and Iron

In this narrative, Che occupies the place of the theoretical subject who defines his surroundings, occupies the place and the position of authority; but this political authority is hidden behind poetics, the use of the first person narrative, which gives the appearance of a narrative of subjectivity, and of personal sensitivity—a diary, an autobiography, a testimonial. In this narrative, various convergences are authorized: the first responds to the narrativization of "El Che" by Che, a self-portrait in steel and iron, intransigence in his command and human sensitivity; the second, to nationalism and internationalism, as attributes of the guerrilla; and the third, prejudgments and distrust with respect to the differentiated peasant masses. On the last question Debray is straightforward:

> There was nothing to catch hold of, no way the guerrillas could break into the surrounding society, which had become a solid mass of suspicion or astonishment, smooth and unassailable at any point. Not [only] did they not have among them, or with them, a single *natural leader* from the area—and even the most backward region has its natural leaders, by way of whom any stranger must pass in order to be accepted and recognized by the locals—they had no one from the area at all. In that sort of rural society, the family's friends and acquaintances, their *compadres* and *comadres*, constitute the first foundations of any political support base. (Debray 128–29)

In this, Che, as emissary, appears almost parenthetical, and the distinction between guerrilla leader and masses is once more emphasized. Without a doubt, first person narratives exclude, if they so desire, commentary by others. Although here we have Debray's analysis of guerrilla struggle, this analysis does not provide us with information about Che himself. Because of this, we are ignorant of Che's foibles, consigned by his companions to secrecy, and oral history. But the narrative masculine I who keeps a lookout on the troops is turned on itself as well: Che includes himself in his narratives of bodies and words, registering his own dizziness, his hunger, the swelling of his limbs, his illnesses, along with his conversations with his companions.

That is, he includes himself as body in descriptions of corporal fragility and vulnerabilities—among which are days of "burps, farts, vomiting and diarrhea" (185) and not only dizziness, fainting, but also waking up "much relieved but soiled like an infant" (187). Still, this masculine I is never an undisciplined or heroic collective subject: it is always a masculine, singular I—even in self-criticism, when he notes that he has been severe with his companions. In its representation of the others, the diary permits him his own self-representation.

Although the exploration and demarcation of the terrain more accurately constitute geographic narratives, domesticity, the intersection with the feminine, prevails, and the psychology of the combatant occupies the center. The syntagm registers one childish incident after another, swaggering masculine behavior in confronting deficiencies at home, economies of partnership, friendships in the face of scarcity. For instance, "A disagreeable incident was provoked because the rearguard ran out of sugar and suspicions vacillated between not having gotten a fair share or certain liberties having been taken by Braulio" (109).

The presence in the Mountain of "daily" and "domestic" problems, from the search for food to personality conflicts among the troops, in effect, once more—as in Cabezas—demarcates a feminization in the writing and, therefore, a sensitization, located irrefutably within the realm of the feminine:

> Finding food, cooking it and transporting it from place to place, thus became almost the prime, relentless, obsessional function of the guerrilla column, absorbing most of its time and all of its members. . . . If they did not eat, they would die of hunger; if they went looking for food they would almost certainly be in danger of death from being betrayed to the army or discovered by them. Guerrilla-peasant contact; purchase of food; contact between peasant and the nearest military detachment; detection, pursuit and encirclement of improvised camp with the cooking pot on the fire in the middle; breaking through the encirclement, often at the cost of dead or wounded guerrillas; and a precipitate retreat—until such time as hunger would once again become so unbearable as to start the wretched cycle once again. Such was the pattern of events, each episode following the last one, whereby the rearguard had to twist their way, saved by a hair's breadth each time. (Debray 118)

In the face of such conditions, Che demonstrates an enormous sensitivity, keeping his eye on the behavior of the troops, allowing us to enter into revolutionary "morals" as economies of guerrilla domesticity. Che here is leader—but "mother" as well, in Kristeva's use of the term. She casts the Mother as idealization of relations, as paradigm of the complex relation between the masculine (Christ/troops) and the feminine, *tendresse*; as a point of convergence of humanization; as representation of poverty, modesty, humility, devotion, and as emergence of a function that is "'Virginal Maternal.'. . . In the symbolic economy of the West . . . the Virgin Mother occupies the vast territory that lies on either side of the parenthesis of language" (110).[4]

These narcissisms, and these ambiguous masculine-feminine relationships, harmonize as much with the patristic series defining the guerrilla as with the nimbus or aureole that, according to Che's companions, surrounds his figure.

In Che's narratives there is an inversion: guerrilla sociology is a psychology of the guerrilla, a constant evaluation of the negative aspects of his personality, of that which interferes with and threatens the formation of the collective, that records a sad panorama of Arturo's aptitudes . . . ; Marcos seems to be hurt by the reference to his errors . . . ; they both told each other to go to hell. . . . These disagreeable incidents among us keep holding up the work. . . . Loro is incapable of getting these things, looks very disorganized. At dawn yesterday I heard Marcos demanding the shit out of someone and during the day someone else. . . . and Marcos had given him peremptory orders, threatening him with a machete and hitting him in the face with the butt of it . . . shoving him around and ripping his clothes. (Guevara 57, 53, 92, 93)

The negative psychology affects the sociology negatively. It intrudes on and threatens the formation of that desired collective subject that demands self-control, asceticism, and so on. In other words, the formation of the desired collective subject demands the growth and discipline required by socialization, living with others in a domestic community in which all the participants are men (genuine democracy?), and, as such, the absence of women does not permit the exercise of patriarchies or tyrannies. At the same time, it demonstrates male frustration at and within domesticity, lacking house and woman, someone to order about, somewhere to unload, "repose."

The Guerrillas (Troop/Base)

Nonetheless, in recording the psyche of the troops in terms of bad behavior and bad upbringing, Che reveals a fundamental comprehension of, and tolerance for, human nature under pressure—that quality of his that is called "sensitivity" or understanding and that, according to Debray, he didn't possess: "Che's own writings, and the memory of his conversation, of his Leninist capacity for self-criticism [meant his subjecting] the progress of the revolution to the most merciless and objective judgements with a sarcasm which spared neither himself nor anyone else" (Debray 9).

However, throughout his observations on his comrades-in-arms, on the actual guerrillas in his struggle, one perceives an almost tangible exercise of *tendresse* (love) together with an always implicit comparison between what is and what should be (discipline), the revolutionary "mystique" always haunting the guerrilla encampments, (con)fusing discipline with tyrannies and authorizing the New Man's uncontrolled exercise of power.

As his narrative shifts from an account of the downtime of exploration—during which Che records a plethora of domestic concerns, childish behavior, the effects of demoralization, illness, and hunger—to times of combat, the "swaggering" subject himself, clumsy in human relations, gradually changes his tone and "becomes" heroic. Che's forbearance of daily shortcomings finally pays off, as acts of bravery and the willingness to fight (to push oneself) take the place of pettiness and lack of discipline. The presence of death, dead bodies, spilt blood marks all subsequent moments. The will to die, to offer and to spill one's blood, and the body half-buried in the ground signal the exit of the feminine and the entrance of the masculine, proof of the guerrilla's transition to "guerrilla." Birth of the masculine from the masculine is military; baptism in blood. The phrase that marks the transition is enunciated precisely by the most undisciplined, by the man who has been the object of the most critical attention, Marcos: "I exploded and said to Marcos that he would certainly be thrown out of the guerrilla troop and he answered that he would rather be shot to death" (122).

This phrase signals combativeness, putting the body in the line of fire. It is more manly to be vulnerable in the face of weapons than to withstand hunger, or carry out the duties of a woman. Various texts present willingness to risk one's life in guerrilla warfare as the ultimate heroic act—a stance reiterated in other texts, among them, for example, Juan Almeida Bosque's.[5]

In the definitive moment of combat, everyone is a hero except Che, who no longer remarks on the contrasts between his behavior and that of the others. For the others, heroism occurs for the first time in their military deeds, but for him—for Che—there is continuity, and his behavior, whether masculine or feminine, is thereby always heroic. He alone suffers no transformation under fire but instead remains integral, from beginning to end. His guerrilla training took place earlier, in the Sierra Maestra: the lyrical subject of the composition is therefore the one already trained, the transcendent, the guerrilla with something more, the "guerrilla" graduated beyond guerrilla. Furthermore, his position of narrative authority is located on the margins of self-inclusion in a de-heroicized domestic morale, hence that "most unusual" quality of his, the aureole. The first part of guerrilla life— domestic habits in living together—and the second—the realities of armed combat—are equally heroic and relevant. In both his words and his actions, this is what Che is saying.

His personal trajectory is from the most heroic and controlled to the least, in contrast to the others' run of play. The others, the troops, begin in petty "corruption" and in embezzlement, in weakness and demoralization: when he demands everything, they give little. But later he needs to ask them for nothing because their behavior adjusts to the circumstances of combat operatives, and so of heroism. It is then that his own body fails to the point of making him totally vulnerable, but only as inscribed in the third person. This inscription comes not from the perspective of his own self-constructed masculine I but from the masculine I constructed by another, by Fidel Castro, when he records Che's death, in the third person, at the hands of the enemy, "blasting him with submachine-gun fire from the waist down. . . . They had instructions not to shoot his chest or his head so as not to cause gushing wounds" (Castro xxviii).

The blasts to the lower abdomen, besides signaling a slow and painful death, direct the gunshots toward his masculinity. Castro declares that one of his major faults was temerity; "excessive aggressiveness, his absolute disdain for danger" (7) was his Achilles' heel.

Only as a leader, or as a military chief, and not even as these, is Che able to intuit himself strictly within his prose, that steely character and iron will emerging nowhere else. When Monje questions his leadership, he affirms, "As to the second point I could not accept it in any way. I would be the military chief and I would accept no ambiguities in that" (Guevara 47).

On very few occasions, if, in fact, there are any other occasions that demonstrate such energy, does he use such blunt language. But in this case, the discrepancy arises first between the Party (Bolivian Communist) and the guerrillas, and second between the national administration and either the international administration or the international proletariat—a Latin American revolution that begins in Bolivia and can count on very few Bolivian combatants and, furthermore, begins in a marked discrepancy with regard to Che, the person in charge.

In breaches of discipline and errors of conduct lurk contrasts between nationalities, Cuban versus Bolivian: "Of all the things we had foreseen, the thing that went the slowest was gathering the Bolivian fighters" (74). And one of the things that distressed Marcos is "that he got criticized in front of the Bolivians" (58). From the perspective of national composition, the guerrilla group thus constituted is perhaps representative, a nucleus of a kind of denationalization of the subject, and of the regrouping of the same under other flags. In the same process of denationalization, Che comes to represent a paradigm and a vanguard. He has transcended the Argentine, he has affiliated himself emotionally with the Cuban and is not inclined to submit his leadership to discussion, leadership originally Bolivian but with a continental geopolitical reach.

One of the components of the "most unusual" could be, then, this combination of the revolutionary subject as transcendent subject that is unconstrained by boundaries—whether of gender or of country—and that nonetheless executes actions both within and without these frames. Che embodies the spirit of Bolívar and would occupy in this century the place

Bolívar designated for himself in the previous century: that of transcontinental leader—albeit of a small international guerrilla group, whose number will never exceed half a hundred:

> Vanguard: Miguel, Benigno, Pacho, Loro, Aniceto, Camba, Coco, Dario, Julio, Pablo, Raul—11 total.
> Rearguard: Joaquin, Braulio, Rubio Marcos, Pedro, Medic, Polo, Walter, Victor (Pep, Paco, Eusebio, Chingolo)—12 total.
> Center: Me, Alejandro, Rolando, Inti, Pombo, Nato, Tuma, Urbano, Moro, Negro, Ricardo, Arturo, Eustaquio, Guevara, Willy, Luis, Antonio, León (Tania, Pelado, Danton, Chino—visitors), (Serapio—in hiding)—24 in all. (136)

This guerrilla army was surrounded not only by an enemy army but by a sparse and scattered populace called the *campesinado,* who will always remain distant, detached, estranged from the guerrillas.

The Guerrilla and the Peasantry (People/Masses)

How are these popular subjects constituted? What is their true place in heroic guerrilla narratives?

Sometimes they are "mountain men, youths, unmarried men; ideal for recruiting" (6). At other times they are "poor laborers . . . out for a walk," "suspicious" (13), or Amerindians, "an Aymara campesino who appears to be quite healthy" (65). That is, bodies whose names vary according to their agency and social place.

The dominant paradigms of class analysis paradoxically interdict uniformity; they are not the masses. They have different economic means, and their real and virtual alliances with the army give them both security and fear:

> Acting as Inti's assistant I went to speak with the campesinos. I don't think my performance was really believable because of his shyness. The campesino itself is within him; incapable of helping us but incapable of anticipating the dangers that he brings and for that reason potentially dangerous. He gave us some information about the campesinos but it was hard to be sure because of a certain insecurity. . . . an average campesino whose daughter is the girlfriend of a member of the army. . . . $1,000 was lent to the campesino so he could buy pigs and fatten them; he has capitalist ambitions. . . . they're poor campesinos and quite frightened by our presence here. (81, 84, 87, 153)

Within these observations lie conspicuous distrust, misunderstanding from unfamiliarity, from prejudice, and from fear, and precaution, which their condition obligates in them:

> One of the sons of a campesino had disappeared and could have gone to give warning. . . . Of all the campesinos we saw, there is one, Simon, who seems cooperative although fearful and another, Vides, who might be dangerous; he's the "rich one" of the zone. . . . We pressured Rodas' son and he confessed that his brother and a laborer of Vides had gone to get the reward which varies between $500 and $1000. (154, 155, 157–58)

Their mutual relation is fraught with stealth, pretense, theatrics, and simulacrum. And the worst is that

> mobilization is nonexistent among the campesinos except for acting as couriers which bothers them a bit. . . . This is a Guaraní community whose inhabitants—rather shy—speak, or pretend to speak, little Spanish. . . . Still short of complete incorporation of the campesinos, although they seem to be losing their fear of us and we've even managed to elicit some admiration from them. This work takes time and patience. . . . The boy who was guiding us began to complain about strong smells on the wind, whether for real we don't know. (172, 197, 201, 209)

Thus, the *campesino* is constructed—first, as a distinction between peasant and Indian, peasant and Bolivian, peasant and laborer, peasant and mountain man, and, most relevant, between peasant and guerrilla; second, as cunning and shrewd and thus susceptible to manipulation; third, as a fox and catty, *ladino*, Güegüense.[6] The battles are, for him, something that happens around him; the theater of conflict is within his terrain, but doesn't concern him. Such battles bring together two alien groups, soldiers and guerrillas. Both get him involved. He is not an agent but an object of something dangerous that happens, that occurs in his environment and that is not of him, nor does it represent him. This is precisely what testimonials of the *campesinos* involved in the Nicaraguan counterrevolution reveal.[7]

Distrust predominates in every gesture or word. Che considers the *campesino* untrustworthy and reads cowardice, fear, lack of commitment, alterity in his mien. And this subject, supposedly, is precisely the focus of the *guerrillero's* struggle. As we will see in the next chapter, Che's peasant remains as unknown, for Che, as Ramírez's for Ramírez, except that in the difference of thirty years, consciousness of alterity mediates, and here the parallels between the two universes come into view.

With reference to this question, Debray illustrates how this theoretical problem adversely affects reality. In the case of Bolivia, he explains how the guerrillas needed to be adopted by a social class, a class that would feed and harbor them. In Bolivia, there was no harmony between the social being of that class and the political consciousness of the Vanguard. From one side to the other of the central cordillera, miners and guerrillas "watched without actually seeing each other, like beings from two different worlds" (20). The Bolivian peasants were indifferent to guerrilla heroism. The guerrillas were unaware of social divisions among the people, for instance, those among the different population groups living in different regions, speaking different Indian languages. Errors were made both on the part of the *guerrilleros*, in their conception of the people, and on the part of the theoreticians, in their belated awareness of the guerrilla. Debray warns:

> The social individuals who make up the class force are not an inert mass, nor is their dialectical interaction like the coupling of two motors.... [And as René Zavaleta Mercado put it, the] Bolivian Che did not always stick to the rules of the theoretical Che, either generally or at specific moments, so that it could be said that Che actually denied the general theories of Che. (23)

The distance established by prejudices or unfamiliarities makes impossible the convergence of that masculine I-guerrilla and that collective subject-Masses/peasants, in whose name the revolutionary processes of agrarian societies speak. Consequently, as a goal, democracy fails, because the masculine I remains forever distant and split from the collective subject, or constructs the power of the institutionalized group as the collective subject. That collective subject—guerrilla => vanguard => party => army => bureaucracy—mediates between the masses and the government leaders of revolutionary societies.

In this manner, a stubbornly masculine narrative constructs the three subject-protagonists between which we originally wished to distinguish: the leader, the guerrillas, and the peasants, leaving aside the composition of the enemy soldiers, equally profiled, whom novelists like Manlio Argueta will later take up. In composing the leader, the narrative subject identifies with him, and commentaries on who he is become scarce.

However, implied commentaries emerge in Che's judgment of the behavior of the others, primarily in the first exploratory stage, when despair prevails, when

> the people are still weak and not all of the Bolivians will resist. These last few days of hunger have shown a lessening enthusiasm, a decline that becomes more evident when we split up ... when even the Cubans ["all Cubans are exemplary in combat" (232)] have not responded ... [when the people's morale is low, when] they have to rough him up [Rubio] even though they're not convinced he was the guilty party ..., [he keeps himself strong, an example, despite the fact that] in the last few days the orders that I give are repeatedly ignored. (98, 116, 131)

Here opens the divide between the leader and the rest. In these instances he demonstrates one of the aspects of the "most unusual" that separates his individual masculine I from the collective subject. The guerrilla is, with respect to him, a difference, a learning, a becoming; and the *campesinado*, more an object than a subject of the revolution, a perpetual alterity, the Other of guerrilla discourse in the mountains of Bolivia.

The *campesino* is the entity who is evasive, slippery, escapist, treacherous, fearful. Woman, in a parallel position of alterity, is a name (Tania, Hildita), a familiar feeling ("repose of the guerrilla?"), someone's wife or woman (El Loro "the Parrot" "confessed that he had visited a woman he knew there" [61]), a teacher (also an object of distrust)—although the feminine is present within the social organization on the exploratory level, in the guerrilla encampment, and in the leader's maternal *tendresse*, above all, in the face of human frailty and the failings of his companions.

Epilogue

Today in Havana, the vigilant eye of El Che lingers. Driving from popular neighborhoods toward the center of the city, coming via Santa Catalina Street, as the car bears right to turn to Boyeros, a faded poster of Che inscribed with Castro's declarations on the paradigm of manhood stares at the passersby. An enormous and perpetually renovated poster of Che, covering the building of the Ministry of the Interior, overlooks the Plaza de la Revolución and confronts the impressive white effigy of José Martí. Multiple images of a dynamic Che painted in different colors cover the walls of the main reception room of Casa de las Américas. The function of Che in revolutionary narratives and iconographies has been that of a lay saint embodying something that was not of this world, the unusual virtues of beings constructing utopias. I have argued throughout these chapters that in formulating this image as paradigmatic, a concealed, perhaps even unconscious, convergence of maleness and femaleness was being proposed, an androgyny necessary for the building of a new society. While these enormous images stare down at the now indifferent youth, in the minuscule private spheres of their impoverished houses reserved for the family's intimacy, the Cuban youth repeats sotto voce an unrecorded phrase, "Dicen que el argentino no era fácil"—"They say the Argentine was not easy."

CHAPTER SIX

Constructing People/Masses as Subaltern

"Little Man"/New Man

No soy un hombre, soy un pueblo.
(I am not a man, I am a people.)
Jorge Eliecer Gaitán

In the program we had anticipated that a campesino native to Morrito
would publicly hand in his rifle to me. A wasted, forlorn little man climbed
up to the platform, poorly dressed, looking like a plucked bird. . . . Facing
that little man . . . dazed by the spectacle he was entering briefly, only to be
mute, exiting as silently as he had arrived. . . . I then had a thought that
has been on my mind throughout these years: What world was in his head,
and what world in mine? What was the connection, the lost thread
between those two worlds, if indeed any existed?
Sergio Ramírez, *Confesión de amor*

In all earnestness and with sincere humility, after the Sandinistas' electoral
defeat, Ramírez, the intellectual and ex–vice president of the Nicaraguan
revolutionary government, poses a question relative to the distance between
himself, the leader of the revolution, and the "little man" of the popular
masses.[1] Speaking as a writer, as an intellectual, and as an ex–vice president,
he registers an awareness of the divergence of visions: the *campesino*'s possible vision of himself and the intellectual's nescience. The quotation makes

clear the intellectual puzzlement of a thinker trying to discern the subaltern. He confesses he cannot see the *campesino,* and he candidly speaks about his bewilderment. Indirectly, he is stating that to see him indistinctly is worse than not seeing him at all, or worse than mis-seeing him, or seeing him as another, because he is the social subject over whom the revolutionary epistemologies were to exert their power. He incarnates the person whose life and destiny the revolution had promised to change. Yet the *campesino* is shrouded.

Ramírez's question, formulated and constructed in several ways, is perhaps the question that most succinctly expresses the doubt besetting the construction of revolutionary narratives that intended ab initio to answer the question of the nature of the popular subject. But, well intentioned as the leaders might have been, their provisional written constructions of the subaltern were later reified in the printed word, and on the basis of these definitions real politics were engineered. For instance, the Nicaraguan Institute of Agrarian Reform proposed and implemented forestation and coffee cultivation programs in unconventional ways that were contrary to the construed "popular mentality" and so wound up overwhelming it. These well-meaning politics, then, directly interfered with the life of the popular masses, and, at the macropolitical level, such projects moved in exactly the opposite direction they had intended, becoming antipopular, or supportive of pretexts that were clearly antidemocratic. In these instances, the narrating masculine "I" took the place of authority and distanced himself from the collective subject of the masses. Between the revolutionary government's dreams of justice and modernity expressed in writing, and the daily life of those *campesinos,* there opened an abyss. Unfortunately, power intended to take root in this abyss.

All of the narratives of the sixties generation—in Central America the generation of the historic convergence of liberal and/or revolutionary modernity—faced the same dilemma, and asked themselves the same questions: who is the subaltern and what is s/he like? In 1983, speaking as a sociologist, Torres Rivas asked himself again and again, "What will a man—that actual man standing under a tree—think of the Revolution?" And wasn't that perhaps the same question Che was inquiring about, indirectly, in his books, which also called attention to themselves as narratives of authority with respect to guerrilla ontologies?

Little by little the generation continued asking and perhaps partially answering for itself questions related to subject restoration: what was the subaltern like? For that query was related to the question of the New Man—

that man described in religious language, mystical language, that man "without egoism or meanness, willing to give everything out of love for his neighbor, as in the Gospel" (Ramírez 128). "What was that New Man made of?" Above all, the obsession of this generation was how it would build that bridge between him—the postulated new masculine I of the New Man—and that other "little man," the masses, the people, so that they could merge into the revolutionary collective subject—alterity, which in the dusk of the revolution Sergio Ramírez would examine again.

Wasn't that perhaps the very same question Roque Dalton was asking himself regarding literature when his character Alvaro says to himself that

> he was certain that Tata Higinio's visit was not merely a delicious opportunity but that it also could be the last. . . . If I could keep him, make him return one more time to renew with his classic conversations (already barely remembered in their most general outlines, without stylistic handles, clues for appropriate use, spare tones, sweet ex-abruptos on hand for emergencies) the knowledge that what he knew today was so important for his authentic career, that of a writer of fiction. (44)[2]

And wasn't that also the question Miguel Angel Asturias poetically answered beforehand in his book *Men of Maize,* answering it profoundly, and so predicting the guerrilla texts of Roberto Payeras, Rigoberta Menchú, and Mario Roberto Morales—to mention but a few of the most renowned of the Guatemalans?

And didn't all of literary high culture in general propose to investigate beyond the doctrines and the silences, to discover what would be the true essence of that "little man," the true bulwark of democracy? Was it not the revolutionary culture's staunch purpose to forecast the imaginary social and political point where the convergence of the new masculine I (guerrilla and revolutionary vanguard New Man) with the popular masses would be found, in whose coalescence the essence, not only of the New Man but also of the new society would be rooted?

They Would Enter the Scene Briefly Only to Be Mute

The popular masses enter the theater of the state briefly only to remain silent—as silent, as intercepted and interpreted as in the liberal text, and as questioned in their silence. The body of the masses is opaque, not only because it doesn't write but also because it doesn't speak, and it doesn't speak because it doesn't trust; because it does not know how to speak; because it has always spoken in borrowed, foreign tongues; because it is already so inured to remaining silent. Why does the body of the masses not speak, or why do only the silences speak through its body?

By way of introduction to a more detailed analysis of the representation of the subaltern in literature further on in this section, I will counterpoint the cases of Roque Dalton, Sergio Ramírez, and Miguel Angel Asturias with Che's writing to explore the instances of convergence between literature and politics in El Salvador, Guatemala, and Nicaragua, respectively. The first two writers are intellectuals committed to the popular cause of revolution; Asturias is a liberal writer and Che a guerrilla. In their narratives, the struggle to come to terms with the concept of popular subjectivities is central.

In Roque Dalton the popular/poetic subject is made to say: "'You big. And blondy-blondy. Nice and whitewashed. Maybe don't get enough sun ...' while he was moving forward, indecisively, clasping his hat to the top of the chest" (45). "Big" and "blondy" are two adjectives that mark distances, like the interjections "huh," the skipped verb in "you big," and the shrinking of the body.

In Dalton, then, the problem is formulated as an aesthetic problem, as a problem of writing and of representation, but the backdrop is the same. The problem of democracy continues to peep from behind the scenes, and weaves itself through discussions of literary stylistics, such as that of socialist realism, and that of Brechtian relativism. Socialist realism trivialized the problems of subject restoration, constructing heroism artificially, copying the language of religious narratives, underscoring martyrdom, sacrifice, and transcendence very much à la Che. Brecht, on the other hand, in his concept of estrangement, introduced the nuances of contradiction in the formation of "proletarian" or popular consciousness and political commitment. The question is always how to discern the Amerindian, the *campesino,* the little man—militarily, politically, and poetically—when he doesn't allow himself to be represented. Because the only representation is with words, through speech, and "el Tata" doesn't speak. Ramírez's "little man" doesn't speak. Asturias's Gaspar Ilóm doesn't speak:

> Gaspar was once again becoming earth ... which is to say, sleep that finds no shade in which to dream ... and the solar flame of the voice could do nothing, tricked by the yellow rabbits that set to suckling in a papaya grove ..., and faded into the water like reflections with ears. (2)[3]

In Dalton, the "little man" would speak with them when they were children. Communication was established through disparity in age, or between the two conditions of subalternity signed by ethnicity and age. In terms of age, the child (future intellectual and—leader?) and the old man (*ethnie/campesino*) become equals, but now those children "so" big are men, the authority. *Chelitos*, "blond," an impersonal adjective, ethnic, interprets the literary personage of Dalton through Dalton the politician; and "big ones," that is, men, establishes the distances between men (*chelitos*/intellectuals) and *campesinos*.

In literature, the representation of these masses is, then, an imaginary (re)construction of orality, the Amerindian or *campesino* speech heard in childhood, a moment in which these two constructed images, that of the Amerindian and that of the history (ontology) of the Amerindian in his speech, meet. Afterward, this history will manifest itself in the alienation of gesture from word—the literate body and the shrunken body of the "tata." The literary methods register distances and estrangements in "popular" (the other's) speech, in written intellectual language, repeated since the world was, in Ciro Alegría's words, "wide and alien," as a problem of contemporary narratives.

Those who speak, then, become interpreters through their writing. In the first instance is Che, who wants to reduce distances. As we have already seen, in defining the "guerrilla," he outlines the confusion between the guerrilla and the guerrilla-troop; between the armed group that engages in guerrilla combat and the guerrilla army that employs a more extensive concept of that which enters into the caliber of "other" others. For example, the collaborators—people by means of which the group advances, extends and homogenizes itself—are part of but not the same as the guerrilla. Che tells us:

> The guerrilla struggle (is) the struggle of the masses
> The masses (are) the people
> The masses (are) rural agriculture (the campesinos)—the "little man," Tata Higinio, Gaspar Ilóm.

In the copula, unequal terms are equalized: guerrilla and masses; guerrilla and people; people, masses, rural agriculture, and campesinos. The agent is the guerrilla, the guerrilla-troop, the armed nucleus, the vanguard. That is the intended masculine I to which the use of the pronoun "us," of the New Man, refers. But they are and are not at the same time the people, masses; they are agents in the process (both in the sense of "becoming" and "being on trial") of being, upon which revolutionary governments based their concept of democracy. The concept of the guerrilla comes to be more or less a hybrid between the militant, card-carrying member of the Party and the sympathizer, that is to say, the *campesino*, as mass(es).

In Che's *Diary,* the real guerrilla is not yet the New Man. The real guerrilla is swaggering, argumentative, and even a swindler: not very different from the bandit outside the law—remember that in one of Che's analogies, the rebel resembles the bandit. The outlaw and the guerrilla then share essential characteristics, but the former is only "the caricature of the latter, a struggle for freedom" (Che 1972, 180). The real guerrilla, however, already enacts, in the guerrilla-troop, the evils of the state constitution of the guerrillas in the *Sociolismo* of socialism—that is, distortion, nonconformity, and even dissidence.[4]

Che's copula is, then, just a manner of speaking. In all of his formulations, a sense of detachment between the two terms of the equation persists side by side with the sense of process. Che's aim was to render the copula a reality and unite the masses with the army and the Party. In this way, his revolutionary theory would accomplish his democratic mandate constituted by the first series of equalities: masses = troop = party = state: that was the condition sine qua non of his agrarian revolutionary theory, and what underlies the formation of a mass (not a cadre) party. In a mass party, the distance between leaders and masses is theoretically erased. In a party of cadres, the distinction between leaders and masses is overtly maintained. Consequently, the agent who would carry out his idea of transition from a military democracy to a political and economic democracy was, for Che, the *campesino*. The *campesino* was the telos of his other series of equalities: the guerrilla struggle = the struggle of masses = people = rural agriculture (the *campesinos*). Since women as a gender are not included, the last section of this chapter attempts to unravel their position in Che's narrative.

In contrast, many years later, Ramírez writes with absolute awareness of the separation between the managing party cadre of the revolution (the intellectual and strategist of the new society) and the *campesino*—"littleman," isolated, primitive, miserable, trapped, simple. Therefore, the project of a national "mental [organization] of a dream," which was going to return the land to the *campesino*, delivering the modern instrument for organizing life, produced, instead of the cherished democracy, government by a Party bureaucracy flaunting power:

> The distant and dispersed effort to reorganize his life was worked out from
> the centers of revolutionary power, and that which the agents of that power
> tried to impose on him, regardless of his own concept of individual freedom,
> also directly collided with him, while, in his ears, grew all the noise of propa-
> ganda . . . which equally violated his world without allowing us to penetrate
> it in his elemental simplicity, a simplicity which was at the same time a com-

plexity . . . and the more simple, the more stubborn. . . . Their world was break-
ing, shattered by the crudity of war. The borders of that world of his were not
universal like the ones we proclaimed. They barely extended beyond the palm
walls of his hovel. . . . *The connection between those two worlds, theirs and
ours, was not yet established so that one would flow into the other and nourish
each other.* (Ramírez 120; my italics)

According to this evidence, the understanding of the subject did not
deepen with the passing of time. On the contrary, in the thirty years that
passed between the Cuban and Nicaraguan revolutions, it seemed to have
taken the opposite direction, draining the energy of the vanguard and calling into question its ideology. The gap between the people and the collective
pronoun "us," used by the guerrilla (the masculine I of the New Man, transformed into a leader of government), widens. "For that reason alone,"
Ramírez maintains, "the counterrevolution became a *campesino* war" (121).
The dream of the revolution became the nightmare of war, and the Mountain vacated by the guerrillas was occupied by a peasant counterrevolution.[5]

Ramírez does not explain how the revolutionary government could have
bridged the gap between the administration and the people. He only declares that "it was necessary to get away from schemes and theoretical prejudices, from established truths, and to abandon models" (122). Thereafter, he
acknowledges two of the principal strategies of the revolution: the first is to
recognize the need of the administration to establish itself as government
and power, and, therefore, to concern itself with its relationships to other
governments, bracketing the problem of the social pact and stressing international solidarity; and the second is to avoid resorting to left game theory,
to "what if," posing hypothetical answers to hypothetical questions. Those
strategies were the best they could come up with to circumvent intervention
and invasion, thus preserving revolutionary power for the benefit of the
"unknown" masses. My argument here is simply that they wrote the New
Man in an old language; that they dismissed the problem of difference as
marginal, rehashing instead a concept of "difference" that derived from
liberal bourgeois ideology. Consequently, they fell into the same epistemological fissures they were insistently trying to mend.

In thinking the subaltern, Ramírez tries hard to understand the intersection between politics and culture, and his musings illuminate the stylistics
utilized by Dalton in his struggle to construct a subject outside the tradition
of socialist realism. Neither Ramírez nor Dalton was a military man. Their
literary inclinations, coupled with their political commitment, enabled them
to conceive of a more nuanced subject. Both lived the problems of the con-

struction of revolutionary states as well as those of insurgency. Dalton lived in Cuba and traveled to the ex-socialist countries as a journalist.[6] He was stationed in Vietnam as a war correspondent. He also had taken the opportunity to witness the formative years of the insurrectionary/guerrilla period in El Salvador. As a result of these encounters, he had experienced the problems of the constitution of socialism firsthand, and he was very well versed in state politics within both capitalism and socialism. In fact, as stated in the introduction of this book, he died at the hands of a guerrilla tribunal that prosecuted and condemned him to death for his political mistakes. Ironically, in his unjustly ignored novel *Pobrecito poeta que era yo,* he predicts his own death, poeticizing precisely the conflicting nature of youth's political commitment.

Combining all these experiences, Dalton felt compelled to disengage the writing of revolutionary culture from the dry, military, guerrilla prose of revolutionary heroism popularized by Che. In becoming institutionalized, Che's prose had lost the vigor and the freshness of the guerrillas (guerrilla troops), and had become a cliché. Being grounded in the city rather than in the countryside, Dalton pushed aside the patristic orientation of *montaña* literature and embraced irony as a means of recruiting people to his cause, proposing a different literary culture as a means of communication. His festive, disrespectful, and jocular tone highlights a new type of revolutionary modernity, one that bespeaks a generational change that we can interpret today as being on the way to perestroika.

In Dalton there is a clear sense of distancing between that masculine New I and the *campesino* masses. There is no longer the assumption of a ready-made collective subject of which to speak. A classic passage distinguishing the old patristic from a new version of revolutionary culture is: "Socialism should signify progress toward pleasure. And that is where one trips over the impenetrable, knitted brow of the dissident consciousness" (Dalton 246).

Students of revolutionary epistemologies must acknowledge the difference between stages of revolutionary written culture. In Che, the constitution of the revolutionary masculine subject tends to become the New Man and is not formulated as a question but written as a definition. Che is totally acritical. He speaks of what he sees without questioning what he thinks or writes.

Che totally disregards the ideological reproductions of his speech. In him, in any event, it is neither the peasantry (*campesinado*) nor the agrarian societies, but rather the proud military ontology of the rebel that is in question. In Dalton, by contrast, there is a quest, an inquiry, doubt, a search. By the time we reach Ramírez, the question has already become politically acute. The most pertinent questions concerning the ontologies and epistemologies of being and existing for the *campesino* masses, subjects of revolutionary transformations in agrarian societies, had come home to roost. The *campesino*'s relationship to economic changes, the politics of war, and the transition to productive and distributive justice must be grasped. Had the Nicaraguan leadership comprehended what the masses were all about, they would not have been so unfortunately surprised at the liminal moment when the electoral vote so eloquently spoke of mass discontent.

The Collective, Plural Subject

Whereas Che's narratives concentrate on only one of the social sectors, the largest and the one he considers most crucial, that of the *campesinado* living in the rural zones, Ramírez's concept of *people* inscribes a situation of greater political complexity and, consequently, involves a broader spectrum of society. The *campesino* remains an enigmatic referent whose meaning was only carefully sought at the end. In their studies of the intersection between elite and peasant cultures, the Indian Subaltern Studies Group warns scholars against narratives written by the national intellectual elite. They propose to look for the constitution of the subaltern in other types of narratives, for instance in the history of criminality. In this respect, the legal code constitutes a better source, complicating the concepts of peasantry.[7]

In their political analysis, the theoreticians of the Nicaraguan Revolution turn gradually from the country to the city as the site of revolutionary struggle, setting aside the problem of the *campesinos* as a class and turning toward a more complex and transnationally linked population. As the political strategy shifts sites, so does the concept of the *people*, which gradually incorporates a more diverse social universe. This pluralism signals the fact that the vanguard party is entertaining a more comprehensive view of the people than that with which they, as leaders, had previously had to wrestle. Class analysis demanded more nuances, and was expressed as a balance of forces, as the struggle within a sophisticated ideological marketplace. Concepts of ethnicity and gender come to the fore and begin to appear in the written political arena. The dominating groups constituting the "national bourgeoisie," the oligarchy and educated groups, cannot be disregarded. During the last Somoza administration they represented a force. The crux of the matter is, then, that a revised and restored collective had to emerge, and that it became increasingly differentiated within the strictly political narratives.

The base, masses, people, to whom the idea of the "dictatorship" of the proletariat had to be sold, was more contentious, and the political narratives of
the revolution, like those of the bourgeoisie, required a wider view of the
social spectrum in order to gain national and international viability.

The new collective subject expressing the joining of the party with the
masses, therefore, is constituted as the emerging social subject of political alliances. It is a subject who moves comfortably within the space of common
front politics and who connects with similar structures in the international
arena. A paramount example in Nicaragua is the so-called Group of Twelve,
already a governmental concept constituting a provisional state power. This
grouping represents the varied and often contradictory interests of the
church (two priests), industry (businessmen, semiproducers), and the intelligentsia (a lawyer, an economist, and a doctor of education). However, at
the moment of victory, the national collective subject changes its nature.
It becomes richer, adding the components of multiethnic, polyclassist, and
gendered sectors enlarging the group constituting the collective subject. The
base, people, masses, turn into what it is, an undifferentiated multitude, a
term belabored by Carmen Naranjo's novel *Diario de una multitud* (Diary of
a Multitude), an unwieldy reproduction of the national/international con-
glomerate, encompassing

> recently named functionaries, plaintiffs of every sort, relatives of the soldiers
> from the old army . . . mothers of fighting guerrillas . . . mayors from the
> most distant villages . . . new ambassadors . . . owners of livestock farms . . .
> foreign investors appearing out of nowhere . . . campesinos. (Ramírez 123)[8]

This baroque notion of collectivity did not exist in Che's guerrilla narrative, nor did the idea of Government or that of State, just as the idea of government or of state power did not exist for the insurgents at the beginning
of the twentieth century—Sandino, for instance. These insurgent organizations at most developed the notion of *patria*, a proto-state, a familiar notion
of fatherland and brotherhood, a polis with no particular idea of economic
productivity and social organization.

What is in question in this New common front concept of the collective is
the inclusion of nontraditional social sectors, Others. At the crossroads of
inclusion and exclusion we must highlight the structural analogy between
woman and *campesinado*/peasantry, between the feminine and the collective, the revolutionary pursued, as the persecuted revolutionary. Notice that
even in Ramírez's narrative, in which the collective represents a common
front politics, women are excluded. The Group of Twelve, for example, is a

group of men, and their concept of intersectorial alliances remains essentially masculine, phallocentric, accommodating neither *campesinado* nor woman. Doña Violeta Barrios de Chamorro, the only woman in the group, later to become the president of the nation, was chosen at that moment to fill the position of her husband and to represent their class position. Doña Violeta was not chosen to represent women. Therefore, in the representation of the representations, revolutionary narratives, like revolutionary organizations and institutions, are negligent. As we noted earlier, they overlooked the question of "difference," and in so doing, they duplicated the liberal bourgeois epistemes they intended to displace.

Women in the Mountain: The Proto-State

To illustrate this neglect, the role assigned to woman within the fatherland/ brotherhood polis of the proto-state—for example, within the guerrilla camp—serves as an indicator of a stale and obsolescent concept of women. In the foundational narratives of El Che, as well as in the narratives that reproduce his ontology, women and the *campesinado* are processed in a language betraying bourgeois liberal sedimentation. Both are couched in a very conservative language reminiscent of the religious colonialism that the guerrilla theoreticians seek to reject. They reproduce an attitude hovering somewhere between populism and paternalism, remaining faithful to the old essentialisms.

In the primary organization of the guerrilla army, as in the most complex nuclei of the guerrilla organization in the liberated zones, within a kind of proto-state organization, woman "embodies those roles proper to her sex, for example, in the kitchen, in the infirmary, teaching, sewing, as a courier, a bearer of tenderness" (Che 1972, 122). Woman becomes part of that revolutionary social subject within the organizations of the proto-state as "a bearer of," because she is "less transcendent than." The proto-democratic revolutionary state in the liberated areas theorizes strategically that "it is easier to maintain her in her domestic duties," even when "she can perfectly replace a man . . . even in the case of lack of manpower to bear arms, even though this is a rare occurrence" (124).

As the guerrilla war advances and seizes more and more territorial zones, as it becomes less a war and more a social organization, and schools and hospitals are established, the masculine I, instead of widening, narrows, invaginates, begins a process of reversal during which women are separated from the circuit of the New heroic economies. Che's openness, and his shifting from an epistemology of exclusion to one more democratic, rests in the reassurance that women do "not create . . . conflicts of a sexual sort," and that they can transport "objects of a certain size, like bullets . . . in special belts they wear beneath their skirts" (123).

In the proto-state governed by the revolutionaries in the liberated areas, hospitals and schools coexist within the military organization. These provisional bureaucracies will then become the permanent structures of the revolutionary government, ordering civil life. Developing out of these proto-structures cultivated in the Mountain, in these bureaucracies women already reoccupy their traditional conservative positions. Thus, the revolutionaries easily and thoughtlessly reproduce repressive social structures. In the hospitals, for instance, no woman is mentioned as nurse, much less as doctor; and in this silence, women are nowhere in evidence. Whenever she is briefly permitted to enter the scene of heroics, the conceptual/syntactical structures reproduce Ramírez's "little man": her participation is minimized ab initio. Women, like "little men," transport weapons, circulating within empty epistemological spaces.

Carrying the explosives around her sex, in the lower abdominal area, the same place in which the army was ordered to shoot Che, is described as merely an expedient method. Like Ramírez's "little man," woman enters the scene to be mute. Woman is inconspicuous, invisible, and therefore, presumably, she can escape aggression and violence more readily than men. Woman's entrance into the heroic economies, loaded with bullets beneath her skirt, clearly demarcates a separation between the people and the masculine I of the military strategists writing the texts, whose author(ity) is exercised in and through the reproduction of ideologies and the dynamics of power, his power, which by definition is control and exclusion.

The authoritative guerrilla narratives of El Che are, in this sense, for women, as the writing of his diary was for the campesinos, traditional authoritarian narratives. For, in representing women and peasantry, revolutionary thinking takes the same path, and reproduces the preexistent epistemes. Women are, thus, quasi men, incomplete men, and sexuality continues to be a danger zone undermining "the morale of the troops." Therefore, both women and guerrillas must be policed. The eroticism of the revolution, we can say in passing, is born with its hands tied, militarized, authoritarianized, and, like the guerrillera, Christianized. The phallus and the logos maintain their hegemony.

This apparent excursus draws an analogy between two empty spaces, that of the perception of gender and that of the perception of the campesinado, during the processes of the constitution of the proto-state, at the moment of insurgency. The traditional concept of women becomes a conceptual lacuna inscribed in the formation of the proto-state, later reproduced by the state. During the 1992 elections this negligence became negation.

At the moment of casting the vote—if there is ever a "popular" election—or at the stark level of the open expression of feelings—when this is permitted—the voice of these subalterns emerges as a surprise element. Error becomes obfuscation, a change of perception. Losing gives focus. It is stunning that a political organization, born tied to the masses and purporting to represent those masses, could be so startled. For that surprise betrays the anti-popular element of their founding concepts, and of their paternalistic, populist exercise of power, as exemplified in the sudden realization of

> schemes of popular convocation no longer functioning, aging or never correct styles of authority, above all in the rural areas committed to the war; improvisations, arrogance, loss of the perception of substantial elements of the political reality. (Ramírez 147)

So there are, in the language of Dickens, "times of madness" (117) or an "epoch of incredulity" (127), the belief, in *Popol Vuh,* that "always dawns." At the Party or intellectual level, this popular process of "deception" or "treachery"—of whom? against whom?—was christened in Nicaragua with the name of Güegüense. Güegüense is a play staging the revenge of the *ladino* masses upon the Spanish government. The name of the protagonist, Güegüense, has served to designate the behavior of the "hypocritical" peasant masses who stabbed the revolution in the back. That is to say, the revolutionaries went back to the first instances of literary representation, to the classical literature of the colony, to borrow figures of speech to signal the rupture between the government and the masses. Güegüense, as a historical term defining the essence of *mestizaje,* covers up the lack of popular representation in the *Frente.* In this figure, a sentiment already narrated by Che was reproduced. The revolutionaries retrack and retrace the colonial mentality, and the relationship between the Crown and its vice royalties with their colonial subjects. The old colonial epistemes were again retrieved and recycled, as was the sensibility representing the *campesinos,* the Indians, and the creoles, as Severo Martínez Peláez says, in their fatherland. But also the question is newly stated: how was it that the voters elected "the trifling alternative of the right"? (Ramírez 146).

Between speaking the deception and the deception itself, the same process of literary construction serving the anonymous author of *Güegüense* mediates here to illustrate the government's method of managing the problematic distances between the anti-popular leaders and the masses. Around the corner from the revolutionary processes, the revolutionaries leading the vanguard come across an unknown national collective subject. The revolutionaries discovered they had not known the collective subject, constructing instead the concept of mob, crowd, of intrasectorial, amorphous masses, and a concept of pluralism that aims more at the mediation of the Party with the other Parties than with the masses, the Party and government as mediating administrative transnational agencies. The concepts of mass, people, women, the subjugated were left behind. And in the representation of themselves, they reproduced those social subjects as subjects of alienation and estrangement.

In the arc described by the first and last Latin American revolutions, in the distance covered by the question in Che's texts through those of Ramírez, there is always a distress. In this chapter I have pursued an investigation of the nature of the responses given to that distress; a distress—if not the most legitimate distress—peculiar to the sixties generation. My dilemma was multifaceted: my aim was, first, to demarcate the moments of conceiving the transition between the masculine I and the collective subject in the constitution of the revolutionary subject as epistemology of the revolution; second, to underscore the transition's tensions, blank moments, empty spaces. Apart from those indicated above with such clarity by Ramírez, where the masculine I of the revolutionary and the collective subject of the peasantry part company, the most profound are those of gender, located exactly in the same place. In the symbolic processes, masses and people merge in the feminine, as representation of the unincluded subjugated, as the unasked. In these moments, as Ramírez says, word becomes flesh, body; but whose flesh, whose body? The collapsing of peasantry and the feminine is not very evident, for literature has granted the peasantry—that is, class—some respect. However, in representing them, doubt, distress, and confusion predominate.

In addition to the processes of representation of women and peasantry, there are those related to culture and politics, the written and the oral world. Ramírez is more correct in that which he makes explicit, when thinking that in literacy campaigns "the two Nicaraguas" were encountered for the first time, and, falling once again into the copula as idea of belonging and procreation, he would say that "one was entering into the other in order to give birth to the new man" (128). And in the formation of the guerrilla and of the Party, in the revolutionary organization, had they not perhaps thought of schools?

In recycling old epistemologies—for example, Christianity—and the patristic prevalent in the narratives of and about Che, we find more than one code and one clue: the New is constructed with the language and logic of the old, and the subjects meet again in the territorial maps of the phallocentric logos.

CHAPTER SEVEN

Politico-Military/Poetic Narratives

Who?

As far as I'm concerned they can cut my head off. . . . I've fallen into the
hands of these people because I was stupid, irresponsible, fearful, because
I drank too much beer, lectured, ate shit, because I was candid, antihistorical,
I volunteered too much, was undisciplined, disoriented, and crazy.
Roque Dalton, *Pobrecito poeta que era yo*

Almost twenty years after Che wrote his elegiac definition of the guerrilla as
social subject of the revolutionary struggle, Roque Dalton published his
novel *Pobrecito poeta que era yo* (Poor Little Poet That I Was) (1984).[1] In contrast to Che's military prose, Dalton's is an experimental novel about the
eclectic ways of constituting a revolutionary subject. Dalton was a literary
man, an outstanding poet and an excellent prose writer. He was very well
read. He read any and all Western literatures, and, like most literary men
from El Salvador, he was in awe of Salarrué, a Salvadoran prose writer
considered the founder of modern Salvadoran literature. As we pointed out
above, Dalton was interested in the polemics surrounding socialist realism,
in particular the Brecht-Lukács debate. The climax of his novel, when the
character is about to make his most vital decision, what could be called
the "free land or death" moment, is a tribute to Brecht. It is at this liminal
moment that the protagonist antihero enters into a dialogue with Brecht in

which the subtleties and doubts besetting revolutionary decisions and consciousness are underscored. Brecht and Salarrué, then, are the two figures lurking behind the difficulties and nuances in representing popular subjects. The fragment used as this chapter's epigraph is one of the many instances in which the engaged militant of the Party racks his brain, faced with the inevitable question of whether to surrender or die for his beliefs. In this, Dalton and Ramírez find themselves at a cultural crossroads, between literary and political constructions of subjectivities. Between this antiheroic subject and the earlier hero, as between the earlier hero and the "little man," there is a chasm. This contrast serves to mark the separation of politico-military narratives from those that are strictly poetic. Literature intercepts politics and strenuously competes with it in the formation of "national revolutionary cultures."

In reading Dalton's narrative, what first strikes the political reader is the drastic change in tone. All the solemnity of the previous heroic-military prose is gone, and, in its stead, a Salarruean jocular, jeering note establishes the priorities of an antiheroic common man. The great Western traditions of the patristic encoded heroes are neglected. Earthly and flawed characters come to take their place. His style, then, immediately speaks to and comments upon the need to polemicize the constitution of a politico-poetic subject, and to grapple with a more complex man than that postulated before by both militant and standard revolutionary state literatures, for example, Soviet socialist realism—a narrative style he derides. The argument for making a distinction between these traditions—Latin American, Soviet, Western—based on this critical position is only possible after glasnost. However, arguing that fiction writers and guerrillas have a different political stance, the former a more pronational (Salvadoran) or continental (Latin American) one and the latter a more pro-Soviet one, is gratuitous; as Partha Chatterjee would advise us, it does not deliver us from the cultural geographies of the Western traditions.[2] On the contrary, it makes criticism veer in the direction of the hazardous zones of "bourgeois humanism," and the "imperial subject."[3]

Yet, what makes for stirring reading is that Dalton runs the entire gamut of Latin American literature, using any and every historical style to frame his protagonists. His style is grounded in the practice of the Salvadoran writer, Salarrué, whose method is to listen to, and then write about, the people. With this as his touchstone, Dalton soars over the European debate entertained by Brecht and Lukács on how to write the revolutionary heroes, secularizing them. It is clear from his gleeful scenes and dialogues that he forswears Soviet cultural politics. For him there is something fundamentally wrong with their simplistic construction of heroism, which is likely to disintegrate as socialism unfolds. He does not agree that the representation of the hero should exclude all petty human traits. We can perceive in him some alignment with the happy formulation of Althusser's concept of ideology, which, if applied to socialist realism, would come to be the imaginary relationship of the poetic with the real subject of revolutionary processes:

> For me, socialism remains a bourgeois phase in the Marxist history of humanity. And I purposefully say that on a morning in which I find myself particularly lucid, since it's been almost a week since I've had a single drop of alcohol. (283)

The substitution of elegy for farce results in a jocularly festive presentation of the urban guerrilla, not as leader-vanguard-cadre, but as militant base. The revolutionary is, therefore, a stammering subject, improvising upon entering the scene. No longer is he the guerrilla of the first Che, all sacrifice and discipline. Neither is he the wearied New Man of Omar Cabezas. He isn't the hallucinating guerrilla analogous to Borge's conqueror, nor the brave one obedient to every test of Ramírez/Rivera's.

He is a frightened man, half-base, half-cadre, who revels in displaying his fear, his astonishment; a man whose comfort has ended and who, with a heavy heart and terrible anguish, gives himself up as lost: "I've always been for compromise, I don't need to repeat it. The only thing is, there are compromises and then there are compromises. The compromise that I love is the most splendid exercise of liberty" (270).

He is also a man with a sense of humor who delights in showing the reverse of the heroic subject and looks around him wondering fearfully about public opinion: "What's Schaffick [Haendal, the leader] going to say?" (391). In other words, this is a blown-up Marcos, the despondent Cuban whose profile and character Che discusses in his diary. The other is now either boss, partner, another militant/friend, a consciousness of the collective in the masculine I, a collective subject before whom he, the base, must show—or appear to show—integrity. Dalton stresses that man is not made of wood and does not start out by thinking about "the affront to national sovereignty [but] about his own skin" (416).

His peculiar way of approaching the issue of subject constitution, however, must not be explained solely through his poetic bent. The years he lived within socialist societies, his grappling with the cultural policies of revolutionary states, coupled with his experience as a journalist and a militant of the Salvadoran insurgency, bestows upon him an experience from which other Central American male writers will later also profit—for example, Morales, Arias, Ramírez. In this way one can argue that Dalton's novel is a sample of revolutionary writing situated at a fertile crossroads, simultaneously benefiting from the experiences of socialist state building by the revolutionary group(s), and by urban and rural insurgencies. In contrast with the literature written inside the revolutionary state—after the vanguard party has become administrative government—this narrative sets itself up as an example, negotiating the plotting of the relationship between a heroic clandestine subject in the mountain (that is, Che's *guerrillero*), and the flesh-and-blood, antiheroic party militant engaged in the urban struggle organized by the Communist Party in El Salvador. Dalton's pages are fraught with images of the formative process of the masculine I-as-clandestine-militant-revolutionary postulated as Marxist-Leninist (Morales's Machista-Leninist).

In considering the problem of the constitution of the masculine I from several positions, Dalton runs the gamut of a literary scale that ranges from the sophisticated perspective of the prose and the epistemes of the double in Jorge Luis Borges to the most simplistic formulas of socialist realism, reviewing, on the way, the narrative adventures of Batman and Superman, Elastic Man, the Invisible Man, Kafka and Camus, and the narrative structures of detective novels. Any sense of authority representing the revolutionary dynamics between the masculine "I" is circumscribed within the poetic terrain to which politics subordinates itself, and is true to the problems proper to writing representation.

As the poor poet that he was, Dalton willingly addresses the question of the constitution of the subject as a militant intellectual, the member of a social sector not necessarily perceived by the Party revolutionaries as revolutionary—all the more reason, then, to attempt to grasp or suggest an explanation for their political commitment. Dalton's lyrical masculine I is concerned with the following questions: Why does a writer want to be part of a bloody insurgency? What propels him to act politically? What is the point at which intellectuals bind themselves to class struggle, and why and how do they disengage from the revolutionary processes? And, in passing, what are the problems pertaining to their self-representation in literature? Many of his characters are politically engaged Salvadoran poets, like himself, and their discussions reproduce, without drama, the troubles of a generation, Dalton's own—politically very well informed—generation:

The writing of literature in our countries implies, to a certain degree, the betrayal of the fatherland. . . . In writing modern literature . . . we are translators . . . of forms elaborated by others. . . . That's why I can dismiss the accusation against me that Roberto and José have made: that of being an alienator, one who looks to Europe, a victim of colonization. The only response I have is that it is my fatherland that has alienated me. Once again, the communists have surprised me with their contradictions: What's the point of internationalism if, while seeking more effective levels of expression, thinking and writing, in a sense, from there to here, they accuse us of being victims of colonization? . . . The only thing that exists in this world as literature is bourgeois literature. . . . When they speak of proletarian literature they always call to mind Gorky, Babel, Brecht, Vladimir Mayakovsky, Nazim Hikmet. . . . None of them, as far as I know, lived on a factory worker's salary, none of them made bricks, nor did they habitually haul bales of cotton on the docks. (283)

After much ado about participation and a savory, humorous portrayal of a political debate with others as well as with himself, in the chapter entitled "José," intellectual commitment finally skirts the edges of prison, torture, treason, and death—the spaces and proofs of the heroic posited by the military narratives. In order to engage himself, José must first surmount the geographical boundaries of his native mountains, home to the *campesinos,* where, according to those military narratives, the creation of the New Man takes place. He must travel abroad and learn the social realities of other regions, in a habitat out of all proportion to his native region. His journey traverses a geography that is mapped as mountain becoming city, and world. Its range includes the social topographies of the socialist countries and the advantages and disadvantages of international solidarity, as well as the cultural geographies of Western societies, both capitalist and socialist. But, although the character is projected against a broader physical and cultural backdrop, he is finally brought back home to his own national, urban geography. The final trial, in which he ultimately commits himself to die for the revolution, is staged in a tiny prison cell in El Salvador.

José and his ilk never openly bear the name of the New Man, however much his character, pointing in the same direction, appears as a troubling representation of the New in Man. There is no question that the poets are not guerrillas of the mountain but rather devoted intellectuals who wish to escape the easy political schemes traced out in the theoretical map of the novel. It could, perhaps, be said that Dalton wants to make do with human frailty and make political matters an everyday affair by casting them as being in the interests of the masses. He wants to strip political literature of all its elementary solemnity in order to de-sacralize it and convert it into a com-

monplace matter, and a subject for internal debate. Thus, in order to construct his partisan narrative, every aspect of heroic life—courage, bravery,
theoretical knowledge, sacrifice, schemes, the sacred, and, above all, the Party
organization—is subject to ridicule. That, I argue, is his way of facilitating
the bonding with "masses"—his method.

In order to get some bearing on these difficulties, Dalton's political characters seek pleasure and look at the joyful side of political commitment.
They take the arid political pamphlets with a grain of salt, and regard their
ready-made answers and clichés as good fun:

> Did I tell you about Bebo and Pablo Armando? . . . In London they were, for
> me, ancient postwar Ottoman emperors. . . . I always felt like a bumpkin next
> to them: they spoke French and English, their hats fit properly, they'd been
> reviewed in the *New York Times,* and they supervised Cuban offices, which in
> Europe are resplendent. . . . If I mention them . . . it's because I'm thinking
> that since I insisted on writing an article, through it we could send a letter to
> that imbecilic, presumptuous, and opportunistic young clown, that lousy
> poet with the cute wife, Yevgeni Yevtuschenko. (131)

Dalton expresses pleasure mainly through self-deprecating humor. Irony
turned inward is a strength that helps to resist tyranny—of the government
and of the partisan structures. But irony as Dalton uses it, and as style, is
double-edged. When he attempts to speak more broadly for the collective in
theoretical form, his stylistics get stuck in the spaces between fiction and the
elements of his own biography. The implications of his characteristic style
become apparent if we accept the argument that Dalton died at the hands
of a guerrilla group in El Salvador precisely because they misunderstood
and/or rejected his playful irony:

> I had to prepare a response to ridicule Chano, knowing that he would try to
> smash me in public for arriving late. . . . He has managed to establish the
> thesis of "organic anticommunism," that is to say, the thesis according to which
> there are certain people (among whom he includes himself, of course) who
> are anticommunists from birth. (33)

Dalton's poetic-political narrative is not naive. It is far from being the
candid narrative of the first insurgent moments in which an authoritarian
and definitive prose displayed in its seams the crudity of its theory. Che's
prose demarcated the first moments of a thought, a simplicity that evoked
the complexity of an episteme. Dalton's, on the contrary, is a narrative of unrelenting argumentation and discussion, of dialogue and problematization
of what it meant in 1965 to become politically engaged. The intentional irony
and the bawdy spirit deceive, for they make us consider heroism as a depre-

ciated commodity, when he is indeed showing us precisely the opposite. Heroism is a transaction, serious business. His writing is a narrative of the heroic last stand brought into the everyday and on its way back to thinking about the individual. For at the same time the protagonists speak—supposedly in the name of the collective, the Party, and the Organization—they focus on the concrete situation of the masculine I as an individual being. That is, they individually return again and again to take a closer look at that "(petit-)bourgeois individualist" subject. Perhaps the genre compels a representation of the individual in his relationship of repression and confrontation with the body politic (and its attendant body-politics) that "national" and international state powers exert over him. How must such an individual react in the face of those pressures so that the enemy does not catch him? Is he, at least in fiction, allowed to cave in? Or must he always make do with sacrifice and proletarian internationalism? In no other way could we understand his invocation of Brecht in what man is, or should be, in his individual drama, reminding his dear comrade Brecht of "the dialectic of my moments and your moments, within our limitations as unrepeatable beings" (428).

Pobrecito poeta que era yo—Poor Little Poet That I Was—is, then, only in appearance a complacent text. Dalton writes the will to heroism as a paradoxical and mind-boggling series of decisions, such as come to bear on the mind of the individual. In doing so, he avoids some of the pitfalls of Che's representation of his *guerrilleros* and their heroism, coupled with the consequent projection of their behavior in the unexpected realities of *Sociolism*, that is, a government by *socios* (buddies, cohorts). Sidestepping the theoretical thinking of the hero, he writes to make acceptable some of the human traits the guerrilla will bring to the formation of his state-building process. His New society, therefore, will not have to contend with the public, long-lasting negation of some of the all too human traits the antihero brings into its constitution. For the hero is enveloped in both self-pity and self-aggrandizement, and in glossing the suffering of the body and putting the body in the place of words, he agonizes dreadfully.

To talk it as they walk it, with black humor and irony, is the strategy that produces the centering of the subject as a split individual, which justifies Dalton's bringing myriad stylistic devices to bear upon its representation. Thus, for example, to convey the experience of being a political prisoner, he believes there is no style better than that of Kafka and Camus. If the writer is to plot persecution, arraignment, debriefing, and cross-examination, the structure of the detective novel finds no parallel. As far as the writing of revolutionary utopias is concerned, the revolutionary models offered by Batman and Superman are unbeatable. For discussing the relationship of the individual to his social environment, there is no better device than Borges's idea of the double.

This secular example illustrates, concretely, how the relationship between the lyrical masculine I and the partisan collective is stated through polemical, argumentative, linguistic strategies. Bringing the history of literature to bear on his text locates his narrative in a dialogic position with Western Literature. Supported by the prestige of scores of literary strategies, he scoffs at the allegedly reactionary character of literary forms, as diagnosed by Lukács (Kafka vs. Balzac), and joins the debate on how to treat revolutionary themes. In his characteristically iconoclastic vein, he comments on ready-made phrases and clichés, for example, "in order to speak as a Marxist" (403), "Engels backed me up with his pounding away in his theses about the transformation of man through work" (410), "in order to avoid making myself look like a Lukácsian rationalist" (413), "and here I believe what would be Marxizing would be to speak of my petit-bourgeois prejudices" (417). Mocking the sacred, or subsuming drama into the comical, is the index of his freedom as a revolutionary writer writing within a revolutionary state. I have no doubt the audience he has in mind is made up of a familiarized left-leaning elite—the nongullible left—who understand, and even appreciate, the in-jokes. In this respect, his prose addresses the initiated, those few who know who is who and what to mock from within. In other words, it indicates the addressee is a member of the famed collective subject. This could perhaps be one of the best interpretations of "within the revolution complete freedom; against the revolution, none."

It is his speaking from within that permits him to play with the utopias of the construction of the masculine I as "anti-imperialist champion[s] at the level of Superman or Batman or Captain Marvel" (414) and also to parody insurgencies, such as the projects to liberate Brazil, using comic hyperbole—the liberation will be undertaken "by means of a collective trap for his ten thousand generals, who had been invited to a colossal banquet financed with the robbery of the central safe in the First National City Bank of New York" (414). Displacements, games, and familiar geographies, James Bond-style, permit him to project a lockup in which the insurgents will poison the enemy with filet mignon, taking them to a concentration camp in Albania "anesthetized with the drug that can be injected into champagne . . . that which would implicate logistical problems complicated enough so that they would enrich the dream" (414).

Nevertheless, self-directed irony is not relied upon to the exclusion of other methods. It is only one of his many literary devices. What the novel plots, indeed, are scores of genuine doubts about the difficulties of bringing revolutionary epistemes to bear on life. His posture against bullheaded, facile, blind radicalism is very clear. In a minor key, I can suggest that in the refined cuisine of the bourgeoisie, for instance, he underscores utopian elements created in counterposition to the long narratives of hunger and difficulties, to those scenes where the guerrilla provisions are very scarce in the Mountain, and the guerrilla starves in the narratives of Che, Cabezas, Payeras, and Borge.

In its literary-political foreplay, everything is subject to contradiction. For instance, the committed masculine cadre entertains the idea of the Party as a possible alterity, as a contradiction. The Party is not only not a given but also in some cases very much a becoming; not fact but practically counter-fact. Within the representation of the human psyche, there are cases of re-version, as when one of his alter-egos, Roberto, is weary of the military and entertains the idea of the demilitarization of Party structures, or cases of un-foreseen or unexpected commitments stemming from psychological needs, for instance, the behavior of the prison guards. In the novel this paltry police force most approximates the popular. However, they are the popular and the antipopular, that is, that which is repressive. It is certainly uncanny to have one of them unexpectedly ask the political prisoner what Communism is, and what it is like. Needless to say, the protagonist skips the answer.

In constructing alterities—the Other, stranger, enemy—there is concern. He is no longer the incarnation of the dumb and evil. On the contrary, a respectful realistic prose delineates a respectable enemy. The CIA agent is his equal, his homologue, the first real contender introduced to him in the prison. He is a man "speaking a language very close to that of cheap detective novels, and there is no doubt that this language is very effective" (424). The language of the CIA adversary is, then, very different from that of the John Q. Publics who guard him, very different from the muteness of the "little man." Before him the guerrilla-prisoner must be on his best behavior. He must learn how to speak. He must be at his peak, on a par with his prosecutor, searching for a "Spanish as expressive as it is refined, that might offer [one] advantages in the dialogue" (419), in order to establish and sustain a linguistic duel, for the fellow knows how to cut him off, reducing him to "an almost syllabic babbling" (419).

It is beyond irony that in the duel between the guerrilla-prisoner-protagonist and the CIA operative, the latter comes to represent national legitimacy, the only Salvadoran voice, national force before the "national" forces of order, more of a man than the "little man," and the guerrilla-New Man put together. The narrative is cast in accusatory legal prose the moment the law is reduced to detecting anticommunist plots, and in this moment the urban guerrilla, José, comes to occupy the place of the people. To paraphrase Guha's dictum, the subaltern appears in print only when he can be narrated as a criminal.

In tracking down communism and communists, the republic displays its faltering autonomy and legitimacy, the caesura in the codes embodying national sovereignty. The CIA operative shows him clearly the processes of denationalization, that the republic and the nation are in vain, for the crimes against "Salvadoraneity" are spoken by a North American, and, as an even greater luxury, they are spoken in perfect vernacular, although with a strong English accent. Spivak's idea, that it is "through accessing the cultural aspects of imperialism [that] the colonized countries accede to national sentiments" (245), finds in these discussions of nation and "nation" its counterpart.

I am of the opinion that in considering the construction of the revolutionary masculine I, Dalton provides a better methodology. His departure from individual self-doubt, frailty, and vulnerability, rather than from all the strongholds of Che's ontological taxonomies, the masculine I of the religious patristic, makes his revolutionary a more credible construction. In their literary games and replays, Dalton's protagonists manage to demonstrate the nuances of the difficulties of conjoining those two social subjects—the flesh and blood and the ideal New Man—and to postulate that only through contortions of mind and body can that masculine I reach an approximation of the collective by inversion.

Who Is Who?

Ascertaining the sex of the writer is as difficult as ascertaining the sex of the angels, says de Certeau. Franco affirms:

> It's not about ascertaining if the female writers have [sex] specific themes or a style different from that of male writers, but about exploring the relations of power. . . . [T]here is not ONE feminine writing yet there is . . . but yes . . . intertextuality is necessarily a battlefield where woman confronts the exclusions and the marginalizations of the past. (1986, 41)[4]

In this respect, to maintain that the guerrilla texts, in their majority, are spaces resolutely masculine, is to state the obvious. From there "the gaps, the silences and absences of discourse and representation to which the feminine has traditionally been relegated can be seen" (Showalter 37). In my readings of these texts, I have been arguing that the copula individual/collective is an unstable representation. It raises severe epistemological doubts, not only in its claim to represent the subaltern masses-people-troops-base, but in the analogy between the subjects of these terms and the place of the feminine. With respect to the politics of gender, we have already observed how the inclusion of women occurs at a metaphoric level, as the

> figure of woman is pervasively instrumental in the shifting of the function of discursive systems. . . . Should one notice this metaphoric division of sexuality (in the woman's case, sex is of course identical with selfhood or consciousness) as property to be passed on or not from father to lover? (Spivak 26–27)

Woman, as a symbolic object of exchange, cannot be overlooked. Woman is like the feminine in the Mountain, which the guerrillas mention but do not pause to reflect upon. Thus, rapture and rape are the conditions of the birth of a nation; or, rather, the feminine is track and trace of the family. In the work of both Dalton and Mario Roberto Morales (about whom more later), I wish to argue the hegemonic presence of woman as a masculine construction and, therefore, textual construction as sexual construction.

In Dalton, all subtlety breaks down when woman comes into the narrative. Woman exists pejoratively in the text as an organ for male sexual satisfaction. The representation of woman as vaginal is extremely deceptive, for it does not address any question pertaining to women's sexuality. In woman as "revolutionary pussy"—the pejorative phrase repeated ad nauseam by the guerrilla revolutionaries we are about to explore—there is very little that is womanly. Just to give an example, the relation(ship) of, say, the vagina and the clitoris as agents of feminine sexuality is totally unknown to the revolutionary New Man. The proof is that they receive no mention at all in the text. As a matter of fact, if we push the argument and if we are to judge by the positioning of the names and adjectives, woman puts in an appearance as metaphor for homosexual relationships or, worse, as a metaphor for national rape. Men speak of women's sexuality mostly describing the back and not the front of the body. Woman is, therefore, nothing but a "sweet butt," a "kissable little butt" (35), a "torso, waist, curved perfection of a thigh . . . and the firmness of the right breast," in sum, "a beautiful and healthy Salvadoran sex" (37), "whore," "friend." Woman is thus an outline, a sketch, a morality, and as we saw earlier in Guardia's portrayal of nation, a metonymy.

In the moment preceding torture, woman is a palliative, fulfillment of desire and masculine expression of bonding and solidarity, the only moment where all men are equal: "If you want to be with a girl one of these nights [the 'little policeman' advises the antihero], it will be sufficient that the Mister know. We are all men and you have to understand these things" (Dalton 433). And, as in Borge, in Dalton there are affections that kill: "using her nightgown as a thick rope, he began to squeeze, laughing hoarsely—I should strangle you, you silly fool—" (38). And all women open their legs: "The women scatter themselves in ones, twos, or threes on the sofas, or the rug, opening their legs like someone complaining about his own history" (47).

In this sense, the masculine sexuality of the revolutionary flaunts its ignorance by revealing anxieties about death, faintness, and failings, the *petit mort* (de Certeau's play on words, remorse, *remords*) of orgasm, but all his eroticism is separate and apart in his unswervingly masculine revolutionary narrative, in which militancy and insurgency are a man's thing and the construction of the New nation something completely phallic. Man, here, means men.

In closing, I want to call attention to the body as a masculine body and extrapolate it, in its sexuality, to the feminine. In the very first place, the body of the hero is represented in all its fragility and vulnerability. The speaking I is the feeling I, and therefore is the I of the enduring and suffering body. That is the urban guerrilla subject position. Within this representation of the body and of fear, the choice of smells and the selection of body parts represented stands out. In general, men have no smell in guerrilla literature. They go around filthy, like walking wounded, as if hallucinating, ragged things, but they neither smell nor stink, or they smell or reek of backpacks, leather, hammocks. Man is in general modest with respect to the smells of his own sex: for instance, the reek of sweat, smegma, or testicles is never mentioned. Odors are, as a rule, reserved for women, who smell of brine, permanganate, blood, fish—rotten.

In Dalton, the representation of the world of the prison—more in the language of Hieronymus Bosch than of the Soviet novel *This Is How Steel Was Tempered*—frames a dirty body of acidic aromas, urine, dirt and fifteen-day mustaches, a body like the one in that single instance, in Che's diary, of "burps, farts and vomits and diarrhea" (1968, 185); that is to say, a physicality, not a sexuality.[5] Or the body "more exclusively aromatized" (417) like that of the CIA operative. In prison the "other" was distinguished by his odors; because he smelled like a respectable man, "I hear only the voice of the boss, who comes smelling of lotion," says Morales (12).[6]

The mouth is a privileged place: it is the place of speech but also of hunger, that which ingests the policemen's leftovers, a place of nausea but not of rankness. In the representation of the masculine body, the mouth is the voice, and the voice is the place of courage. "My voice tended to shake, even becoming shrill, although opportune coughs saved my dignity" (423). The voice is the signal of manliness; the voice is not voice but "balls." To speak with a high-pitched voice is to be a faggot. To "have balls" is not to be afraid and, consequently, to speak with a strong voice. "Sons, I need to be brave; I need balls" (122). The voice-balls-manliness, masculine topoi is reiterated in Ramírez when Paul Oquist declares to him the percentages of the vote, and he asks him:

> "Can this tendency be considered irreversible?" . . .
> "Yes," he replied without hesitating, making an effort to make his voice heard with firmness, "It is irreversible." (Ramírez 148–49)[7]

Or in the declaration made by Daniel, who "spoke with firmness and serenity, with aplomb" (151).

In the same way that the voice is the site of masculinity, curiously, for a man, the site of emasculation is the ass(hole) and the buttocks—which in women are "sweet butt," a "kissable little butt"—parts of the body that he extrapolates from himself, from his own body as a masculine body, to the body of woman, and from patriotism to eroticism. In Dalton, as in Martínez, a woman is "a sweet butt" and making love is "butt slamming." However, when the *guerrillero* is captured, Dalton uses the language of homosexuality to signal his loss. Denationalization is centered in that expression: "The orders were coming from Washington and the Salvadoran government would do no more than bend over" (425). To be "assholes" is to smell bad to the revolutionary nose. "To kiss or lick someone's ass" is to be an opportunist. Front and back, Vanguard and Rearguard. The front is the phallus; the phallus is voice; and the voice is fundamentally "balls," the proper place of masculine sexuality, of manliness. The ass is behind, social emasculation, surrender. "Taking it up the ass" or to "bend and spread" are expressions of cowardice and defeat.

In summary, Dalton's representation of the revolutionary subject as an imperfect human being, as a man who is capable of making mistakes, accounts for his desire to build a political narrative very distinct from the heroic constructions of military narratives. I believe he succeeds in portraying an all too human revolutionary, a more credible persona than Che's idea of the *guerrillero*, but that in so doing, he, like all others, creates a parenthetical world for women to inhabit. Women, in Dalton, are not revolutionary masses; they remain "revolutionary pussy," sex objects for the satisfaction of the urban guerrilla's sex drives. Must there be in revolutionary literature a woman-separate domain? What the relation might be between Woman as object of devotion, and women as family members (daughters and widows) and as people acceptable as leaders of insurrections and secular authority, remains, for guerrilla literature, in obscurity. Only women writers address the question of the constitution of the subaltern as (sexed) subject, when the exploitation of sexual differences seems to play so crucial a role for insurgency on so many fronts. For other matters, mainly those concerning male sexualities, women can always rely on our representations as outside the "revolutionary democratic" narratives, and inside the perverse ideas of male sexual or political power.

PART III

(Wo)man

CHAPTER EIGHT

The Masculine "I" as Other

The Formation of the Revolutionary Couple

> I like my drinks strong, my women weak.
> Jamaican proverb

By the 1970s, revolutionary writers were attempting to plot women within the narratives of political struggle. In his novel *El esplendor de la Pirámide* (The Splendor of the Pyramid), written in the 1970s but not published until 1986, Mario Roberto Morales purports to narrate the revolutionary couple.[1] This novel relates the story of a Guatemalan revolutionary who is helped by a Mexican woman he symbolically nicknames Pyramid. Pyramid brings the revolutionary to her house and shows him the way around Mexico City. Sharing a house, however, leads inevitably to seduction and to lovemaking, giving birth, through purely circumstantial events, to the classic, clandestine revolutionary couple. Besides making love, the two protagonists engage in a vehement dialogue, bluntly discussing the greatest theme of revolutionary love, that of political engagement. Obliquely, they also discuss one of its most important topoi, the masculinization of woman.

One striking feature of this frustrated love story is that it takes place in the shadow of another frustrated love story. The latter is played out within the war zone in Guatemala and, hence, is more legitimate than the one taking place in Mexico City. The protagonist's suggestion to his new mistress,

Pyramid, that she transform his story into a film script (constituting self into a multimedia enterprise that projects the *guerrillero* beyond the purview of guerrilla literature) situates him both inside and outside this second narrative. Predictably, the narrative ends in betrayal, in woman's disloyalty to the *guerrillero* and, through him, to the fatherland. The text ends by unblushingly demonstrating her inability to become a true New Man.

Within the purview of feminist theories, the poetics of this novel make the cogent political point, so explicit in other texts, that in learning political commitment, woman must once more pass through the crucible of male sexuality. The text consequently becomes a vehicle for exalting woman's sensuousness and man's boastful display of his lovemaking savoir faire. The masculine tongue spends pages going over the female body—primarily her toes—and we are frequently besieged by moans of orgasm, a veritable "Karl Marxutra" (16). Woman continues to be portrayed as the object and realization of erotic desires, "revolutionary pussy," but she is already situated in a semidialogic position within the space and possibilities of insurgency. Thus, the vocabulary of erotica was to make its way into the political debate of the period, making the Marxist-Leninist label undergo a dialectical transformation into "Machista-Leninist" to indicate the absence of revolutionary sentiment toward woman within revolutionary epistemes.

In this sense, the text plots burlesque erotica ("momentary impressions") inserted into a masculine patriotica ("very sapient questions"). The mattress on the floor is the symbolic place of an exchange dividing old generations of guerrilla fighters from new ones, and it is also the site of the surrendering *guerrillero* "conquered" by love. Better still, it stands for the space of reconciliation and dialogue between two potentially compatible sensualities. Predictably, however, the mattress is the place of man's conquest of woman. She is made to express her surrender straightforwardly: "This is how I feel when I let you do me, you turn me to you, you lay me down, sit me down, do with me whatever you want, I am your object and I like that" (26).

And then, to round it off, compelled by the masculine epistemes the text flaunts, she speaks her thoroughly masculinized desire for self-destruction: "I tried to leave to do awful things, to get raped, so they'd spit on me and hit me, so they'd protect me and love me, I wanted to say the hell with them, cheat them, I wanted to lose myself to find myself" (26).

Erotica, as the expression of masculine subjectivity, often entwines the civic ethos, lovemaking, and male sentimentality, and commits the error of presuming that men's sexual pleasure equals women's sexual pleasure. In this narrative, the constitution of woman's self, and woman's expression of sensuality, defuses any tendency to pathos, expressing instead an unbearable stupefaction. Woman's erotica is simply part of an ontology of woman as a cultural landscape. Woman simply mirrors male narcissism as insurgent and revolutionary—"woman," the "feminine," metaphor of reading and topography of writing, meandering through the morass of the patriarchal imaginary. No less *machista* than her interlocutor, however (both products of the same author), (the) Pyramid also contributes to the reproduction of passé concepts of possession and jealousy coupled with seduction charted throughout the urban Mexican landscape. Lovemaking and discussion compose the bulk of this narrative, but not what is most essential. What is most essential, in my view, is the attempt to pry affect from the personal and fuse it with politics. In other words, there is an attempt to narrate the imagined processes of constituting the revolutionary collective subject by departing from the man/woman copula and from the effort to instruct the woman in the debits and assets of the revolutionary insurgency, thereby entwining civic and sexual fantasies. However, as a construction of woman, Pyramid has not passed through the crucible of feminist thinking.

In this respect, "splendor" and "Pyramid" are key words standing for the hypogram of a relationship that tries to unite, synthesize, harmonize what I shall call, for short, the gender struggle at home and the intimacy of battle. Both words demand the revision of previous definitions of Che's *guerrillero*. Drawing on Indian mythologies, the *guerrillero* must be like a Pyramid, boulder, building, monument, mausoleum. As such he must possess the attributes of serenity, arrogance, immobility, slenderness, verticality (the masculine), but also a broad base ("masses"—*masas* in Spanish also means "buttocks"—the feminine), or, as the Jamaican proverb has it, "strong men, weak women." This is, perhaps, a shot at describing the New Woman as the New Man.

How clear a witness this bears to the legacy of "men's inevitable, universal, eternal perception of the female body as an absence" is marked by the author's perception of Pyramid's political illiteracy (DuBois 13).[2] She is "a lack . . . , wounded, deficient, defined by absence of the phallus" (13). In fact, what is new about the text is a discussion of woman's liability and the elements of her liberation. The guerrilla says, "Look, Pyramid—this is how we should be, like a pyramid. Firm and broad at the base, erect, vertical, quite tall and above all pristine, transparent" (Morales 78). There is little doubt that, in addressing her, he is persistently making himself a conduit and a filter, stressing and stretching the same code of honor regulating the behavior of one of the instances of Che's *guerrillero*—purported asceticism which here is far from meaning carnal abstinence.

The problem is that, for woman, being vertical also invokes the realities of domestic emotional economies. It means single-handedly confronting the politics of domesticity head-on and transcending them, that is, managing the ideologies and legal practices of divorce—the ex-husband's claims, the kids' needs, the aunts' and uncles' reproach—where conservative elements and the intervention of the state ambush woman on the path to liberation. In fact, divorce sets loose another figure and underscores other, more tangled genealogies and etiologies. No one doubts that the family is one of the sites of women's oppression, but the *guerrillero*/lover makes family affairs appear simply as woman's personal problems, as part of the constitution of her psyche, hence depoliticizing the issue. Within the purview of revolutionary epistemes, divorce is neither a state mediation between men and women, nor the legal enforcing of male supremacy, but the woman's subjective-psychological business. Whose voice, if not that of transcendent male acumen, speaks when the *guerrillero* appraises coupling, as follows?

> The possessor is dependent, the one who gets jealous is dependent, the macho is dependent, always going around looking for his goddamn mother, a mother who'll go to bed with him and once in a while glances at her kids. (34)

Dependent, yes, but the person who is chastised in this forceful and apparently liberatory diatribe is not the husband but the wife—Pyramid. The dependent figure the narrator addresses is that of woman, being liberated by the male guerrilla in exactly the same way as Latin American nations (Woman) are liberated by the *guerrilleros*. In this paragraph, woman is again and again mother/lover, the figure originating in other texts and reproduced in other domestic/symbolic arrangements in guerrilla literature, for example, Cabezas. Morales situates this question on the level of the everyday—the house, the couple—not the Mountain—for the house has already become a site of political struggle in urban guerrilla affairs—woman escorting the new urban transnational guerrilla on some local outings. It is perverse that, by counterposition, in the inner sanctum of the home, the couple he brings into the discussion is distressingly at odds with the concept of the New Man, he who "wants serenely, without possession" (42).

Discussion infringes upon the agendas of women's liberation, and feminism is expelled from the insurgent epistemes, only to be cursorily sketched in, and superseded by, "real politics," those of endurance, willpower, sacrifice, the masculine tenets of the insurgent body outlined by Che. As I will discuss in subsequent chapters, testimonials, such as Alegría/Flakoll's, are beset by the same anxiety, and partially bemoan the portrayal of woman as insurgent and as woman, or, what is the same, the portrayal of woman within military narratives.

In Morales's text, the new male formulation of woman's liberation consists in removing woman entirely from the realm of the institutions—family or state legislation—and reducing or inscribing liberation completely within the individual psyche. Like man, woman needs to transcend herself in order to be worthy of entering the sanctuary of the rebel Mountain. Maternity takes a leave of absence or is totally annulled. However, in contrast to men in the (male) narratives of insurgency and nation building, woman is left alone, and feminism is nothing, a private effort, woman's volition. In short, gender is subsumed under patriotica—with a concern for women's issues seen, most likely, as a *gringa* subject.

Nevertheless, what signals a generational break with Che in the formation of self is, first, the presence of mass media, particularly rock and protest music, the Beatles and Violeta Parra, the Chinese Cultural Revolution, and, perhaps even more important, the fact that Christian epistemes begin to be challenged by oriental philosophies of contemplation. The ego's desire is regarded as the root of all evil. This text thus relocates the model of the guerrilla from one of Christian patristics to one of oriental philosophies, in which asceticism, paradoxically understood as sensualism, is the essence of the *guerrillero*. Oriental philosophies will be in charge of addressing three main concerns: the oppression of woman in the family, the oppression of man in society, and the oppressiveness of Christian epistemologies. However, the documents from the mountain reiterate Che's religious principles:

> Woe to the comrade who, while performing a task, tells himself, "I can't take this anymore," or, "What an indomitable will I have." No, Pyramid, what fortitude can you communicate to, and inspire in, the comrades in your charge if you continue to conceive of yourself in such weak and egotistical terms? One should celebrate and bless the moment of challenge, rise to the occasion with joy; there is no need for sacrifice to be blind suffering; rather, it should be a motive for exaltation and satisfaction, of the total realization and unfolding of your capabilities, and that is no more nor less than pure joy. (Morales 124)

But within the hegemony of oriental epistemes, the woman is all the more to blame; she is responsible for her situation:

> "Come on, Pira, you're not going to go on thinking that they've been doing it to you all your life. You chose the path, you, the deformed little girl, you,

the tomboy, the conniving goody two-shoes, you chose your husband."
(Morales 79)

With the shattering of the *guerrillero*'s personal hopes, however, he tor-
pidly comes to the conclusion she is unremittingly mulish. The narrating
masculine I articulates his exasperation when he comments on the liberal-
minded qualities of the New Man in dialogue with woman: "You have in
your hands a true love story, totally legitimate, and yet you don't know what
to do with it" (45). A true love story is predicated on the entwining of the
twin graces of civic duty and sensualism. In predictable male fashion, however, the necessity of recording the story as History and converting both into
multimedia propaganda is assigned unilaterally to her. The *guerrillero,* in his
turn, is entrusted with more sapient questions—politics—thereby evading
all responsibility for the personal and appointing her to bear the brunt of a
political relationship aesthetically recorded.

Small wonder she is baffled. In a total quandary, she doesn't know what
to do with love; she doesn't know what to do with politics. One is led to suspect that her perplexity, when she is placed in such a textual predicament, is
related to men's lucidity. They "already" have a legitimate and authentic love
relationship (the erotica patriotica), or they always "love" (fuck) freely—
that is, unencumbered by possession or the responsibility of legitimizing
the possession of the body. They don't have to worry about maternity leave
to go to the mountain, as do all *guerrilleras* recorded by Randall and
Alegría/Flakoll.

What mars this analysis of woman's position is that it rests upon the age-
old ideology that posits free will and that, worse, assumes that the self is
male. There is no question but that the adage "The power to define is the
power to control" is here given full play. Moreover, Jardine's unraveling of
Lyotard's concept of metadiscourse, which defines itself as "a functional-
true discourse, that is, as discourse that authorizes itself to say what it says as
true" (42) holds equally true here. Therefore, in Morales's narrative, woman
is ignorant because she is defined as such by a self-constituted "non-macho"
male who is not a macho because he is a *guerrillero,* and because he says he is
not a macho. In fact, his constitution of self and others shows the contrary.
His strategy of collapsing his love for woman into his love for country, or his
civics into his misogynist aesthetics, allows him to explain away his rejection
of woman on the basis of his patriotism. It is in his love of country that he
locates his studied definition of freedom and free will. He extrapolates from
the practice of free will as political commitment to the practice of free will in

individual relationships, the former foregrounding the constitution of the state as power, the latter glossing over it.

It is worth asking where and how, in this brief masculine narrative, the history of woman's empowerment is buried. As I aim to demonstrate below, in Oreamuno, the empowerment of woman is a liberal concept, located only partially in the professionalization of woman; in Naranjo, wealth—or, as we will see, homelessness—is what permits woman's unfettered behavior. Thus, these two women writers postulate the economic bases of woman's power. Here, however, it is purely a question of willpower and political commit-ment—of no gain and therefore no game.

Political devotion is the midwife engendering the text as both masculine and feminine. In this narrative, woman comes into being only by meeting two male challenges: first, that of becoming author(ity)—writer, as well as protagonist, of their love story as movie script—and, second, that of becom-ing writer of her own story as History. Nothing wrong so far. But a caveat should immediately be added to this sentence, for woman's being is a hy-pothesis, a test, a laboratory. She is a kind of guinea pig, a marionette, very much in keeping with her role in Oreamuno's deployment of the father/daughter relationship. The latter is a relationship that depends on a double dare, in which the daughter is a half-being, a (wo)man. We are to conclude that as expression of desire, Morales's text aims directly at subsuming love-making into militancy, and indirectly at positing the continuation of loving other men—the people in the Mountain. It is, therefore, phallic and logo-centric. As I will explain further on, the narrative strategy of alternating the omniscient narrator masculine I with the second person "you" dictates the direction we are compelled to follow.

From Sexuality to Legality

In line with the dialogues established between the *guerrillero* and his woman, Pyramid, I want to move to a second instance of meaning and argue that Morales's text is also a legal text, the accusatory and probationary text of a crime—woman's defection and betrayal—in which the institutional posi-tion of the subject is masculine.

In the second part of the novel, "Pyramid in the Shade," the narrator-*guerrillero* calls himself to order. Dialogues are interrupted. The pleasure of heterosexual interlocution and interaction is curtailed. All entertainment dissipates. The narrator supersedes aesthetics, the idea of making their love affair into a movie script as a competent construction of narratives of erotic free love, and returns to the well-trodden conventions of realism and the journalistic prose of political pamphlets. The erotic skit played on the mattress to music—of Willie Nelson ("All of me"), Liza Minnelli ("Someone to Watch over Me"), Carlos Puebla ("I'm Bringing a Song from Cuba"), Soledad Bravo, the Beatles, and Violeta Parra—gives way to a linear, "realistic" narrative to better enable the expression of Historical events, thereby foreclosing on the possibility of plural interpretation.

In this second part, woman is put on trial; she sits on the defendant's bench. The masculine casts doubt on the feminine. The masculine subject occupying the narrative omniscient masculine I, very much as in *The Death of Artemio Cruz*, addresses woman, speaking of himself in the second person, as a "you," "your actor," words always addressed to Pyramid's actions, disguising a political reprimand in a pseudosentimental narrative charting her downfall. Man is here permitted the possibility of speech, the entering into the symbolic community that empowers him to speak of absences and lacks, and, as such, in this narrative "the phallus is the privileged signifier of that mark in which the role of the logos is joined with the advent of desire" (Lacan 287).[3]

To build his political case, in Morales's logos, all elements of misjudgment and error are credited to her. Whatever is dysfunctional is her fault. But misjudgments, errors, and faults are not part of the dialogue; they are either encoded in his final monologue where, in her absence, he recapitulates the relationship, or in her soliloquies recorded in her asides. Her flaws are all political, beginning with the issues of divorce and self-pity and ending with her politicization, which she paradoxically accomplishes not through dialogue and discussion but through reading, through minding his business, perusing the secret commands of the Organization in his absence. Just as a jealous woman would examine and smell her man's clothes, and look for scraps of paper in his trouser pockets, she reads his guerrilla communiqués when he is not home and she is alone. In silence, Pyramid breaks the law, instructing herself on the *guerrillero* maneuvers. Her reading of History is a clandestine act of self-instruction, the only way to learn about transcendent events. While she reads, she comments. In her asides, the writer writes woman's self-denial: "The impossible desire to be or to have the phallus is analogous to the desire for the consumption of signs" (DuBois 13). All the same, while she reads, she invokes the classic epithets involving the verb "to fuck," and all the Mexican allusions to "mother"—*de poca madre, ni madres, mamadas, hijos, jijos, hijin, hijole, puta madre, no mames, que chingaos*— "motherfucker," "I don't give a shit," "it sucks," "sunufabitch," "son of a bitch," "sonofabitch," "oh my god," "your mother sucks," "don't be a sucker," "what the fuck." Such are her commentaries on his text.

While she secretly reads the documents in solitude and in violation (hiding her fingering of forbidden male writings), readers could notice that the documents are written in various voices. One of the voices is that of the omniscient narrator, intervening to comment on the same documents, informing us of those episodes in history that the documents do not reveal. Among these is the commonplace story of a failed guerrilla love affair in the Mountain. Thus, love story is wrapped around love story, and woman's betrayal confronts woman's betrayal. Historical documents are once more read as the intersection between History and story, reiterating that the masculine I personal is political. History is both private and public, erotic and patriotic. The voice of the masculine I narrator/clarifier emerges as interference, deus ex machina, autonomous, uncommitted voice, unfettered by the intersection between story/History, in which she, Pyramid, is a total outsider. It is then by reading the documents that Pyramid fully realizes, for the first time, the nature of her predicament, that is, the implications of having shared her bed with a clandestine man.

While she lives her own fantasies of love and commitment through the fantasies of the "real" failed Mountain love affair, behind her a family portrait articulates her own past life story as an abused wife. Woman's family history and the country's patriotic History position themselves as stories of the fucked mother-fatherland. The *guerrillero* is simultaneously rapist and liberator, a double image that characteristically haunts guerrilla ontologies and epistemologies.

Just to contrast briefly male and female narratives, in Yolanda Oreamuno's women's soliloquies and asides, the commentaries of women on male sentences, actions, or writings serve a totally different function. There, the asides are postulated as a *pris de conscience,* as internal monologues serving the agendas of resistance and empowerment. Here there is a privacy where masculine ontologies are laid bare and elucidated, an area where genders clash. In Morales they represent masculine interference, penetration, areas of doubt, responsibility, and, even worse, guilt, cowardice, self-denial, accusations, and put-downs.

This scene in which Pyramid is portrayed as secretly reading the classified documents must be kept in mind at the moment when the repressive practices of the state intervene, forcing the narrative to fold over onto itself, when the narrator forgets the artistic, and submits entirely to the fallacies of mimesis or realism. For, as in innumerable and unrecorded instances of lived political participation by women—manipulation by the *guerrillero* leads directly to prison. In woman's incarceration what is visible is precisely what Morales fails to recall in fiction: male political neglect, when not outright abuse and battery.

In prison, and in danger, the ideal of the couple resuscitates the topos of the resting place of the *guerrillero*. It emerges in the conditional as a utopian time, expressed in self-pity and belated sentimentalism:

> "And how I wanted to begin to live a life, Pira . . . like a quiet pool, like a pool, of clear water that doesn't move at all, even if the whole city moved." (98)

Upon leaving the protected space of the house—"the place of woman is at home," "resting place of the *guerrillero*"—we enter the space of politics and are fully present at woman's trial and sentencing where she enters, shadowed by suspicion.

The contrasting scenarios make for disquieting reading, the author's intention signaled by the shift in discursive style. But woman indeed is beholden to no one. In this sense, the space of the prison, where the two lovers are now located, and separated, is hopefully a bridge between home as sanctuary and the Mountain as the site of exercise of one's free will. That is the New Man's best bet. The dialogue has been cut off, and in his innermost feelings the *guerrillero* prays and pleads for her endurance and commitment. Upon her faithfulness to the struggle (as love for him) now rests the safety of comrades and of the Organization. Enduring fear and accepting punishment, a test he has chosen for her, signals the end of the *guerrillera*'s apprenticeship, her graduation, the hour of reckoning when she will show herself worthy of belonging to the heroic pantheon of the fatherland. But it is easier for a camel to pass through the eye of a needle than for a woman to be saved.

While the examination is in process, we are never reminded that she has not been duly instructed. We just bear witness to the voice of author(ity) talking to himself and to his peers, preparing the brief against women by juxtaposing and inserting narratives of events, as History, within narratives of events as stories—a collage which includes motherhood, children, the family, "women's concerns," the objects of sexual liberation and feminism. But feminism and patriotism are separate and counterposed agendas that the *guerrillero*/judge submits to the test by enjoining woman to resist in silence.

In prison, as in the Mountain, the intersection of History and story is no longer art but History—a script, hopefully, with which they both still struggle. But her double bind is that in this same intersection she is to write herself as a subject on trial within what, for her, is the unknown legal code of the guerrilla. In the meantime, preparing for the impending attack, in his jail cell, he implores her not to surrender. But his entreaty can no longer prevail. His main argument to her is that patriotic love and the endearing memories of lovemaking are the same—sentimental capital not to be forsworn out of fear of torture. Now the etiology of both affections is mixed and truly engendered. Would it not be evil at this point to ask if this is perhaps a real appeal to the "vaginal solidarity" of the "revolutionary pussy," or must I be more generous and consider this plotting a begging of the real question, an alternative configuration of the couple?

Is it not ironic, for once, that the first lesson taught to woman should be delivered within the inner voice of a monologue, and that woman's real importance should be recognized only when he is locked in? At this hour, what mentors are to teach the lessons that might prevent woman from falling into the argumentative traps of the system? Who is to teach her not to believe in the state's predicates? Who is to instruct her, now that state repression in prison is the same as believing in the husband again, in the children, in the shrouded aunts? To the *guerrillero*'s chagrin, it is too late. The man, now, holds forth in judgment, and realizes that his security depends on her, a woman lacking in political savoir faire. Blatantly leaving her to grapple with her own self-teaching, to test her own feminine liberation, to enact her freedom in private was not wise, and now becomes a liability, their shared plight a textual quiz that both must fail. Tormented by the consequences of his own negligence, he must now expiate his loss. Woman's place is, thus, once again, at the locus of betrayal and cowardice—Malinche's right flank, masculinity's waning quarter.

Like Ramírez's "little man," woman is also shrouded. Her only profile emerges through erotica, a genre that revolutionary epistemes show themselves unable and unwilling to transcend. Passing the legacy from one generation to the next, say from Che to Morales, does not enable the *guerrillero* to cast woman in a more favorable political light. She must always be first the object of his lust, a vehicle and filter for his self-construction. In this light, the juxtaposition of the omniscient narrative masculine I with the you of the addressee as intended actor creates a unit: the actor/protagonist of a story narrated as History, that the narrator induces her to write, is a "your actor," who is none other than Morales in the position of the subject as author/actor/narrator of the patriotic Histories and of the erotic stories. This is essentially the same author/actor/narrator who appears in the accounts of the *guerrillero* produced by Che and by Cabezas. Woman is persistently placed in a double bind, in her role as a marionette, ordered to write, read, grow, become informed, know herself, and "be free," all by herself, in contrast to the *guerrilleros,* who are born into a political life and go through their training as a team.

The main slippage of this text is between overtly positing love for women and covertly disparaging their abilities. The gist of the matter is that Morales's view is not divested of reference. The unremitting lustre of this genre founders on the discursive tradition of Che, generally reckoned as the classical source for the discussion of any issue pertaining to the self-formation of the *guerrillero.* The liability is that the representation of woman is not easy to assess. The asset is that the figure is likely to fracture as we women grow. Woman still comes into being under considerable pressure and within the purview of males jockeying for position within the national pantheon. From the outset, women have borne subjection, antagonism, and retaliation against their own mock(ed) deliverance. Feminism might be considered the watchword that would lend credence to the attack, generally undertaken in a certain bantering tone disguised as concern or self-pity. If the formation of the revolutionary couple continues to be couched in such undertones, any formation of the collective subject will be hamstrung, and any real discussion foreclosed. I propose, in closing, to let Pyramid speak and to urge her to give us her own account of his story.

CHAPTER NINE

The Body as Excess

Yolanda Oreamuno's text *La ruta de su evasión* (The Route of His/Her Evasion) is the first serious Central American feminist novel.[1] It enacts three instances of male/female relationships: the traditional man/wife couple—Teresa/Don Vasco; the ideal love affair mediated by the daughter/father relationship—Gabriel/Elena's father/Elena; and a very novel lover/mistress coupling—Gabriel/Aurora. However self-evident these three forms of plotting gender exchanges might seem, the dialogic nature of Oreamuno's discourse nevertheless thrives on logical perversion. In order to untangle the web of relationships, she places men and women in untenable human positions, the specter of women's rights haunting every line of the page.

The title itself immediately places the critic in a dilemma, since gender relationships are enmeshed in the ambiguity of the possessive *su*, which in Spanish means both "his" and "hers." Thus, the masculine and the feminine are welded together, inhabiting exactly the same place in the syntagm. The constitution of the subject and the determination of gender depend upon a homonym. If I take *su* to mean "hers," the theme of the novel is defined in terms of the always desired definition/possession of woman by man (Teresa by Don Vasco) and, therefore, her evasion. If I take *su* to mean "his," the theme is defined in terms of the perpetual persecution of man by woman (Gabriel by Aurora) and, therefore, his evasion. Consequently, the narrative is perpetually slippery, and the identity between the referent—the relationship man/woman—and the signifiable—possession—is never completed. Entrapment and contention, as the objects of textual/sexual desire, neutralize the possibility of a loving relationship between man and woman. In this dispute, grammatical coupling precludes his/her possession.

In questioning the logic of the formation of the couple/copula as a dynamic of possession/evasion, companionship is dislodged from the emotive, and expressed through metaphors of disease and the symbol of death. Death again impregnates the corpus of feminine literature, and death, it seems, is a gift to fend off opprobrium. Death, either as biological process or as metaphor, forestalls any personal fulfillment within heterosexual pairing.

Earlier I observed that the texts by Borge and Ramírez eroticize the death of woman. In women's texts, on the other hand, death is patrioticized (politicized). Representing woman as dead, or dying, Oreamuno deploys three distinct strategies, which correspond precisely to the conceptualizations sketched by de Lauretis in her succinct "Gramsci Notwithstanding." De Lauretis's narrative of the Schucht sisters outlines three of the roles permitted to women in Western societies: "service functions within male structures, adherence to the feminine mystique of charity, sacrifice and self denial, and madness" (de Lauretis 89).[2] I want to read Oreamuno's three instances of coupling against the background provided by de Lauretis to signal the ubiquitous transnational character of the reproduction of ideas of marriage and coupling.

Case # 1: The Feminine Mystique—Madness

Within the feminine mystique of madness, both fiction writer and critic chart traditional patterns of coupling in which woman is all givingness and therefore all self-negation. The metaphor for self-negation in this case is silence. In the relationship between Teresa and Don Vasco, as in that between Gramsci and his wife, woman, as subject, is constituted as silence. In Oreamuno's fiction, the relationship has been so mismanaged that Teresa is in bed, dying of verbal abuse. Dialogue has never been a prerogative of coupling. Talking is masculine—Don Vasco's language being honed into the sharpest instrument of patriarchy, constituting woman's subjectivity in subjection as the object of male enunciation.

In this first example, only men talk, and their conversation is beyond the pale, defining woman's likes and dislikes. The story finds its purchase in men's hypothesis that woman likes to be quiet. For that reason, they speak about her in front of her, referring to her in the third person: "she." Male speech transforms woman into a referent, a grammatical category, a pronoun. The mythic version also resorts to finding where heterosexual coupling locates itself under patriarchy, whether in speech or somewhere else, for instance, in service and sexuality. As in previous guerrilla literature, Don Vasco's pleasure in conversation and interaction again circulates communication as homosociality.

In writing this first instance of coupling, Oreamuno uses two typographic conventions to signal split enunciation: one is written without quotation marks to indicate sound, the other in quotation marks to indicate silence. The first represents voice, the second, thought. The first is plotted as intercommunication between two men within fiction; the second projects itself beyond the margins of the text, into the void where lies the possibility of intercommunication with an absent reader. Are readers posited as woman's interlocutors? (En)gendering meaning through mitosis (one side masculine and the other feminine) is once more presented as a narrative ambiguity, for what is presented as real, masculine speech is fiction and what is presented as imaginary, feminine speech offers the "real" possibility of communicating with others through writing. Admittedly intersexual heterosexual economies are not given enough credit. The silenced logos of woman is presented in opposition to the masculine logos, as the locus of the symbolic.

We are to conclude that, for Oreamuno, intersexual communication, as heterosexual, occurs against the run of play. The authoritarian voice of Don Vasco, who, tangentially, is involved in clandestine arms deals for the insurgents in neighboring countries, defines male insurgency and future nation building indirectly by defining women's conversation as "a senseless screaming of animals," reducing the feminine logos to sounds (the speech without writing Derrida analyzes),[3] to orality (75). He never answers the question of whether she, shadowed by the suspicion of her gender as species, likes to listen. Instead, Teresa, the dying woman, addresses the same question, thinking about like issues in reverse, racking her brain to figure out "what men speak about when they are alone," a question that Naranjo answers: they talk about politics because politics is female and so they can fuck her. Teresa, in turn, expresses her desire to hear them speak about anything except politics.

Woman, set up to lose, is the much abominated "angel of the hearth" who loathes disturbing him, and would rather eat her heart out than tax his brain. Her dilemma is "what to say not to disturb him" (76). How to say what he wants her to say? How to guess what to say to cover him, to not negate him, to support him, her man, in front of the other; how to announce "something little, something ordinary, something feminine, beyond every kind of judgment" (77)? She decides to say, "[We] women are curious about what men think. We are curious about everything. Perhaps it is a form of entertainment. For me to hear you speak is like seeing you eat. If it pleases you, it is all right" (76).

Through this carefully prepared strategy, Oreamuno reiterates, with characteristic acerbity and bitterness, a definition of heterosexual relations as negative for woman. As in Morales, woman's speech is a male pre-scription; her words are spoken to herself, or only to him in private. This is exactly the case of Gramsci's wife, studied by de Lauretis. For her, Gramsci's wife, like many other women, lived her life a recluse, in the total passivity and silence of madness. To be *in articulis mortis,* the metaphor Oreamuno selects to represent muteness, stands for the absolute catatonia of the ventriloquized woman.

Case # 2: The Feminine Mystique—Sacrifice and Self-Denial

The second instance of coupling is the metaphor of a ménage à trois played out by Elena, Gabriel, and Elena's father. Here, two men vie to dominate and explicate woman. "What shall woman be?" is the question, and whatever the answer, woman must first pass through the crucible of male ideologies. Elena's father hypothesizes that what fetters woman is precisely what defines her as an emotional, tender being, capable of loving and feeling. Consequently, man must set her free. He must prepare the ground for her to learn how to rid herself of emotion. The means is complacency; Elena must have all her wishes met, for only in satiety, in the absence of desire, can she accomplish his wishes and her own apotheosis.

The model for her liberation is the demise of femininity, woman becoming man. Man is defined by freedom, and woman can be free only if she can be made into a man, into a (wo)man. The father sets out to win over his daughter by prying her away from womanhood and fusing it with manhood. He makes a reasoned case for this hypothesis and undertakes to make his daughter his guinea pig, proposing nothing less than her defeminization. By force-feeding desire he allays her scruples, seeing satiation as the key to her "liberation" into manliness. According to this model, woman's liberation rests on stripping away whatever is "female" in woman, having her become the clone of a man.

In this second instance, the issue of marriage is definitely sidestepped, and women are considered capable of bearing defeminization. Woman is thus first presented as a hypothesis, as an exercise in male hermeneutics, and as a laboratory. The father could not be suspected of bad faith, although he is the instigator of his daughter enacting her own self-denial. In this quandary, Oreamuno seems thoroughly to enjoy teasing out the significance of man/ woman relationships and seeing how one half renders the other obsolete. A merely overburdened daughter enjoys herself to death, and is quite ready to take part in the game. Oreamuno has gone one better than Romanticism, a set of beliefs she reverses and derides, for if feelings—love, passion, *tendresse*— defined woman in the past, now those very same definitions define a woman's lack, hence satiation of feeling is postulated to constitute her as full.

The dissolution of masculine power over a feminine body is, from the masculine point of view, paradoxically, only realized when (wo)man transcends her love and need for man. Elena is assiduously monitored by the father who does not permit a ripple seriously to disturb her wishes. In the process, he plays havoc with her life:

> I have believed in woman's freedom, and you must prove my theory. You can't say you lack anything. . . . Everything is possible if you do not succumb to the stupidity of falling in love, marry, and place my dreams [in another] man. (205–6)

Losing all sense of propriety and decorum, pleasure and satisfaction enables a woman to become a worthwhile interlocutor for men, solving several problems at one stroke, not least of which is the problem of how to become deserving. Admittedly, this definition of woman negates woman's self and postulates a double male bonding, first between father and lover and, then, between the two of them and a masculinized Elena. Following in her father's footsteps, for instance, Elena succeeds in making Gabriel, her lover, believe that she can never love, while in her interior monologues she explains her inexplicable behavior to herself, for her words are spoken as self-negation:

> Elena struggled between contradictions; she debated and searched and she tormentedly reached the bothersome conclusion that she did not know who she was: the powerful unique woman of before [her father's (Wo)man], or the submissive hurting woman of today [woman without masculine agency]. (204)

In order to be a woman and to constitute herself as woman, Elena oscillates between the masculine ideologies of the feminine and the masculine/ feminine practices of the feminine/masculine. Feminine desire for emotional expression and satisfaction and masculine denial of that desire lead woman to paralysis.

Oreamuno buttresses her analysis of the relationship between Elena and her father/lover by duplicating the idea of woman as laboratory, in an episode in which what happens between man and woman is replicated in ethnic relations. Oreamuno plays with the theme of the relationship between white and indigenous women, portraying the latter as the laboratory of the former, thereby duplicating the daughter/father exchange in which the former is also a laboratory for the latter. The framing of tyrannies and patriarchies, moving from the father to the daughter and from the daughter to the Amerindian, is thus reinforced. Dissecting the body of an indigenous woman (the Other) symbolizes this hermeneutic.

Feminine willpower materializes when Elena, a medical student, decides to bring home the body of a dead indigenous woman to practice dissection. The appropriation of ethnicity is part of a woman's fulfillment of her desire and part of the process of setting her free. Desecrating the body is also part of her schooling, but desecrating it through the mediation of the lover unfolds into another metaphorical ménage à trois between Elena, Gabriel, and the dead indigenous woman. Thus, necrophilia is re-inscribed in Central American belles lettres, making the death wish a not exclusively male patrimony.

In exercizing her willpower, Elena succeeds in using the dead body of the Amerindian woman as an instrument for her own liberation, at the same time facilitating Gabriel's construction of his own erotica as a ménage à trois. If by carrying out her father's wishes, Elena better enables him to succeed in making the living body of the mestiza woman the confirmation of his hypothesis of a masculinized (wo)man, then executing the woman's will further enables him to take possession of the Amerindian woman. The hypothesis that woman is man if she is stripped of emotions is demonstrated through the collaboration of father and lover. The hypothesis of freedom as the essence of man is again construed in the repossession of woman as ethnicity. And both possessions are achieved through the collaboration of father/lover and (wo)man-daughter. The trinity is as follows: father proposes, lover agrees, woman disposes. If fulfilling sybaritic postulates, such as satiety, is the essence of freedom, then willpower and satiation are synonymous, masculine essence and ethos.

Indulgence has no bounds. Hedged with potential conflict, the body of the indigenous woman in the house recasts public and private spheres. The bedroom is simultaneously autopsy room, morgue, as the bed is operating table—a metonymic syntagmatic chain beset by conflict. In this confusion of public and private spheres, man and woman will hammer the scalpel into the Amerindian woman's belly and butcher ethnicity and past (History). The privatized public space has been transformed into *oikos,* a domus analogous to society. When the couple enters the scene, house/bedroom/laboratory/hospital/morgue, the space is immediately eroticized. The masculinized living (wo)man, somewhat de-eroticized, and her lover will dissect (rape) the eroticized dead body of the Amerindian woman.

On this body—of woman as Amerindian—man reconstructs his erotica, one in which he revives the other. He begins with the smells—a synesthesia of the feminine body—"a strange smell," "a smell between sweet and acrid" (118), embodying and enveloping the feminine and ethnicity in death. Into the productive belly (uterus/maternity/womb), in the "powerful breasts," or in the ripped neck (like Borge's Madame Bovary's) he projects his sexual excitement. Through the smells the two women merge in one, the aroma of one prevailing over the rancid pestilence and stench of the other. The mestiza takes the place of the Amerindian with her intoxicating sexual aroma of wealth created, in contrast, by expensive chemicals, perfumes "fresh and healthy, penetrating and persistent, salty and iodized, intoxicating and maddening" (118).

This second instance of coupling is no less problematic than the first. It is also a split narrative where the juggling of sets of meaning is less evident but where the woman-daughter Elena, representing a marionette, is no more entitled to speak than Teresa. When Elena speaks, her father speaks through her. If, in the first instance, the dialogue was carried out between two men, and the difference between man and woman was signaled by typographically separating the writings, in the second, the apparent tolerance of the father is a ruse of concealment. At the same time, the apparent complacency of the daughter becomes deceit and evasion. She is all sacrifice and self-negation, like one of Gramsci's sisters-in-law.

Here we find once more an instance of how, on the live body of woman as daughter, man, as father, practices his own corpus of antifeminist hypotheses. The solution to the problem of constituting gender as difference or as neutrality remains couched in evasion, represented as death. Evasion, skewing the body, is the trace of men and women dissecting their relationship.

Case # 3: The Feminine Mystique—Charity

Of the three cases presented, the most extreme is the third, in which woman, Aurora, is all charity, all piety—the third of Gramsci's sisters-in-law. The third case brings to mind the writings of Simone de Beauvoir on Jean-Paul Sartre, in *La Cérémonie des adieux.* Alice Jardine retextualizes fragments of this text "of writing-*qua*-oral-history" (Jardine 91),[4] in which Simone reconstructs, as in plastic surgery, the moments of deterioration of Sartre's body:

> 1972—more politics, more voyages, until Sartre finally begins to wet his pants and leave brown stains where he was sitting; ruining his clothes; acting like a child, just before he's off on more trips, seeing more people until finally he begins to lose—his arteries, his veins, his nose, his skin, his head. He forgets. He can't get it right, and finally, he loses his eyes. While "eating messily"— "his mouth soiled with food." . . . And his bladder and intestines are completely out of control. (Quoted in Jardine 92)

In spite of all this, Simone expresses her desire to lie by him all night during the first night of his death and to stretch her body out next to his, but she cannot

> because of the poisonous gangrene that has taken over this textual cadaver. Incest is denied because of the poisoned body—she does lie down next to Sartre, but separated from him by the thin white sheet between them. She sleeps. (94)

Naturally, Jardine wonders about this textual extravagance, and, with her, I wonder the same in relation to Yolanda Oreamuno and her need to make her character Aurora exact precisely the same vengeance upon the body of her beloved Gabriel.

Perhaps what is at stake in both Oreamuno and de Beauvoir is to strip the veil from the thesis of "male sublimity." As in de Beauvoir, on this textual site Oreamuno expresses her bitterness and anger at what she calls treason and, in fact, models her example on the parable of Judas:

> Judas Iscariot did not betray Jesus. He had been a rich man who left everything to follow him, it is futile to think he would sell him after for thirty dinars. What he asks from Jesus when he surrenders him is tangible proof of his divinity, something akin to: "Save yourself from them and let us see you are God." (Oreamuno 309)

In this third instance, it is woman who constructs a hypothesis, the hypothesis of male superiority as "masculine sublimity," which man must prove. He must demonstrate his divinity, that is the omnipotence and omnipresence of his power. Woman, Aurora, puts herself in the position of Judas, demanding, as Judas demanded of Jesus, that Gabriel prove his superior divinity. Man, who has lived all his life demeaning woman, who has made that humiliation his essence and his discipline (*tendresse*), cannot allow himself tenderness. He asks,

Do you want to be a man's mistress, his lover, his darling, his bitch? Do you
want to be the one who is always under his shrieks, the one who deserves his
rage, the one who annoys and is not wanted? Do you want to be the one
he uses with disgust and leaves in remorse? Do you want to be the one he has
between his legs only when he so wishes? The one that is no more than a
chair, or a rug, or a handkerchief? Do you want to be next to me without my
seeing you, walk at my side without being spoken to, that in caressing you I
caress somebody else, that I insult you after you caress me? Because I am that
man . . . I do not love you, nor will I ever love you. (270)

And she said yes, but under one condition: that he remain identical to
himself, that he would never allow himself to feel love or be tender. Here,
the inverse of the second example is presented. Women must not fall in love,
nor must men show their tenderness. Those are the instances of absolute
masculinity; but to know the veracity of these premises, both must be put to
the test, and for that, they must be pushed to their limits—death, treason,
contradiction. Truth can only be found in the total negation of those feelings. However, Gabriel falters and Aurora calls him to order. The bitter irony
of this formulation falls within the mortification Jardine identifies in de
Beauvoir:

> Gabriel was no longer sure of his words and attitudes. . . . He had passed into
> disorderly interjections, into inconclusive thought. . . . Aurora was not used
> to having compassion for him. . . . She had made of the loved one an arrogant
> being, majestic, omnipotent; a lord of life and property. . . . When she com-
> pressed herself, he became big, pitiless but secure. Seeing him so majestic, so
> full, produced in her soul a double satisfaction: that of her own lack of tran-
> scendence. (310)

We are before narratives that signify by inversion and demand a reading
against the grain. Here Aurora has taken the subject position of the father in
the second coupling. She formulates the hypothesis of male superiority, and
Gabriel must test it. She has also used her own father as an example of "masculine sublimity." She makes her father and husband occupy the same position, and she demonstrates how woman drifts from one tyranny to the
other. From her father Aurora learned to respect that virile sublimity in simple gestures, such as running his hands through his hair. But that gesture and
the memory of an instant of tenderness when her father calmed her fear,
came together, and she also remembers that when she caught her father in
the sexual act

> he did not seem to mind his nakedness, nor the shortness of his shirt, nor the
> absence of pants, nor the ugliness of his legs. . . . He was natural and in no

hurry to get rid of her or to start that again (she did not think what that was, but she felt something), which the girl had interrupted with her sudden appearance. (277)

Thus, a gesture, a nakedness, and a misconduct come to be the synecdoche of Man. Nakedness "without trousers" and tenderness suggest eroticism, incest, and, in the sensuality of fathers toward daughters, the threat of rape.

Used to being small, "soaking up humility," Aurora accepts superiority, but also demands consistency. In the narratives of desire for revenge, woman compares the two figures of patriarchy, that of the father and that of the husband-lover, and, in asking for consistency, demonstrates the inadequacy of both. Gabriel, however, complies and gives himself to her in death, and Aurora, like Simone, lies down next to him, stretching out her body next to his.

In these three examples of masculine–feminine interaction, Oreamuno shows the absurdity of definitions of gender and some of the contradictions of its construction. If the text is to have a kernel of value, it is that the Romantic gendering of woman that we outlined in the beginning finds its nemesis here. Unlike the *guerrillero* text that reproduces the ideologies of Romanticism, women's literature takes issue with it and grudgingly takes it to task. With a heaviness of heart and terrible agonies of mind, they decide to cut off access, and no entreaty can prevail. The implosion of gender relations is based on a logic of confrontations and limits in which, by using like premises, patriarchy is put down. The text is argumentative and one of the most intelligent and incisive on questions of gender. *La ruta de su evasión* (The route of his/her evasion) is also a writing of bitterness, rancor, and revenge. Like many brilliant women of her generation, Yolanda Oreamuno committed suicide. In her life and in her work, she recorded instances of woman rotting within the husk of patriarchy. She stood up, looked around, and stumbled upon horrific remains.

CHAPTER TEN

Implosions

Narcissus Becomes a "Signifying Monkey"

The first moment of European intellectual fascination with the prose of Jorge Luis Borges is one of pleasure. Foucault rejoices in reading the classificatory system of animals that mocks his own paradigms. The second moment is a revulsion: Baudrillard discovers with horror that Borges's map is identical to his own geography, that is, no longer Borges's conceptual map itself but the inner map of European epistemes.

The transition from Foucault's to Baudrillard's reading of Borges suggests a new credit system of cultural exchange, and the unfolding of a denationalized, transocietal subject. In this new exchange, Narcissus implodes into a "Signifying Monkey."[1] I want to argue, first, that this epistemological recognition could be construed as marking the borders of the constitution of a central subject—national, hegemonic, universal—and, second, that culture is no longer concerned with validating environments by establishing equivalencies or reciprocities, for knowledge has been wrenched from the primary order of the natural law of value (analogies), and from the secondary order of the commercial law of value (equivalences), to be placed within the tertiary order of the structural law of value (simulacrum). At this epistemological moment Carmen Naranjo's narratives come into play.

"We are not who we were and we were a pretense of being"

If in her previous narratives—works such as *Sobrepunto* (Stress) and *Los perros no ladraron* (The Dogs Did Not Bark)—Naranjo has already addressed questions of vacant spaces and wasted time, in *Diario de una multitud* (Diary of a Multitude), her rhetorical exercise becomes a virtuoso re-presentation of social meaninglessness.[2] *Diario* is divided into three segments. The first, entitled "Hilos" ("Strands"), is a masterful representation of various unraveling events. The second, "Claves" ("Leads"), constructed as a series of paragraphs beginning with "It is about," and "It is not about," attempts a hermeneutics. The third, "Tejidos" ("Weaves"), returns to the same themes, and finds in politics, in the representation of a street demonstration, the apotheosis of maelstrom.

In these three segments, *Diario* reproduces a wide range of detached voices and scores of fragmentary exchanges between people. The fragments are not logically organized. They do not correspond to or produce a taxonomy. There is no sequence; there is no plot; there is no story; there is no individual protagonist. Reality is no longer a privileged referent, an uncontestable primary order. Words do not approximate reality, neither do they cause a reality effect; they only simulate conversation. As in Borges, in Naranjo paradox is set at the center of the cultural discourse, highlighting one of its fundamental operative functions, that of locating difference within identity.

Naranjo reproduces people's speech, writing, and reading in order to stress that the popular character has lost its unity, its individuality. The popular character is not here the poor little man of Ramírez and Arias, or Argueta's lovable peasant woman; neither is s/he Asturias's or Dalton's humble Indian, let alone Morales's or Borge's heroic *guerrillero*, nor for that matter does s/he embody Che Guevara or Alegría/Flakoll's massacred people. S/he is constituted as a popular non-subject—assorted, eclectic, disparate, dispersed.

It is worth noting in passing that Naranjo's text is not a postmodern text but a text of Central American modernity, a period already licensed for the anonymous representation of people. This plotted anonymity could be understood within the purview of an alienation related to economic determinism, to ideologies of progress, and to the economic exchanges of common markets and import substitution programs. *Diario* collapses denationalization with nonrepresentation in both politics and poetics. In placing the paradoxical logic of the constitution of the popular subject at the center, *Diario* renders dividends in two alternative historical moments.

The Collective Subject = Zero

In *Diario* we read words uttered by a subject whose only identity is the voice. This subject, disembodied and deprived of a family environment, speaks profusely but has no story to tell. The linguistic sign is dislodged from the body, and the social subject is constituted on the basis of uttered nonsense. As Deleuze and Guattari would have it, human stories become autistic narratives in which floating signifiers braid the strands of a drama in which human beings are inconsequential. There is agency but no telos.

Diario illustrates chaos by constructing it through the tangling of logical and illogical propositions. The voices in the text speak disorder. Systems, taxonomies, classifications are no longer part of the everyday. Enunciation takes place within a vacuum and words are tautological, in an account that is sketchy and divested of reference. In Naranjo's narrative of fragments, causality has been thrown out the window and replaced by the casual encounters of the "multitude." In this way, the text endorses Baudrillard's logic of nonreferentiality, of simulacra, because in it,

> the whole traditional mode of causality is brought into question: the perspective, the deterministic mode, the critical mode, the analytical—the distinction between cause and effect, between active and passive, between subject and object, between ends and means. (56)[3]

In some cases the words narrate aggravation, abhorrence, and bewilderment, but in both monologues and dialogues the referent is an empty space, a perpetual delusion—at best, tautology, self-referentiality. For example, the angry voice never tells why it is angry. It just starkly signifies anger. Irritation, annoyance, vexation, exasperation, the whole range and variety of feelings are signs signifying themselves, and the total solitude of the speaking subject. There is no question that something happened to someone, that something was the matter, but that "something" occurs surreptitiously, in the void. The disembodiment of the subject is notable not only in the profusion of monologue, but also in monologues impersonating dialogues: here one and the same subject asks and answers for him, her, and the other. Problems are settled by argument, lies, character defamation, false arraignments, and counterfeited depositions. The whole text is an orchestration of empty words and of emptiness, for example: "Are you ready? Ready! Really ready? It seems incredible but it's already ready!" (15).

The social situation of the protagonists is that of players in a deadly game. Who is the speaking subject? At times an office clerk, a four-year-old child, a woman in a beauty parlor, someone tormented, two deaf people, a married couple, an unknown man/woman of indeterminate age, two old holy-rollers—that is, Borges's classificatory system that so enthralled Foucault. However, Naranjo's taxonomy is not an abstract listing of real and fictitious animals; it is the inventory of social inanity. In some instances, she tallies telephone conversations, or records the cramming of cheap philosophies, un/ethical aspects of consumer society copied verbatim from propaganda blurbs, regurgitations of TV soundbites, syllogisms, metaphysics, vulgarity. It resembles the baffling encounter between two illiterate people staged in Clarice Lispector's *The Hour of the Star*, where the only conversation possible is the repetition of information learned from an all-news radio station, conversation raised to the power of paroxysm by the multiplicity of voices of the crowd.[4]

Whatever the case, an unidentified speaking subject keeps us at bay. The reader is given the task of putting together, by means of free association, the series of spoken non sequiturs. We may surmise a man is advising a man on how to deal with women, take a peek at a sexual incident, witness adults evading a child's question—all instances of overlapping discourses, used to simulate and manipulate narratives of events like that of stealing a cat in the street just to get the reward, cases of resignation, of anger, of self-commiseration, crude cynicism, separating the speaking I from itself.

This gibberish, however, lets the reader intuit miscellaneous discourses: the economic, the positivistic of discourse progress, the impudent, parroting others, the financial, articulating risk and bankruptcy, that of the client, that of hearsay, that of commerce—reiterative double diction, evasive and authoritarian communication. The nihilistic discourse thrives—dialogues about time, stories of depressions, confessions, moments of intimacy between seller and beggar, advertisement, drifting news reports, visceral, deep-seated reflections on everyday topics rendered innocuous, moral and social judgments of people.

Within the fragmented prose of the text, the popular subject is undetermined. The substitution of being for speech (whose?), the reduction of life to the diexis (the here and now of the moment of speech), is structured in the narrative contracts of fragments. As Gramsci says of the history of subaltern groups, the history of the subaltern is "necessarily fragmented and episodic" (Forgacs 54), hence, so is its narrative.[5] Any intention of unity is disrupted by the hegemonic groups. However, in Naranjo's narrative, this dichotomy has also been sundered. Here, as in Borges, the sign is permanently discovering its own negation.

The Servant/The People/The Rally

Nonetheless, there is another way of reading *Diario*. In this reading, people, the servants of the sign, distinguish beginning, middle, and end of a text concerned with plotting vacancies. In the tripartite organization of the novel, we could collate servant with "Strands" (primary order, individualism), people with "Leads" (secondary order, collectivism), and multitude with "Weaves" (tertiary order, transnational subject constitution). The vanishing national socius, later charted in Naranjo's extraordinary story collections *Nunca hubo alguna vez* (There Was Never a Once-upon-a-Time) and *Otro rumbo para la rumba* (Another Route for the Rhumba), is entirely transnationalized. Paradoxically, the Aristotelian dicta for the perfect literary composition are entirely satisfied in a story without a story.

Embodying and naming only take place at the beginning of the text, in the inaugurating epigraph. Here we are introduced to an urban social subject, "Juana Sánchez, the Perez's family cook," through which the voice of the multitude is once named. Juana Sánchez's paradoxical statement triggers the text:

> At night I dread reaching the morning awake, and in the morning I am scared of continuing to sleep and not waking up on time. How to get rid of this fright? If I sleep more or I sleep less, the situation is the same. One cannot quit sleeping nor can one stay endlessly awake. (7)

In this epigraph, the transgression of logic is obvious. Paradox is the expression of Juana Sánchez's one affliction, that of sleeping or not sleeping. Fatigue and insomnia due to overwork and an unrelenting work schedule and anxieties about keeping her job and coming through for the boss substitute the metaphysical and logical problems put forth by the characters of Borges—or of Shakespeare—who probe the logical perplexities of paradox. Juana Sánchez describes an unremitting fatigue making her dreadfully anxious about sleeping or not sleeping, that is, afraid of being helpless and losing her job. She cannot quit sleeping, neither can she stay endlessly awake. Juana Sánchez is situated within the space of double negatives. Sleeping (rest) is traversed by an ambivalence: to do it or not to do it: when she is set to do it, she doesn't do it, and when she is set not to do it, she worries how not to do it.

It goes without saying that this open contradiction bespeaks the presence of a hierarchical social order. Notice, however, that her voice is strategically situated outside the corpus of the text, in an epigraph. The enunciating subject is thus placed outside the cultural hegemonic discourse, or at an intersection, a crossroads, thus invoking the marginal nature of the representation of the subaltern—people, masses, bases => become the multitude. Juana Sánchez is an invisible, nonexistent maid. In "Strands" the main concern is precisely to plot people like Juana, that is, those located beyond representation. "Strands" dramatizes the unsigned nature of "social types," for the major concern of this narrative is all and every forgotten one whose embodiment is not registered by Culture. Juana Sánchez's logic, transcribed in the epigraph, inscribes the character concurrently inside and outside the cultural text, the position of a maid in the socius. In "Leads" the author will plot precisely the ambiguous, indecisive, and confusing positions of the voices of all the other characters in the fragments of the text, who, like the maid, are nameless. Their unassigned, impersonal worries, irritating for anyone, occupy the subject position of anybody, a subject position assigned by the reader.

The feeling of ambiguity, the confusion of opposite meanings in every sign, the alteration of signifiers, is the micro-representation of the macrorepresentation of Naranjo's *Diario*. The multitude is none other than the social subject we have been looking for—people, masses, troop, bases. Their representation is that of the "subject position to be assigned" whose sign, multitude, nothing/no one, is its privileged signifier. Nonetheless, the sign *Diario* takes a position and it is here that simulacra are located. A diary—*Diario*—is an individual, personal convention indicating a bio-graphy and even an auto-bio-graphy, which now comes to represent a socio-graphy—the coveted aim of revolutionary narrative. Carmen Naranjo has no interest in the primary unity of the subject—Juana Sánchez. She is, rather, concerned with the representation of the transcended and dissolved subject, for example, domestic workers. Her position converges with Baudrillard's, because in representing the crowd through its speech, Naranjo privileges the paradox—Juana Sánchez's allocution. In doing this, as in Baudrillard and Borges, the interior and the exterior map come to be one and the same. There is no longer

> subject, focal point, center or periphery: but pure flexion or circular inflection. No more violence or surveillance: only "information," secret virulence, chain reaction, slow implosion and simulacra of spaces where the real-effect again comes into play. (Baudrillard 54)

It is thus that in Naranjo's narrative the cultural subject finds itself simultaneously inside and outside, represented and unrepresented.

Fatherland/Politics

There is a very beautiful woman . . .
her breasts bared, in a white gown
holding the national flag
very confidently in her hands

> . . . a naked woman, large
> and so beautiful like the other . . . on each side
> a soiled worker, a few coffee trees,
> and on the ground . . . serpents,
> and deep inside . . . a few trees with parrots
> and fruits.
> (Naranjo 128)

If Juana Sánchez's epigraph enjoys a comfortable position marking the liminal moment of the text, the meeting of a crowd (people, masses, bases => Zero) at a state office marks almost exactly the middle. In the gathering of a few nameless folks, the reader confronts the inevitable inclusion of the state within the narrative as the ordering principle of cultural discourse.

The fatherland, the nation, has never been marginal to Naranjo's interests. But in this particular text, the fatherland finds its underpinnings in the representation of the state, and the narrative underscores, for the first and only time, plot and story. Both constitute history. For the common folk, story and plot as history reiterate lacks, negligence, belittling. This fragment epitomizes, once more, the story of the non-representation of the people by the presidency, or the president's simulated representation (democracy) of the people. In turn, people's history is plotted as the micro-history of a nameless town, and as people's oral story—that is, as their determination to remember verbatim what transpired at the state office in order to recount it at home. Both their tiny, nameless town and their story act as pivot, one of the possible leads for reading *Diario,* that is, one of the many daily instances of the state disregarding the claims of the people.

Within the office, the state-nation is represented in three different frames. The rural folks make up one, and the paintings on the walls compose the other two. The three images are images of power. The first is a live picture of the misrepresentation of people by the state, a sign of their denationalization. The second is an iconography of the country: a woman with bared breasts firmly holding a flag in her hand. The third, one of the fatherland: a very beautiful woman, two soiled laborers under her arms. In these three instances of socio-political representation, the distance between people-masses-base-troop and fatherland is asserted. However, only the narrow space of the office, where people wait, invokes the state. The people and the state are situated in different loci within the laws of value. Within the sign "people" there is no room for analogy or equivalency for they are situated in an outer-space, or in an insignificant non-citizens' space (their own town), in the void assigned to them by the structural law of value, rendered visible in their lack of representation by the state signified by their waiting. The space of the people and the space of the state are cut off, non sequiturs somehow converging within the same political loci—"the nation." The theater of the state, reduced to the waiting room of the office, is concurrently a metonym of its power, and a metaphor for the overlooked.

The country/fatherland/state represented in the three frames could also be construed, first, as the representation of the unrepresented denationalized masses within the state, and, second, as the masses as troops fighting the wars of Independence, and, third, as the masses as laborers validating the Republic. Notice that the three figures representing the fatherland are anonymous. The pictures on the walls are unsigned, and the people in the room are unnamed—representation of the representation. If we attend to the pictures, one of them frames wars, blood, battles, the struggles for Independence. The troops in battle are positioned "below" the country-icon-woman who presides over them, and is positioned "above." In the other, anonymous peasantry (peasantry of the coffee ad campaigns) are positioned on the same horizontal plane with the woman/country, one on each side. The levels of subordination and equality suggest the transition from the chaotic nation-building wars to the ideology of democratic order, positivism, production, and progress. Coffee trees, parrots, fruits, and serpents foreground a tropical cornucopia and paradise. It may seem odd, but the national iconography reproduces images reminiscent of the Second Napoleonic Empire, perhaps the bourgeois taste and sensibility of the Latin American *independentistas*. The ashtrays' golden border, "surely gold, . . . pure gold as appropriate to a respectable and symbolic place" (128), bolsters the image of Napoleonic Europe, and contrasts with the subdued bearing of the people in the waiting room. With the help of these images, the founding fathers stressed the power of the fatherland over the country, iconographized as a hyperbolic European-looking woman. Within the purview of Latin American ethnicity this woman is a detached figure. Her size and beauty recall an image from distant geographies and ethnographies, perhaps a Renaissance Madonna, a Greek matron, or a Rubenesque blond beauty. Is it surprising that woman, troops, peasantry, and scenery are the same compositional elements of the fatherland that guerrilla literature underscores?

The woman/country is then a hyperbole. She is signaled by the superlative "very." One woman is "very beautiful, very," and the other "so large and so beautiful" (128). *Very* and *so* are distancing adverbs gauging the gap between the contemplating eye and the woman (mother) country. The country thus represented is, consequently, a superlative, a transcendence, that which is above. The woman—beautiful, strange, and distant—parallels the country. That is how the compositional elements are displayed in the office. The space of the office is scanned by the contemplating *pueblerino* eye. The eye contemplates the two pictures, the office's interior decor—the table with its glass, "the large rug," the "impressive ashtrays" (128). "The room was examined carefully by each of them, until they had a complete inventory and capacity to later describe in detail everything in the room" (128). This careful gaze finds everything imposing, handsome, strange, and distant—like the fatherland.

Juxtaposition indicates a dislocation of levels—from Europe to Europe via Independence and Progress—and the difference between codes, the spaces allocated to the state and government. We cannot help but notice the size of the woman and the size of those battling below, the tidiness of the woman, her beauty, and the filth of the workers by her side, the fractured and dividing positioning, below and to the sides, of those who fight and work, and above, the icon woman/fatherland. The unseen position of those who govern and those who make art should also be borne in mind. Like the woman whose figure intersects transnational cultural, historical, and national spaces, the painters (culture) and government are all transcendental signifiers.

The beauty represented and the breadth of the scene exert a crushing power over the people. When one of them dares eroticize the fatherland, "such a huge woman"—"he would not be so passive, simply sitting, looking ahead, like that worker, with such a huge woman by his side" (128), he is immediately reprimanded by the others, and he complies. The *güevos* as metonymy of courage, masculine structural law of value, do not play a role in this dynamic of sanctuaries, in which the state is temple and church, symbol of authority, transcendent entity. *Güevos* and "in men's terms" (132) signify, as in Argueta, working the land, knowing "how to cut the toughest sticks, and to remove from the land the heaviest boulders, with one's own hands, as appropriate to the distance between them, in which one is alone with one's conscience and one's strength" (Naranjo 132), like José in *One Day of Life*, like Nachito Catín in *Tiempo de fulgor*. The *campesinos* are assigned signifiers such as humble, timid, patient, silent, forgotten, servile, ethical, and "very honest."

These structural juxtapositions are rare instances of straightforward speech in a text where no one has a story to tell and the story to tell is about nothing. The last representation encoded is a corollary of the lack of political representation of the *campesinos* at the office, which is now translated into a mass unrest and demonstration. Politics is expressed as disorder, looting, and death. No one represents anyone. No one organizes anyone. The words *communism* and *justice* mix with bombs in vacant lots, with the invocation of Che Guevara and Fidel Castro. The aim is to have "the power in one's hand" (134)—but whose hand?

Bloomingdale's after Selling the Rain

It ought not seem odd to have Naranjo plot popular insurrections as chaos, for already by 1965, in *Sobrepunto* (Stress), the revolution is problematized. In this novel, the representation of woman as dead and the interpretation of her voice by a man indicate the same obsession with absence and presence observable in other Central American works, and, indeed, it predates them. *Sobrepunto* was finished in 1960 and published in 1980. The passing of twenty years between writing and publication of the text causes the decades of the sixties and eighties to merge in a continuum and juxtaposes gender relations in traditional and insurgent societies. In 1960, Naranjo had already observed and recorded the discriminatory treatment women experienced at the hands of poetic and political revolutionaries.

In *Sobrepunto*, women's traditions are written as absence, death, silence. This representation concurs with the values enacted by insurrectionary, revolutionary men in their politics of national formation. It is not accidental that the zero point of woman (death) is symmetrical with the representation of the nation at the point of revolutionary transition. Whilst the revolution is excitement,

> a grand party in which they [the comrades] wish to participate, that way our group, a group without boss or party, appears to be an alliance of fifteen-year-olds who have exchanged an afternoon of adventures for preparation for igniting a fire. (19)

Woman is unwieldy, capricious, mercurial, desperate, alienated, and, ultimately, suicidal. Speaking of herself, the protagonist of *Sobrepunto* explains, "I have been a chain of stupidity" (52); "That is me, a poor little spoiled animal, stranded" (93); "pale, submissive, animal-like," with a body reeking of poverty or permanganate. Not without profound irony, Naranjo makes her male character say, "I haven't put a label on your back, but I have created a story for you" (45). In *Sobrepunto,* suicide, punishment, and self-punishment prevail, just as in the construction of the New nation the name (of the father) prevails over and against the revolution.

In this novel, the politics of poetics and of language demand that women's suicide emerge, as Guha states, more as case history than as social logic.[6] Nevertheless, if social logic is not part of erotica, it is part of patriotica, a set within the politics established by oligarchic family codes. In a novel that plots social change, the essence of the revolution is the transformation of the state, and, insofar as women are concerned, transformation implies changes in the dynamic of family/capital/state (Germani passim).[7] However, the representation of woman through fractured speech, her incoherence, is a signal of her political disbelief. For women, the creation of the New modernized or revolutionary state is a non sequitur evidenced in language like the following:

> What do men talk about? About women, my dear, about women and politics.
> And do you know why they speak about politics? Because it is female and
> they fuck it and transform themselves into eternal fathers. (127)

Fucking women (erotica) and converting themselves into eternal fathers (patriotica) does not tally. How does "politics" transform a being from lover into father? It seems that for the feminine imaginary, the father and the lover occupy the same place, and one is reciprocally the other. In this narrative, the father, the daughter, and the lover are disjointed, as much as the people, the state, and the fatherland are severed from each other in *Diario.* The family constitutes a poetics in which Oreamuno, Belli, Alegría/Flakoll, and Guardia meet. In all these fictions, the functional oligarchic family is a premodern leftover. As a matter of course, the plotting of women in *Sobrepunto* is just an exercise, the pre-history of the feelings of a disappearing nation, nationhood, and nationality, which at the end of the 1980s constituted the profile of globality.

The title of this section, "Bloomingdale's after Selling the Rain," invokes two short stories, one narrating the predicament of a homeless Costa Rican woman in New York, and the other ironizing the selling out of the national territory through a story strategizing the government's sale of rain. In the eighties, Naranjo sets out to construct immigrant characters. In her book of short stories *Another Route for the Rhumba,* the trauma of the immigrant has captured her attention. Transnationalism and consumerism join to shape the destiny of a street-woman who literally makes Bloomingdale's her home. Here consumerism is simulated: since the ideal consumer is a person who virtually lives in the stores, this ideal is paradoxically met by a homeless woman who literally lives in the stores but who, in order to stay in the store overnight, must impersonate a robot. Humans become the simulacra of machines, and the (re)production of simulacra is presented as the only way of living and making a living:

> Simulation is characterized by a precession of the model, of all models around the merest fact—the models come first, and their orbital (like the bomb) circulation constitutes the genuine magnetic field of events. Facts no longer have any trajectory of their own. (Baudrillard 32)

In the mall, the woman organizes her own laws of primary accumulation, investments, sales, circulation of merchandise, and anonymous societies, that is, a complete reversal of the situation in which capital generates its own simulacra. Following the same logic of the story of the hero and the traitor in Borges's short story—where hero and traitor exchange places constantly until the two are no longer distinguishable from one another—the story of the immigrant in Bloomingdale's juxtaposes the terms *homeless, immigrant,* and *elegant consumer,* the house refurbished daily by conspicuous consumption and the furnishing department converting itself into home. The store's simulacrum of a house is the consummation of the ideal home, one which woman can refurnish daily. Every day the woman/robot/homeless person/ shopper chooses the bed she will sleep on and her bedding. Instead of leaving the house in the morning to go shopping during the day, she leaves the shopping center in the morning to take care of her business outside, coming back home to the shopping center at night. The story ends with the homeless woman's proposal that all the homeless take over the malls. The individual solution becomes a collective solution. The story amply fulfills Baudrillard's dictum that

> it was capital which was the first to feed throughout its history on the destruction of every referential, of ideal distinction between true and false, good and evil, in order to establish a radical law of equivalences and exchange, the iron law of its abstraction, disconnection, deterritorialisation. (43)

Only a woman, and only a woman like Carmen Naranjo, could push those limits of causal logic to these extremes. After *Diario,* Naranjo intends, in her writing, to return to common places, but habit, custom, style, and a very highly articulated sense of the zeitgeist concerning the logic of the socius won't let her. In her work it is obvious that the signifier has been infected with the mortal virus of simulation. Naranjo's lucid dialectics operate on the impulse to try to retain the unrepresentable. Reality and realism are long gone. The logic of globality has snatched the signifier from the socius—people, masses, troop, bases—and located it in multitude, crowd—the collective subject = Zero. The misrepresented people have been displaced from the peasant structures of Costa Rican society and thrown into the phony world created by Bloomingdale's. Away from the nation and the state, peasantry and servants are located in the mall, a final and fatal irony of Naranjo's constitution of the popular subject, roboticized humans who have no place in the narratives that affectionately recreate social types and/or position them in insurgent revolutionary geographies.

PART IV

(Subaltern) Nation/(Subaltern) People

At the head of everything is God, Lord of Heaven.
After Him comes Prince Torlonia, lord of the Earth.
Then come Prince Torlonia's armed guards.
Then come Prince Torlonia's armed guards' dogs.
Then, nothing at all. Then, nothing at all. Then, nothing at all.
Then come the peasants. And that's all.

Ignazio Silone, Fontamara

CHAPTER ELEVEN

Them

In one of the most lyrical articles in cultural criticism, "Chandra's Death," Ranajit Guha explains and comments on the transformation of cultural signs performed by legal scripture.[1] The analytical reconstruction of the abortion case of a woman named Chandra, her punishment and death, leads him to explain convincingly how an act of solidarity between women is converted into a crime, filial/parental love toward a woman into masculine solidarity, a loving sister into a murderer, all of the actors in this tragedy into the accused, and the expressions of pain into legal depositions. Where, he asks, is the pleasure that that man felt for Chandra in the moment of possessing her? Where is the love and passion of which lyrical Bengali poetry speaks?

In reading the legal fragment that registers the case of Chandra's death, Guha demonstrates how love, understood as sexuality and the fulfillment of pleasure and desire, is subordinated to the legal writing of the civil code that regulates customs among people. Legal writing has the power to edit narrative sequences in order to make them permeable to judiciary logic, in which the transformation occurs. In obedience to the laws that sanction this privileged connotation, the real history of the subaltern community is transliterated in an abstract moment of legality; and the will of the state, with its piercing voice, interrupts and contains the will of the social subject expressed in moans, sighs, and murmurs.

On another level, Guha's writing about legal scripture re-presents for him one of the signs of the inability of the "local bourgeoisie to speak for the nation" (Guha 41), their inability "to understand and value the articulation of the masses of this nationalism except negatively, as a problem of law and order" (39), a historical incapacity, whose study "constitutes the central problematic of historiography of colonial India" (43).

In "Chandra's Death," the sign of woman is situated at a series of inter-sections: masculine desire/sexual exchange, simple facile virtue/patriarchal knowledge, feudal ideology/masculine fantasy, colonial anthropology/penalization. By virtue of this semiotic any event can convert itself into a case, any disobedience into a crime, any enunciation into self-accusation. By means of this hypothesis, or the assimilation of one order into another, the masculine subject has the property/liberty to situate himself as the masculine "I" of discourse at any one of the enunciating levels.

Patriarchal concern to exercise maximum control over female sexuality, the gold standard and base of communal contracts, is entered as evidence in these anthropological sites across which the patriarchal subject moves with impunity. The two terms in the enunciation are refuge and sanctuary for the masculine subject position. The transition of that masculine I, from lover to custodian of patriarchal ethics, becomes invisible. The relation Guha establishes between the micro-event and the everyday, the fine detail apparently irrelevant to social existence and the interrelation between genders, and the extensive drama of this social life itself as an object worthy of historiography, both say something about this historiography. As Foucault says, only when death crosses the path of history does it convert itself into a crime, that is, a relevant event and transcendental signifier. The narrative of the law, which transmutes death into assassination and assassination into murder, "changes the scales, lengthens the proportions and makes visible the small-est grain in the visible history" (Guha 139). Thus he explains how legal narratives play "a role in the exchange between the familiar and the extraordinary, between the quotidian and the historical" (139). The moral and the political find one of their saddest convergences in the judicial in this case, that of the administration of sexuality and, with it, of emotional life within the context of nation.

"I can see the morning star through a little hole"

The morning star, and thus the evening star, is called Nixtayolero. So it is called by Ernesto Cardenal, who appropriates an indigenous term to replace the name of Venus, goddess of love. Because twilight frightens her, Guadalupe Fuentes waits for day to break through a little hole left by the branches of the *tihuilote* tree, with which José built his and Lupe's ranch. Ernesto Cardenal's *zanate clarinero* "flies over our hut saying clarinero-clarinero" (Argueta 3).[2] The watchbird announces the hour of daybreak. At half past four in the morning José has to run like a thief so he will not be seized by the "pohlice." The voices of the *Popol Vuh*, who have asked for centuries what must be done in order for day to break, are invoked and answered by Lupe, José's wife, Adolfina's grandmother, Justino, and María Pía's mother.

In Argueta's narrative it is a woman who speaks; women validate her courage, her feminine authority declaring decisive judgment, her verdict condemning the forces of law and order. It is a woman, Romelia, who tells the story of the protest in the bank, a woman, Adolfina, who organizes and who protects a woman retreating, and a woman, María Pía, who tells the history of the torture. The masculine voices—José, Justino, Helio, Ramírez—are sparse and are all placed in quotation marks. Women (Lupe, Adolfina, Romelia, María Pía, Romelia's mother) come to occupy a central or radial point of reference in a narrative of nationalities in which the major Central American voices converge. Those of Cardenal conjoin with those of the *Popol Vuh*, with those of Salarrué, with those of Asturias, in the representation of the sign of Woman and people, as historical subjects of the other Central American historiography. The masculine voices are also theirs, and they are the army, the authority, and the law. This is how, within the macrosystem to which Guha refers above—law and order as constructions of the national masses—Argueta constitutes "the politics of the people" as "autonomous" dominion which "continues operating vigorously" in spite of the resistance offered by the paradigm of Nation (Guha 40). The relationships between legal culture, popular culture, and high culture are called into play in a testimonial narrative through the writer's writing as a scribe.

To Guha's question in search of the desire, the attraction, love, and pleasure that that man had felt for Chandra in the moment in which he possessed her (that is to say, before creating a child engendered by his own semen and converted into a legal case, rendering her pregnancy an object of legal prosecution and the death sentence, or driving into exile the woman who did nothing more than give him pleasure), the Central American text responds. It responds from the marriage bed of the poor, inside the *tihuilote* ranch, as Lupe puts it in opening the testimony of a single day of her life:

> When the big star gets to the little hole . . . , it's four in the morning, and by
> then I'm awake . . . pretending to be asleep, snuggling up to José when it's cold
> or my butt pressed against him if it's hot. (Argueta 4; translation modified)

Then in the silence of dawn, when Minerva's owl prepares itself to take flight, she serves him his coffee and his beans, and "while [she] watche[s] him eat in the candlelight [she] keep[s] quiet, not saying a word. It's time to say goodbye" (51).

"Goodbye, José," she'll tell him at 4:30 in the morning and again at 2:30 in the afternoon, when the army officials come to show her his disfigured body, the body of the man who was her only companion, and whom she has to deny, in order to show him, in his hour of death, nothing other than her absolute and unrestricted love. His unconditional love is shown with the painful opening of his only good eye, as a sign of complicity, understanding, and love between them, conveying their final pact before death is consummated. With this gesture the absolute dividing line between solidarity and venality is traced:

> I have not failed you, José. I understand that you were saying goodbye when
> you opened your eye, and besides greeting me, that you were proud of me, see-
> ing me standing, with my arm around the shoulders of your granddaughter.
> (192)

Can you identify this man? asked the authorities.

> Then I said no. It had to be no without any quavering of my voice, without
> the least trace of doubt. And at that moment the good eye was opened. (192)

The aestheticization of mass repression reaches a climax in this eye, which sees because it is seen, as José de Jesús Martínez would say, repeating the poetics of Machado. In the shift from the possessive "you" in "your eye" to the impersonal "the eye," and from the active "you opened" to the passive "[it] was opened," and in this complicit look a pact and the equality between man and woman is established. Two consciences stand united before officialdom.

Neither Lupe nor Chandra is alone: they are accompanied by a chorus of women situated on the sidelines, horizontally, as Guha says subalterns organize themselves. In one of the most accomplished acts of solidarity in the history of loving in Central American representation, in the patriotic eroticism of the subaltern, the granddaughter first, then the grandfather and grandmother remain serene and firm before the threat of power. In contrast to Chandra, labeled as a criminal in the state's narrative, the literary environment of the testimonial confirms Lupe in her self-generated literary representation, situating her at the center of her community: with her neighbors, her daughters, but most of all her granddaughter, Adolfina, and Adolfina's friend, María Romelia. The representation of the subalternity of these women, through their own testimonial voices, passed through the sieve of Argueta's literate culture, constitutes, in the writing, the political representation of the possibility of common cultural fronts between two kinds of subalternities, that of the male and female peasantry and that of the literate intellectuals, the former excluded from, and the latter disillusioned with, the liberal/colonial historiography of the oligarchic Central American elites and their concept of nation.

As in the case of the writers analyzed earlier, Argueta and his informants try to embody the other concept of nation, the other patriotic love. In the case of the testimonial narrative, the contesting concept of fatherland speaks of democracy, civilization, *mestizaje,* and communism. Somehow, I suspect that there are, in all these analogies, dreams of liberalism that Central American nations never had. Perhaps "communism" is the expression of an anti-oligarchic stance, against daily repression, a way of phrasing social-democratic aspirations. Caricatured in the discourse of one of the guards, in the historicized confession of a friend, in unpolished rhetoric, and also, for this reason, popular rhetoric, the voice of the subaltern is reproduced; one who, like Chandra's lover, has decided to support the vertical power-narratives of legal prose.

The (de)eroticization of the Masculine/Feminine Body: Solidarity in Affinity

Romelia and Adolfina, thirteen and fifteen years old, respectively, find themselves on a bus going to Chalatenango, Chalate, after taking part in a protest organized by the Christian Federation "to get an answer concerning a cheaper price for insecticides and fertilizer, but the Bank was closed" (37). There are men on the bus, but they begin to be embodied only as dead, disappeared bodies. For instance, nobody knows where Romelia's cousin was lost. María Romelia's voice tells the story in idiomatic phrases, the vocabulary and grammatical constructions calling attention to themselves as peculiar to unschooled people. This is the language of the impoverished, of the "subaltern," of those of "inferior rank" according to Guha. The speaker, Romelia, reveals in her speech "the general attributes of subordination . . . whether they be expressed in terms of class, caste, age, gender and office or in any other manner" (Guha 35).

The rhythm of the young girl's speech is agile and can be considered as journalistic prose in which an informant tells a reporter of a series of events occurring in rapid succession. The here and now link themselves to another succession of events, which together make up a more extensive narrative. Romelia's voice narrates and the words flare up: pohlice, chopper, gas. Along with these are other words: *apiarse, chiquistes, guiste, cipota, guangoche, pisto* (to get off, *chiquistes, guiste*, kid, loose, cash). Both series form semantic ensembles writing the hegemonic tensions of Modernity.

"Yes, well in the past few years things have changed" (Argueta 24). Therefore, the vocabulary of the subaltern has also changed, for in Romelia's discursive voice there also exist counterbalances to "pohlice," "choppers," and "gas." These are "to participate," "rally," "comrade," "rights," "affiliate," "empowerment," "awareness," "to organize," "peace," "christian federation," "farm workers' federation"—these last written in lowercase letters. They are also semantic ensembles of Modernity toward Post-Modernity, each with its own history. It behooves Lupe, the main voice, to make the original list of words untranslatable into the technical languages. Such are *bayunca, perraje, chapin, chacaras, siguanabas, cipitios, encumbrar, machigua, cuche, guisquil, dominguear, chapoda* (rough woman, herd of dogs, Guatemalan, small plots of land, ghost women, kids, raise up, *machigua*, dog, *guisquil*, for Sundays, clearing the land). There are also more complex systems like those invoked by folk medicine, the *infundia de gallina, la manteca de garrobo, los polvos de culebra, las hojas de guarumo, la manteca de zorrillo* (chicken fat, garrobo fat, snake powder, guarumo leaves, skunk fat)—similar to those things Chandra swallows in order to abort. These are words that fail to signify and that signify Indian and peasantry at the same time. They belong to other semantic horizons and other narratives, as is said today. They invoke the first territorial encounters, the first cultural survivals, and the small world, the microterritory that begins in the *hacienda* and ends there.

The radius of action is narrow: Lupe and José's world scarcely reaches the detour, the store, the people. It is no wider than a kilometer. This is why the name and measurement of a kilometer is written in capital letters, like a key referent, signifying that "something more than," not a unit of measurement but a confinement, that Lupe's world does not extend beyond that point. Yet *kilometer* is at the same time a territoriality, signaling the presence and absence of objects and commodities found "beyond," like lime for the corn, aspirin, clothing, the people. To echo Asturias, these products are highly appreciated; *cuche* soap, for example, is a soap that in Nicaragua is called "soap of the happy dog," a soap with a high percentage of lye that is, as in Asturias, "sacred like corn" (8). Beyond the kilometer lies the state farm, cleanliness, land clearing, the day's pay, planting and idle seasons, the owner, the jeeps, pineapple, coffee, latifundio, capital. There is a constant comparison implying a "wide and alien" world, other.

In the small world there is a small utopia: "[to] have some tranquility . . . live in peace and . . . [to] have enough to eat" (46). These are Romelia's mother's desires for her daughter, for her daughter's children, for her daughter's friends. Poor people's love and solidarity in affinity is clearly established between Romelia and Adolfina. It is very similar to that which is established, mindful of the difference, between Fidel and Che, between Cabezas and Ventura, between El Zorro and El Danto, between Martínez and General Torrijos. In just such tones Romelia tells of Adolfina's skill in directing the retreat on the bus, choosing who may leave and from which corners so that the "pohlice" will not kill them, and how, when the "pohlice" encircle them, she remains calm. They push her into the bus through a window and she does not complain. She is not intimidated, for, in the words of her grandmother, Adolfina "is alive and [they] are not going to kill her slowly" (194). When she can, she will sneak away and jump over the ridge. She is only fifteen years old. And the eye that contemplates her is thirteen. The fleeting moment of first person narration ("I was one" [37]) rapidly slides into third person ("the *compañera* let another group off" [38]), allowing the narrator to place herself in the first person plural ("There we arrived at a pohlice checkpoint" [38]). In this conjoining of pronouns, the first, third person singular, and the first plural, solidarity is established between two women, an affinity that ends in Romelia's testimony when Adolfina visits her to take her some crackers and oranges, and "When I see her leaving, I get a lump in my throat" (46).

"Dominus Obispu, On Your Ass I Pinch You": the Voice of Empowerment

Between the semantic ensembles, perhaps, the groups of words that form systems and significations, and the love of the informants, mediates not only the framework of law and order, one vertical and one horizontal concept of civil rights and peace, but also the problem of consciousness—What is awareness? It is empowerment, having one's eyes wide open to see the boss, and not lowering one's head, because looking him in the eye makes you respectable. And, naturally, it is in the human body, the body of the son, Justino, and the body of the husband, José, that precisely this representation of empowerment will come to be presented. Facing these bodies, the woman,

Lupe, mother and wife, is neither *mater dolorosa* nor an erotic object, because "Lupe is so courageous they say she did not even cry, I always admired your grandmother's strength" (46). As the popular saying goes, grief is a private matter: "After what happened to my son Justino, I prefer to stay closed up inside myself. It's not that I get sad. It's something I can't explain" (9). At the end of the novel, after midday, in the dying hours of the afternoon, there is the reiteration of and obsession with empowerment, which is strength, a means of struggle and hope for the future.

In the beginning, conscience is a moral, religious term. When one speaks of the voice of conscience ("Doesn't your conscience bother you?") this is a Christian concept. In Lupe, it is the voice of religion. Conscience, in the beginning, is an authoritarian voice. It is the voice of power. It is the voice that generates fear, a voice threatening punishment. It is the internalized voice of the superego—religion, state, government, law: the bad *Cadejo*:

> The voice is not ours. . . . The voice of conscience is severe, absolutely unpleasant . . . the voice of conscience does us favors, but they're favors that no one asked for. . . . The voice of conscience belongs to one and doesn't belong to one's own. It comes from God knows where. (15, 16, 18)

But to be conscious also means to open your eyes, or not to lower them, to look directly ahead. Consciousness is a glow, an inner light, in the words of Ramírez and Dickens, radiant moments. As in the first meaning, in the second the semiosis of consciousness is connected to religion and to changes in the notion of religion and of religious practice. It is related, within the farmworkers' organizations, to the concept of cooperatives, better prices and administration, initiated by oppositional religious groups. It is a concept that puts the body on the line, embodies itself.

The presence of the physical body slips from the games of popular language, abundant in Central American literary uses of *anus* and *ass,* into severe physical punishment inflicted upon a "faggot" priest. In the feminization of the masculine body as degradation, in the allusion to homosexuality as a weak point and vulnerability, the semantic field of the police and the military impresses itself upon Argueta's narrative. For "them" (the army) social sensibility is effeminate. And that is why "the priest was found half dead on the road to the kilometer. They had dumped him with his face mangled . . . they shoved a stick up his ass . . . and a little further up the frock was hanging all torn up" (30).

In the section on patriotism, as told by one of the guards, the differences are established. The men are divided into two classes, "the faggots and the real men," and "within the real men the truly macho must be chosen: those are the ones for the death squad" (128). In Argueta's section entitled "Them," the treatise on the fatherland is the treatise on "real men." The exchange between this military unit and the farmers' organization, the federations, and the cooperatives is called human rights. That is, that struggle—after empowerment—is synonymous with human rights, as in civil rights, as in the code, as in law and order, "the right to health care, to food, and to schooling for our children," tiny utopias (31).

This empowerment is synonymous with seeing through one's own eyes, not lowering one's head, learning "to look them in the face" (32). It is also the source from which this significance is generated, the translation of words into one's own language: obverse and reverse as in the case of Guha's Chandra, where kindness is not submission, respecting one's neighbor is not respect for the master, respect for the master is simply being satisfied with what he arranges, goodness is not resignation, communism is enjoying the earth and not gaining heaven. Empowerment is, in one aspect, struggle, and in the other, human rights. A glossary of these terms marks their tensions with postmodernity.

At the end of the day in *One Day of Life*, when the sun begins to set at 5:00 in the afternoon, Adolfina Hernández Guardado tells her grandmother it has been a difficult day but it is almost over. Her grandmother, Guadalupe Fuentes de Guardado, asks her what could have happened to the man who was brought by the police, and her granddaughter responds, "Don't think about it, Grandma, he will know what to do" (213), and her eyes fill with tears. With that last phrase concludes the growth of courage between two women, vying to keep the promise to the grandfather, José Guardado, who asked them to deny him so as to avoid the unnecessary sacrifice of more blood. And they have made this request a matter of empowerment.

With this history, Central American narrative reaches a threshold. In the urgency of his need to represent the subaltern, Argueta did not hesitate to gather its words. Seduced by the words of the subaltern, the narrative puts aside the imaginative reproduction of social environments and instead goes directly to the theater of war in order to gather the testimony of its protagonists firsthand. In his fictionalized testimonial Argueta enacts his opinion of the process of representation of a gendered subaltern. His people/informants are not found, I would like to argue, far from Dalton's Tata Higinio, from Ramírez's anonymous *campesino* in Nicaragua's revolution, or even from the Indians in Asturias. Argueta's characters descend directly from this literary genealogy, finding their imaginary history in it, and those characters find in these their modern incarnation. This is not to deny, of course, that the former are fictional characters, who resemble real people in what is represented. In the same way, the modern narrative, whose real voices are directly recorded, has still been processed by the narrative skills of the writer. But after reading the narrative of the voices of the peasantry that Argueta presented with his pen, at least a moment of silence and reflection is in order.

Those whom we find in the intersecting discourses are not ordinary characters. They are extraordinary characters in and for their ordinary role. The extraordinary is that we are confronted in literature with voices we have heard all around us in Central America. In the life of these characters we can recreate in the imagination what everyday life has told us for so long. The last dialogue between grandmother and granddaughter assumes, in the bosom of what is most dear, a political stance that throughout the novel has been defined as a matter of empowerment. The definition of empowerment is not only a string of words written in the narrative but corporeal representation of the physical exchange that occurs when the human body lives that meaning and definition.

Empowerment is the head of Justino nailed to a stake. It is the disappearance of Helio Hernández's body. It is the body of Emilio Ramírez submerged in a bucket of water with a chili-laden toothbrush up his ass. But empowerment is, above all, in the end, the courage to deny, with the voices of two women, one forty-five and the other fifteen years old, with conviction, the most beloved. When José, organizer of the cooperatives, is brought half-dead to his house to be identified by his relatives, both women, in one of the most transgressive acts of solidarity, the younger calling the older to order, deny him:

> How am I going to know him if you bring him bathed in blood! I don't even know who it could be. You can't even see his face, I don't understand how you could think anyone would recognize this man. (190)

Accepting the grandmother's moment of weakness, she calls her to attention: "Grandmother, what is happening to you?" (191) and the grandmother, wife of this mangled, beaten man, denies: "No, I don't know who it could be" (193).

CHAPTER TWELVE

"There Is Nothing like a Man Astride... in War, or in Love"

Asturias's novel *Men of Maize* opens with a war.[1] The cacique Gaspar Ilóm and his entourage are on the verge of betrayal. Woman, Gaspar Ilóm's wife, the Piojosa Grande, intuits woman's treason but cannot avert it. At the banquet celebrating the initiation of combat, Vaca Manuela poisons the nobility, and the struggle for the freedom of the forest of Ilóm is finally ended. As a result, Machojón's son is borne away by hallucination. The Amerindian past haunts him in the shape of swarms of dragonflies, and he dies. Machojón, too, dies of grief. Colonel Godoy, content with having defeated the Great Warrior, is, like Machojón and his son, lured to his death. Rambling and deranged, the defeated skirt the boundaries of their own land unmolested. The damage has already been done. There is no seeking softer surroundings. The destruction of the mythical Ilóm has opened up a rift, at which the entire population takes fright, never to try again, daunted by the failures of the past. Devastatingly depressed, their actions are those of a people coming to terms with a lifelong and terrible premonition. The Amerindians are left without succor. Goyo Yic goes blind and is condemned to look for his wife María Tecún, who has vanished as if swallowed up in the depths of the earth.

With the death of Ilóm, the people of Ilóm are forever routed. There is no attempt to grasp the reasons why; everything has already been explained.

The Indians are simply dislodged from the cultivated areas of modernism to roam the frontiers of progress. They cannot leave the narrow circuits of informal subsistence and seasonal economies, zones barely even patrolled by the state. Literary critics were quick to spot this excess, and conceived a growing antipathy for this kind of representation, which seemed to place a strain upon the fabric of society. Condemning his indiscretion, they immediately excluded Asturias's style from critical consideration.

Modernism/Magic Realism/Positivism

In a polemic between realism and modernism, Jameson isolates the following quotation from Jonathan Culler:

> When a writer such as Baudelaire or Flaubert is "conscious of himself," that is "conscious of his images as interpretation, of his words not as furnitures of the world but as artifacts which . . . are utilized to communicate ends," then the old literary discourse enters a long terminal crisis, from which canonic modernism is the only "solution." (64)[2]

Perhaps, if we avoid using the term *modernism*, to skirt any conflicts within Latin American studies, where modernism means something different, or substitute *magic realism* for *modernism*, the same can be advanced of Miguel Angel Asturias, more than a century later, in his novel *Men of Maize*.

Without Jameson's irony, but with the same historical tendency, this is perhaps the idea that Martin Lienhard's double reading of the text entertains. Willing to heed both sides of the polemic, in his first reading, Lienhard appraises the arguments put forward by those concerned with realism, taking issue mainly with the intersections of literature, history, and anthropology. Then, he turns around and presents a thesis along the lines of literary criticism, mediating between two ideas, both tenable, in order to bring interpretation closer to the mark. His first reading foregrounds the problem of intertextuality, probing the accuracy of code switching and translation, upholding history in particular and the social sciences in general to be excepted from the problems of representation. Literature is not considered capable of the same accuracy, and Asturias is evaluated on the basis of his alleged conversion of history into myth and held responsible for his lack of specific ethnic identification of the "indigenous referent," the knowledge of Mayan culture acquired through his visits to Parisian museums and libraries.

Admittedly, critics are never entirely candid, and the historical arguments hurled against Asturias's representation are an instrument not only to attack him but to construct a larger intellectual argument against the politics of magic realism. To lay bare the essential fictional character of literature is a way of taking issue with writers' proficiencies in managing linguistic codes, a virtuality interpreted as a vote in favor of the aesthetization of life and against social mobilization, based on strictly realistic or naive referential conventions of reading/writing—whether defined as a disjunction between vision of the world/style, or content/linguistic organization. As I will contend later, reading along the lines of argument and plot, stressing event, that is, reading literature as history, is paradoxical, for it simultaneously asserts and denies "reality" by bringing up questions pertaining to the referential, realistic level—granting at the same time that the referential is solely an indigenous myth.

Lienhard's own phrasing of the question proposes a reading against the grain, first granting that *Men of Maize* "could circumscribe itself to examine the way in which the writer converts the historical conflict between Indians and *ladinos* in the Maya area into artistic language" (317).[3] Then, by calling on the character Hilario, the voice who declares himself storyteller, he argues the opposite:

> The author's internal double, "within the text" [is] in charge of demythifying the mythical perception of novelesque reality . . . [and] the demagogic nature [of the text] at first sight, results in a dialectic game of mythifications, demythifications and remythifications, capable of invoking in the reader a liberating reflection on the nature of Asturian "magic realism." (320)

What seems to be at issue here is to discern the clash of two ideas by elucidating the nature of both readings, to determine whether both are referential, that is, imaginative rather than reflexive, or not, and to foreground the hegemonies of representation. In other words, there are two methods of proving the "truth" or narrative "authenticity" regarding the problem of the referentiality of the account of the Mayans and their conflict with *ladinos*. One is to proceed indirectly, by reading the text through other disciplines and thereby moving from history to "Mayan" mythology (passed through the filter of Mexican or Guatemalan culture), from economy to ethnology and from there to literature, that is, from literature to literature by way of other disciplines. The other is to proceed directly, reading the text as literature. For the moment let us just point out the redundancy, and stress that Lienhard aims at demonstrating, first, how Asturias transforms a historical conflict into a literary conflict, and, soon thereafter, how this same conflict rendered as literature constitutes itself by and in virtue of the same literary language, as a liberating reflection of the historical conflict, which is our primary signifier. In other words, he holds both strands of the Culler-Jameson debate in a tight grip.

The gist of the argument between realism and modernism (magic realism), which basically consists of deciding what is the real, and what the mocked, representation of the Mayan, brings other issues into play. Those interested in arguing against realism within magic realism, or in disdaining magic realism, would press the issue of "intertextuality," indexing the transition from history into literature, and taxing Asturias for his pretended representation of Guatemalan Amerindians, arguing that what he is doing "in reality" is transforming them into literature. Those interested in arguing the realism of magic realism will tease out meaning by interpreting it in terms of liberation, thereby studying the predominance and consciousness of form, shunning stark realism—primordially of the socialist ilk—qualifying it as positivistic, and reducing it to just another type of textual reality.

What is crucial to this debate is the question of positivism. On a scale startling to even hard-bitten cynics, the argument is not between literature and the social sciences, but among the social sciences themselves, there, history and anthropology in Paris and history and anthropology . . . where? In Guatemala? The problem of literary mediation can be reduced to a national or regional debate, the proof of the matter residing in the range and variety of empiricism and pragmatism rampantly proclaiming accuracy through proximity—in other words, arguing that direct knowledge of Amerindians in Guatemala yields a more accurate picture of Amerindians in Guatemala.

The act of rendering all writing into textuality, literature and fiction, resulting in the conversion of the Mayans into text, positions literary accomplishment and critical meticulousness within the same interpretive grid. Both signal the textual character of Mayans, whether "represented" or "misrepresented," in whichever textuality, thus highlighting the positivistic nature of both representations. Therefore, as in Culler's argument, in the Latin American polemic, magic realism or the predominance and consciousness of form prevails merely because it signals the constructed—artificial, fictitious—character of the author's constructions, whether of the "classical" or "progressive" positivistic variety, leaving vacant, it could be argued, the place of certainty. Criticism, correction, or adjustment requires loose and blank spaces where contenders can negotiate new contracts of meaning. The shifting and negotiating of positions between the intertextual and the formalistic arguments index an adjustment, the swinging of the pendulum between Marxist modernism and humanist postmodernist interpretations. In this debate, literature goes one better than history and ethnology, for the social sciences are strongly marked by classical positivism, caught up in the mimetic fallacy, whereas literature (magic realism) constituting itself as just fiction, poses no claims on reality, thereby turning the literary Amerindian construct into a sharper representational tool, an indirect instrument for Amerindian liberation. Foregrounding history institutionalizes the representational hegemony of the social sciences to the detriment of literature.

In these redundancies and tautologies, I presume, one can find the underpinnings of other purported ways of seeing and narrating the Amerindian. At issue, here, are at least two polemics: one zealously guarding the gates against the validity of comparisons and concurrences (Latin American magic realism and European modernism) and a performance-oriented one exploring the heuristic assets—and liabilities—of transforming a literary text into what it already is, a literary text. The basic premise of this second position is the rejection of positivistic epistemes among the propositions debating the place of the representation of the social subject of insurgency. The debate stops short of quibbling over the nature of realism—critical or bureaucratic—whose literary representation is kept at bay, holding it in contempt of the court of history. Lienhard's reading is located at the intersection, where both arguments have been shaken to the point of near collapse, each side holding the other responsible for misconstructions, one historical, the other textual, one more "real," the other "unreal."

Considering the oxymoronic frailty of the negotiations, both arguments keep strictly within the margins of verisimilitude, understood as

> the cultural code that is capable of dispensing its contents . . . of reinventing something like Genette's notion of the verisimile, eliminating any recourse to such codes and cultural motivations which are so common to [any French realist writer]. (Jameson 29)

Asturias often achieves this verisimilitude, in fact, above all in evoking Gaspar Ilóm's "indigenous" world. Here once again we find ourselves confronting the problem of the reducible, the redundant and the tautological, peculiar to positivism. Because if Jameson is correct, I am compelled to state that modernist aesthetics, that is, the indigenous world narrated by Asturias in the experimental, self-referential language of magic realism, is more suitable to the indigenous world than, let us say, socialist or classical positivistic realism. Or, not being entirely candid, I could invoke the paradox that the Mayans represented by magic realism are more Mayan than those represented in the realism of the social novel—for example, other Amerindians in

Huasipungo. Thus I could argue that between the two textual virtualities, that which most denies referentiality is the one that most approximates it.

Admittedly, when examined, Asturias's modernist "magical realism" proves to be precisely the ground of his European positivism—the Mayan culture learned in museums and libraries, the Amerindian/*ladino* conflicts aestheticized. However, there is more to Asturias than meets the eye. His obsession with plot and argument, his still identifiable linear narration and desire to tell a story—remnants of other modes of literary production in his literary space—is, on the underside, the voice of *criollo*/Republican/positivism nationally produced in Guatemala. Neither interpretive reading allows us to posit a break from positivism. European modernism (and consequently Latin American magic realism) is no way of transcending positivism, as the works of Irlemar Chiampi and Rodríguez Monegal promised.[4] Instead, Asturias could be situated precisely between two positivisms, one more classically conservative, the other more democratically liberal. Perhaps this is a self-evidently ludicrous position signaling the dilemma of continental writing in its two incarnations, those of the progressive liberal revolutionary and the progressive radical nationalist, within which we literary critics are also situated.

This is why Lienhard's dilemma is particularly attractive, since both readings are not only possible but also advisable—perhaps the embodiment of Barthes's concept of "the writable."[5] The criteria for certainty—which only means we take Gaspar Ilóm's grammatical existence seriously—turn us back to the social existence of Guatemalan Amerindians today, a return that places us again within positivism's affection for content and its belief in substance, that is, the metaphysics of the referent, or what I want to call, for lack of a better expression, the new humanism. Ironically, accepting the linguistic proficiency of the writer is today a way of preserving the social meaning of the text.

Whatever the verdict may be, whatever the outcome of these polemics, *Men of Maize* gives the impression of being an investment particularly dear to the author, an investment that cries out its denotation, in the sense Barthes gives the term. It is not that he is going to be carried away by passion, but the world of these people—be they his major characters, Machojón and Vaca Manuela, Goyo Yic or Nicho Aquin, or the entire ensemble of minor characters that populate his universe—is very dear to him. Gaspar Ilóm's predicament, for instance, invokes nostalgia, indicating that "some process properly allegorical of the past is possible" (Jameson 287), even though here the glossy transparencies of the nostalgic cinema Jameson puts forth as proof of nostalgia are replaced by an equally glossy invocation of courage, defense of what is one's own, of what in the words of the winner Colonel Godoy will come to be, in the last instance, Alas! manliness:

> "That Gaspar Ilóm was a devil of a man." . . . You could never guess his thought, it was wayward as the flames in the clearing fires. Here, there, everywhere his thought leaped, burning, and it had to be put out, and how was it to be put out if it was the thought of a man at war. (75)

This is another dimension, the plea for utopia. The concept of nature and naturalism, the life of feelings and instincts pertains, in Asturias, to a syncretic reconstruction of the Mayan world. This is recreated through the myth of the cave, a European cultural code, which allows him access to the world of the dead, to the past, and to history. The Platonic cave through that strange marriage of politics and eros also represents the vagina of the fleeing woman, in this case, "Tecuna":

> Some have within their secret parts the bodies of small palpitating birds, others the downiness of aquatic plants which begin vibrating as the current of the male swirls through; and the magic ones have sexes like pleated bundles which gradually fold and unfold in the ecstasy of love, there where the blood drives its last living distances in an organism that is possessed, then leaps to become the beginning of another living distance. In the final plunge, love is inhuman like a tecuna. Its hidden snout seeks out the root of life. You exist more. In those moments you exist more. The tecuna weeps, struggles, bites, squeezes, tries to get up, gasps, mouthes, sweats, scratches, and is left like a wasp unable to buzz, as though she were dead from suffering. But she has left her sting in the man who had her beneath the breathing of his desire. Liberation ties them together. (288)

The utopian vision is a method of endorsing the natural to monetarist economies, thereby partially retrieving some of utopia's critical negative acerbity and wielding it as an offensive weapon, as an instrument with which negatively to construct a new vision of well-being and instinctive gratification:

> You should have seen what this land was like when they were cultivating it rationally. . . . Maize should be planted as they used to plant it, as they still do, to give the family its grub, and not for business. . . . They did things in a small way, if you like, but they had all they needed, they weren't greedy like us. . . . I saw the forests of Ilóm burning at the turn of the century. It is progress advancing with the red of the conqueror . . . because it was progress that turned trees into firewood. (253)

The argument for the enacting of a utopian and gratifying inversion, in which an intelligence localized in Guatemala and identified as Guatemalan incorporates the indigenous world into its cultural representation, could be supported by the extraordinary *tendresse* the text displays for characters and story. The Mayans bear the full brunt of history, and, after centuries of being pushed into darkness, they are now poised for the spotlight. The rot is laid bare: all of the human subjects suffer from severe and, it seems, final derangement. Gaspar Ilóm's hand, time and again expected to rip off their concealing bands, is dead. The hallucinations of pain and love have undone Machojón and Goyo Yic:

> Machojon was a man, and his fears were just that, the tremors of an old fool who, because of his age, was starting to be afraid of everything. . . . A swarm of locusts on fire, Machojon thought, and he bowed his head to hide his face from the downpour of luminous insects. . . . Machojon caught a glimpse of the pixcoy to his left and crossed himself with the hand in which he held the rein. "Out, pixcoy, away!" . . . Machojon eyed the flying storm of sparks. It was still growing heavier. . . . The horse, the packsaddle, the sheep-skin cover . . . everything was on fire. . . . The candle glow of the fireflies streamed down from his hat . . . like the light at the beginning of the world. . . . Machojon, anointed with light and water, felt his jaw trembling like a loose horseshoe. . . . As long as he stayed in the saddle he would be a star up in the sky. (27–29)

> "Maria TecuuuUUUn! . . ." shouted Goyo Yic, without breathing, weary of inquiring with his hands, his nose, his ears, in things and in the air, which way his woman and children had gone. Little streams of weeping, like brown sugar water, ran through the dust of the roads on his cheeks. And he went on shouting, in a tantrum. . . . Goyo Yic stood cocking his ear, without breathing, because he was drowning in air and he had to breathe quickly sometimes and sometimes he had to stop breathing altogether. . . . He slapped himself on the face, pulled his own hair, tore at his own clothes, and with no more breath to shout, he kept on, just talking. (104–6)

Both are plunged into agony, walking disjointedly into a life that does not belong and has never belonged to them. They have dropped the reins of their lives, their hearts sagging under the weight of gloom, their eyes unfocused and their faces fixed in the grip of death. All guesses about their destiny have proved to be unfounded. But in their struggle, they never cry off. Those are the rules covering procurement: life is destined to batter them unfairly.

But if the deep fondness with which they are portrayed is not enough, there is also the tempo of narration, the economy with which the story is told, the spiraling form unfolding and sluggishly revealing the links between the characters, the relentless repetition and remarking of each and every episode, the tangling of one into the other. These are not solely the product of artifice, the expression of the will of the writer, but the indigenous world's compelling presence, perhaps the imaginary recuperation and preservation of previous cultural spaces. Asturias could not have learned this anywhere except in the geographies and ethnographies of his native Guatemala.

In the protected areas of the literary reservations, the presence of other ways of narrating the popular can be discerned—the tradition of the *Popol Vuh*, Salarrué, the popular voices of anecdotes and refrains. All these elements give the text a hybrid mestizo character, reproducing the "readable" in the mixture of realism's and magic realism's techniques, the *criollo* side and the European-educated side of the author evidenced in anecdotes and inventive phrases, events and sequences of events, and allusions to the "other," centering nostalgia, while the "other" keeps a distance, his voice totally absent, his measuring gaze perplexed.

Poetic *tendresse* and narrative distancing do not constitute, as might be conjectured, the two opposing poles of a single proposition. On the contrary, they constitute the twin elements of one and the same proposition, which on one hand loves the subject as a literary subject, and on the other knows himself to be alien to his world. This distancing not only assesses the *ladino* side of Asturias, but his creole stand, signifying through and with this a transnationalized cultural production of a class, or group, which, by education and culture, disengages from *mestizaje*, situating itself in a nonnational limbo. By birth and by trade they are neither national, nor indigenous, nor *ladinos*. Perhaps they belong to the transcodified universal as transnational, which is, properly speaking, the locus of the presumed ubiquitous "national" oligarchic bourgeoisie, of the groups holding power worldwide, or of the intellectuals educated in the international centers to compete in the international markets. This cultural limbo (already appropriated at *Men of Maize*'s publication by transnational cultural industries) is defined as a space from which data is compiled, and in the novel it emerges in many places. Among other deeper articulations, it emerges in the minuscule yet pertinent phonetic distinction between the *meiz* of the Mayan ideolect, and the *maíz* of the writer's ideolect, inscribed in the Spanish title of the text, which the English version cannot register. Substituting the phoneme *e* for *a* draws the distinction between the Mayans and the international intelligentsia to which Asturias, the Nobel laureate, belongs.

The presence of *tendresse* draws attention to itself, attenuating his position as the subject of the positivist discourse of progress, which Asturias and his compatriot Cardoza y Aragón learned in Paris, but also in Guatemala, particularly during their elementary education at the beginning of the century. *Tendresse* underwrites his oscillation between positions, appraising the distances between the noun *Indio* and the noun *Indio,* depending upon their subject position as insurrectionary subject, indigenous leader, insurgent woman, wretched of the earth, "little indian." If I argue that the voice of the narrative authority does not seem to have any distance with respect to the ideologies of progress, I am unable to explain how Colonel Godoy, the military character, qualifies the relationship between barbarian positivism and civilized positivism, considering positivism from the indigenous perspective in phrases like "It is progress advancing with the red of the conqueror . . . because it was progress that turned trees into firewood" (253).

Thus literature staggers from representation to representation, one element (form) accounting for keeping the reading within the boundaries of European modernism/positivism, the other (events and plot) accounting for that pertaining to Latin American socialist realism. If, at the beginning of the narrative, what is unintelligible (new codes) or what is writable (the zero degree of writing of the history of Gaspar Ilóm) keeps us alert to the "modernist"/Latin American magic realist canon, in reaching the story of Machojón, his son, and Vaca Manuela, the discursive levels dismiss the argument of modernism with the smallest gesture, a brief interjection, freezing the techniques. In plot and story, *tendresse* heavily outweighs all other techniques, and, considering that the second story is a corollary of the first, the "truth" or referentiality of the first depends upon the second, and that of both upon the subjectivity of the character or characters who tell and retell.

We must keep in mind that Asturias finished his book in 1949—the same year Carpentier published *El reino de este mundo*—but almost twenty years before the publication of what is now called the new Central American literature. Roque Dalton's book is dated 1976, Lezama's *Paradiso* 1966, and only in the works, first of Ramírez and then in those of Chávez Alfaro and Argueta, could one find variations of that *tendresse* Asturias displays for the poor more than for the Amerindians, or shall I say for the impoverished and ladinized Amerindians, a sensibility perhaps born with Salarrué in the 1930s. A tangential look at two of his contemporaries, Lezama Lima and José Coronel Urtecho, gives us two entirely different measures of how the Amerindian masses were represented, their playful and mocking irony contrasting with the seriousness and, above all, the sobriety of Asturias. For instance, one can never find in Asturias a description of the Amerindian as "a precious little Indian, chubby, with fat cheeks, energetic, as if escaped from a Diego Rivera painting" (Urtecho 37) or "the Indian with a hat in his hands, white trousers cut above the knee, a short-sleeved white shirt, looking like a tanned stone" (107), Dalton's taking-off point for ironic distancing in the loving construction of Tata Higinio.[6] But neither can we find him writing the *guajiro* José Eugenio Cemí as "crude but very imposing, having the intemperate presumptions of a handsome provincial; talkative, although with a rich flow of palatals transformed into explosive syllables and swallowing the ends of words" (63).[7]

Furthermore, Asturias's Amerindians, in Asturias's dialogues with whites, creoles, or *ladinos,* rarely speak like Amerindians, using terms like "nuay," conjugating the verb only in the second person singular in an attempt to establish within the verb tense the distance between yours and mine. In fact, the passage from which this speech is excerpted is one of the few in which the cultural codes peculiar to the author and different from those of his fictitious universe shimmer in a speech that is not only that of a Mayan but that of the *criollo* Asturias. True, it is in the most banal of languages, the least magic realist, that socialist realist phrases such as "The Spanish beast resisted" and "They answered him from their beds, in a strange language made up of stammers, and from some houses . . . copper colored faces emerged to greet him without affection or hatred" can be found (280).

In concluding, I should like to observe that my readings of Asturias do not enable me to trace distinctions between Amerindians and *ladinos.* For me both are subaltern social subjects, and for me the problem of indigenous representation is related not only to pre-Hispanic cultures, but also to the endemic poverty of the modern world, the reverse side of progress. Furthermore, this lack of distinction between Amerindians and poor *ladinos,* as they are called in the novel, who in no way differ from Nachito Catín or from the peasant who comes to greet Vice President Ramírez on the stage, is not rendered explicit in any of his characters, except in the voice of the white characters, such as the priest Don Casualidón, or Sicambro.

In their speech, the other characters, poor *ladinos,* reproduce with a certain consistency aspects of the ideolect attributed to the Amerindians, and in their clothing, customs, and myths, the survival of indigenous mores—if positivism and neopositivism left some distinguishable and classifiable cultural survivals. "The natives were poverty-stricken Indians who wanted for everything because their families were large" (281). Let us not forget that this narrative links the poverty of these Amerindians—a poverty represented with the burning of the forest of Ilóm at the beginning of the century—with two types of economy, with the indigenous subsistence economy in which corn is meat/beef/flesh and body—the symbolic in Barthes—and the market economy, which plants to sell. "It is progress advancing with the red of the conqueror . . . because it was progress that turned trees into firewood" (253). In other words, for Asturias, the permeability of poverty, which makes the borders between one and the other type of economy fluid, is what is alien to the narrative persona and to his world. This takes us once more to the representation of the social subject through the characters, to the name and to the noun in which the representation of the civil, the social, the cultural, the psychic, is entwined. In affection, which could be encoded as a theory of sensibility, these characters did indeed invoke the presence of the social subject.

It is worth remarking that throughout this book the popular subject has been invoked as a social subject, cast in essentially political and military narratives concerned with the idea of nation building and social justice. This subject has not been lacking in feelings, but the feelings granted to him have all been negative—frustration, pain, vengeance, and hatred. In the libidinal literary economies, pleasure and love have been subtracted and redistributed elsewhere. That Asturias and the writers we will examine in coming to the end of our journey bestow upon their popular characters the possibilities of a loving emotional life is already an innovative cultural code. Ramírez's Nachito Catín, a poor man, more truly a mestizo than Asturias's *ladinos*, is a man interested in revenge, whereas Machojón, for instance, is carried away by a passion for his son that makes him curse his historical role. Machojón's remorse for his betrayal of Gaspar Ilóm has nothing to do with any political, national, or class affiliation. His obsession with fire, his neither Barthesian nor Lacanian relation to the symbolic dragonflies, the light of the warlock of Ilóm, of the curse they threw over the participants, of the destruction of the indigenous world generating the narrative, signifies only the love alliance he contracts with his dead son. But among the affections, one of the most telling is that of man for woman, singularized in the myth of María Tecún or the Tecunas, women who are said to abandon men, giving rise to a theory of love. Here again it is useful to observe the metamorphosis of a political text into an erotic one. That is why, perhaps, the title of this chapter once more signals that love and war form a copula:

María Tecúúúúúúúúúúúúúún! . . . María Tecúúúúúúúúúúúúúún! . . . [the blind Goyo Yic shouts looking for his woman María Tecún]. A woman's name which all men shout to call that María Tecún lost in their consciousness. . . . Who has never called, never shouted the name of a woman lost in his yesterdays? (222)

María Tecún, woman, becomes a repository for an ensemble of novelties that will be reiterated in Guatemalan literary history. María Tecún is the hill into which Alxit, queen of Tecún Umán in Arias's novel, is transformed. But María Tecún is also the name of the vanishing woman, of women who leave their husbands. In Asturias there are two of them, one whose disappearance is explained through natural or accidental death, and the other whom Goyo Yic finds at the end of the novel. Like Alice Walker, Asturias endows his protagonists in literature with a love that perhaps they did not have in reality.

But, as in the Tacuatzín, a hermaphroditic animal, to be a woman is connected to being a man, a *macho*. "The moon light turned him from a man into an animal, a possum, a female possum" (130). The quotation entitling this chapter reproduces exactly the thematic motif of this book, war and woman, two identical propositions invented by men. The narrative subject of the impersonal phrase, reproduced as a popular refrain, popular wisdom, a common currency circulating, is referred to as a thought by Colonel Godoy, the character positioned at the apex of established hierarchies within the narrative contracts, and who is in turn the highest state representative— if there is one—that Asturias permits himself here, and later these hierarchies are reproduced by the rest. Woman is political betrayer in Vaca Manuela. She is blabber and drool, lies and deceit, artifice (23); she is soothsayer, visionary, concerned about man in La Piojosa Grande. Woman is the ideal woman who waits forever for her lover, who lives for him (43): she is the one who cuckolds, the one who betrays (112).

As a full-blooded Amerindian, as a native and natural to this literary land, woman is the most marginal to the narratives of magic realism. She haunts the margins of myth, but her abode is within the areas of positivism. As can be gathered by the list of her descriptions, her representation is located within the canons of modernity, which incorporate Christian epistemes. Women are absence and war; they are betrayal, the historical site for men to display their eroticism and their dependence, and for the writer Asturias to evoke his own sexuality and orgasm.

PART V

(Wo)man/Motherland

From the turn of the century until this day, [the public mind] was
the object of a cultural and ideological industry that was as
unrelenting as it was diverse: ranging from the school to the press
to mass culture in its multitudinous dimensions.
Gabriel Kolko

CHAPTER THIRTEEN

Case B: Of Testimonial and Diaries

Narratives of Success and Failure

In Gayatri Spivak's introduction to *Selected Subaltern Studies*, one can find a number of ideas relevant to the study of the constitution of the subaltern as a revolutionary subject.[1] For my purposes, the most interesting are those that question the concepts of success and failure with reference to the constitution of the subaltern. It could be that those two words are the loci of positivistic readings of the "development" of the subaltern; but it could also be that their seductiveness is related precisely to the opposite, for success and failure become relative when one uncovers their being as a mark of "cognitive failures." Success and failure are gnoseological concepts—and political concepts, as well. Whether we realize it or not, they punctuate change as confrontation—in which one either wins or loses—or as transition—from one stage to another. Success and failure are thus words framed within the great narratives of the modes of production. There is a certain uneasiness, however, in the use of a terminology that makes us aware of the question of what terminology to use, since we wish both to trace the trajectory of the subaltern-woman-revolutionary on a graph, and to avoid the problems implicit in the idea of "development," implying in turn success and failure.

There is no question that the terminology of "the moment(s) of change [needs to] be pluralized and plotted as confrontation rather than transition . . . and that such changes are signalled or marked by a functional change in sign systems" (3). There is also no question that the terminology of change has corollaries for a theory of consciousness and culture that, as Spivak asserts, brings the hegemonic historical thought to a crisis, and this crisis branches toward the fields of a theory of reading. For instance, in the case of Claribel Alegría and Darwin Flakoll's *They Won't Take Me Alive: Salvadorean Woman in Struggle for National Liberation,*[2] as much as in their *Ashes of Izalco,* the ideas of success and failure could be applied immediately to insurgent guerrilla movements and their current strategies. However, both texts could be read simply as a convergence of voices in a perpetual dialogue, both with the texts written by insurgent revolutionaries and with texts from previous insurgencies, in which woman was decentered and kept on the corners of a social narrative that pretended to incorporate the popular masses. From this perspective, the text contributes to the study of subalternity by presenting us with a reading of woman as a revolutionary subaltern, central to the social text. Success is, then, in this case, securing the convergence of the plurality of voices, masculine and feminine, Salvadorans and North Americans.

They Won't Take Me Alive is a narrative of organization and of incorporation—into the revolutionary struggle—in which the gendered subject is constituted as an equal participant, (sameness). Men and women have "equal" rights and "equal" politico-military responsibilities. From a gendered perspective the problem is the liberation of women. Here, the question is raised in exactly the same terms as that of the liberation of men. The equation national liberation = collective liberation presupposes "equal" representation of men and women within the term *collective,* a kind of "affirmative action" program within the bosom of guerrilla warfare. However, as we have seen, the word *collective* is hollow; it has a built-in void wherein women are placed.

It has been very well documented that the revolutionary leadership always asked women to wait and to postpone. For the sake of unity, they said, for their children's sake, for national security, not yet please. Thus, to say that "it was by means of the incorporation of women into the revolutionary struggle . . . that woman was to liberate herself, acquiring her own proper and just dimension" was only partially true (Alegría/Flakoll 74). It is, in many ways, to constitute her as man by incorporating her to the male field of action, and it is to insert her into power as a man. And what about her femaleness?

Eugenia, the main protagonist of this testimonial, is always portrayed as asserting her feminine being—much to her sorrow. Javier, her *compañero,* tells us that "she was always very critical about all the little traits [notice the diminutive] of male chauvinism coming up in the separation of tasks for women and tasks for men" (74). Because she is critical of the gendered division of labor and gender roles, she is culturally mandated to prove herself as a man. In the process, she disapproves of any "little" deference given to her by her companions-in-arms. For instance, she rejects any "help" in carrying a cache of arms and dismisses her companions when they want to alleviate her burden because her feet are bleeding. Equality, male and female, is defined here as identity (sameness) and comes out in phrases such as "What counts are the capacities" (83), or "She could not abandon the tasks because of her infant girl" (92)—phrases that interpellate women only. The underlying assumptions for this *récit* are, naturally, narratives of modes of production, for they acknowledge the division of labor—masculine/feminine—as one of their primary structures.

Women's discussions and the discussions about women within revolutionary organizations of revolutionary societies, however, have sufficiently demonstrated that even if women's liberation equals national liberation, the participation and incorporation of women within the liberation of the people (read country) never proves a sufficient condition. It becomes imperative, then, to separate the strands and break analogies such as woman equals country, sovereignty, liberation.

Another important question this testimonial raises is related to the nature and logic of the politico-military narratives. As in the case of the narratives of modes of production, of which the politico-military narratives are a subset, the encoding of both these narratives always prioritizes the divisions of class over any other and, consequently, presents them as narratives of progress and of transition, erasing the confrontations taking place in the intra-national/domestic cultural spaces where the constitution of oppressive gender roles takes place. This type of teleological organization does not annul the questions of success and failure, and, consequently, the positivistic patterns are always in attendance.

Anything that follows, particular to the formation of women, is flagrantly omitted, as it is in the other (male) narratives, where men and women are again evaluated on the basis of sameness. Eugenia will never permit her comrades to carry anything for her because that signifies not being equal; not being like a man. The revolutionary sense of worth and of value is instituted in military training and in the military disposition to follow orders. Women and men are equal only to the degree that both are dedicated revolutionary combatants; as such, they must excel in all organizational duties, in the execution of orders, in temerity and sacrifice, in military discipline and a full command of weaponry.

All the women under scrutiny in this text distinguish themselves in exactly the same manner, and all of them are characterized by their capacity to incorporate into their own feminine bodies all the adjectives applied to the *guerrillero* himself in Che's essays on the guerrilla. In chapter 5 I argued that the constitution of the revolutionary subject as a male subject cannot but signify a sexuality, and that sexuality/textuality properly unveils itself as such in revolutionary legislatures, clearly denoting the bracketing of the question of gender as constituted here. The results bear two formidable consequences for the revolutionary state. The first is to alienate women—more than half of the population—and the second, in alienating women, to alienate the masses, for the majority of the masses are women.

Considering the appropriation of the narratives of empowerment by women, and trying to put aside the epistemes of positivism legislating success and failure, I want to suggest that Alegría/Flakoll's testimonial weaves together the dissimilar strands of military and romantic narrative protocols into a narrative of character formation. It is a kind of bildungsroman, positing the convergence of man/woman in women and men, and debating coupling, maternity, and love within the framework of revolutionary insurgencies and revolutionary organizations. The text addresses questions of maternity within the revolutionary processes—or ideas that seem to postulate a role model of/for revolutionary maternity. The formation of gender differences based on the incorporation of maternity into the revolutionary processes, and the androgynous specular image of writing that we analyzed above, are also under consideration. Additionally at stake is a displacement from the representation of women/masses in the house and in the plaza in *Ashes of Izalco* to the representation of oligarchy/revolutionary, plaza/bush, spontaneous insurgency in the mountain/urban guerrilla warfare in *They Won't Take Me Alive: Salvadorean Woman in Struggle for National Liberation*.

I want to begin by identifying the adjectives that engender the feminine as revolutionary, occupying the place of the clandestine guerrilla. The same Christian series, "abnegation," "sacrifice," "heroism," definitional terms taken from the patristic juxtaposed to the series of heroic romanticism, remain positioned within the revolutionary epistemologies. In the case of women, however, "selflessness" and "sacrifice" also belong to matristics. They were, and still are, female attributes defining women—*stabat mater dolorosa*.

Nevertheless, Eugenia is defined by a combination of adjectives, supporting my thesis of Eugenia's simultaneous representation as a woman-man. If we attend to posture, dress, and unconventional speech, we realize that we are facing behavioral patterns classified within "the masculine." The list of adjectives adds to this image: (a) soft, agreeable, an attractive personality; (b) shy, nervous, silent, a worker in several social organizations—peasant organizations, cooperatives, human welfare organizations, women's groups; (c) brave, daring, politically skillful, a leader, an organizer, with a strategist's mind—"She thought forwards, backwards, sideways, centerways" (54).

It is immediately apparent that the heroine is modeled on the image of the hero, but we never find her as heroic in masculine narratives. That is the reason for conceptualizing this writing as information retrieval. The collective author Alegría/Flakoll draws women out from "anonymity" and from the list of the "disappeared," nameless persons. That is why one of so many women serves as a representation of "the thousand girls, women and older Salvadoran women who continue facing the struggle without surrendering" (9). The informants are men and women, among them Marta and Ondina, Eugenia's sisters, María Elena Girón, her friend, and *comandantes* Ana María, Nadia Palacios, and Mercedes Letona. In narrating Eugenia's life they narrate their own, and so the testimonial of one becomes a collective testimonial of the many.

In his article on Rigoberta Menchú, Robert Carr argues against this position. He sustains that Rigoberta is not a transcendental signifier, that she cannot represent "all" indigenous people. Dinesh D'Souza's argument is exactly the same as Carr's. However, the upshots of their arguments diametrically differ: Carr's is one of inclusion and D'Souza's one of exclusion.[3] Alegría/Flakoll try to strike a balance in representing one woman through the voices of many. Thus, the many become one and vice versa. Perhaps the problem is that both critics take extreme positions, and, consequently, neither considers the possibilities and realities of popular and common-front politics. And this is precisely the point of Alegría/Flakoll.

Eugenia, a commander-in-chief carrying out and issuing orders, is a woman who not only merges masculine and feminine in her own persona, but brings together two apparently antagonistic narrative strands. In the first chapter, military language frames the text, but it borrows a vocabulary from romantic language and a story "invented" by Alegría/Flakoll. They imagine how Eugenia was captured. Is it here, I wonder, that success and failure are located?

The authors "invent" because the book is written by using the testimonials of what is fundamentally a women's collective, and because the intention is to make these women visible, to give them voice, to place them in the theater of History and to incorporate them into History through the incorporation of their actions through their voice. But none of these women was a witness to Eugenia's capture. One of them accidentally heard about it on the radio. Thus, these authors invent a situation in which the decisive personality of the heroine is underscored. It is due to her command, and the influence of her initiative and strategic mind, that we see the three members of the operative act swiftly. She is woman, whose feminine intuition is used to detect danger. She can deliver arms from the city to the countryside. She can shout the final defiance: "They won't take me alive!"

Within the logic of military narratives that opens and closes the text, a whole sentimental and emotional life is also being constructed. This sentimental life does not contradict the rules and logic of military life, but it does contrast with them. There is a narrative difference, the difference between the encoding of feelings and the encoding of orders, that plots and assigns gender roles. Is it here, perhaps, that success or failure can be found?

If we now compare the first chapter with the last, we cannot help but compare the difference between narratives of love and military narratives. If in military actions the commandant falls (fails), in love letters she succeeds. Sentimental narratives are, therefore, in this text, narratives of success, framed by narratives of modes of production, which, perhaps, ultimately are all narratives of failure. At the beginning of the text, the type of story the testimonials will tell cannot be predicted, and neither can the narrative mode, but both are insightful and reveal a strategy of inclusion. Thus, both narratives succeed although the political movements "fail"—small consolation for literature to succeed in place of politics.

It is in the interest of both writers and informants to stress the hardships of the struggle—the harshness of discipline, dedication, and commitment—that coexist with masculine/feminine tenderness, the famous *tendresse*, the development of couples and heterosexual love. The collective narrative of Alegría/Flakoll, to which Salvadoran men and women contribute, duplicates the structural dualities in which men and women, with the same strength, reinforce the same sense of commitment and conviction put forth in *Ashes of Izalco*. It is necessary to underline that this testimonial does not display the same contradictions other testimonials reveal. It does not ensnare women and the feminine within men and masculinity. However, the problems of the constitution of the social subject as a member of a couple, and of "revolutionary" maternity return relentlessly.

I have been arguing that the writer's strategy is to show how a series of voices converge to render the presence of women on the historical stage of Salvadoran history irrefutable. This collective subject shows that both Eugenia and the informants are women very different from woman as she was portrayed in testimonials by men. Their actual presence in the struggle is one such difference. Their feminine debates on coupling, home, and maternity mark a second. In fact, if this narrative shocks, it is in the representation of revolutionary maternity. "Revolutionary" maternity is a walkout. It leaves the idea of individual maternity behind and replaces it with a notion of collective maternity. Consequently, family is no longer defined by blood ties alone. Ideological bonds are now paramount, as I will explore in these last three chapters (re)conceptualizing the motherland.

For this New couple, love is predicated not only on sympathy and attraction, but on shared values. It is not a relationship that immediately seizes women but one that develops slowly. Love, marriage, coupling are instances of revolutionary life lived within a revolutionary framework and the revolutionary process, and the revolution is the fundamental and ultimate value. Javier and Eugenia knew they were not going to be together all the time. After all, "marriage was going to constitute the beginning of her clandestine life" (63).

For this "brave new woman," this woman who has proven herself in the military terrain, to extrapolate her "courage" from the military to the formation of subjectivity as "lover," as "mother," is an arduous task. To discern and assimilate what is normal within abnormality must be exasperating. Heroic and commonplace characteristics do not mix. It is easier to accept Eugenia's heroic character alone than to accept that she is a normal human being who laughs, makes jokes, and falls in love. It is odd to see her in full command of weapons and then fully displaying, through baby talk, her emotional vulnerability. The discussion of the betrayal of the leadership based on a cleft between private and public does not hold here.[4] Eugenia is not two-faced. Her man/woman nature, her rating as a third sex, excludes her from any a priori gender roles.

Conventional mores make it difficult to evaluate her ideas on child rearing. One might surmise that the concept of revolutionary maternity would be rejected. Bringing up children as revolutionaries from an early age, enrolling them in revolutionary activities as informants, might not easily be accepted. The idea of children growing up within a collective, confined to a party cell, explodes bourgeois ideas of maternity. However, for those who reject monogamy, the nuclear family, and bourgeois morality, this is presented as both an alternative and a product of sheer necessity. The constitution, structure, and strategies of the family as a social organization are targeted.

The New behavior is mandated by regulations that mothers and fathers—mainly "revolutionary" mothers—must acknowledge. Freedom to have children means freedom to have them live on the edge of death and danger. It means to consign them to the care of their grandparents, for these children's parents live as if sentenced to death. In this struggle between prior private and public categories, the military and the romantic narratives seek to strike a balance. For to accept one set of premises—military insurgency, for instance—is to accept the other—children on the verge of a nervous breakdown. "The boy or girl must live in a secured house, under risks, the possible fall of their parents" (68). Eugenia's ideas on maternity are that "our son [where is the daughter?] would also be the son of the organization, a son of all the *compañeros* with whom we would share more closely the different moments of war" (68).

It is not without irony that, in portraying this process of improvisation, the new testimonials become narratives of success and not of failure. For they narrate the difficulties of a trying process; the difficulties of the moment in which transition as confrontation is displayed; a moment in which weapons mediate between human beings as masses, and human beings as Army. From this perspective, patriotic narratives about women are always narratives of war. They are, consequently, situations of embattlement that jolt the foundations of social institutions—the family, child rearing, and maternity, not to mention the nation-state. Under these circumstances, to ask about success and failure in the positivistic sense is almost meaningless, as it is to be concerned with strong positivistic ideas of "improvement" and "progress." What is being represented is movement and confrontation. Better and betterment, improvement and development, are locked in hope. Betterment, success, and progress do not carry the same meanings in revolutionary narratives. In fact, the word used to signify "success" is *triumph*, which within revolutionary codes is a synonym of *apotheosis*, that is, a point of culmination and, therefore, of departure.

Alegría/Flakoll have come a long way in the history of their literary representation. If, at the beginning of their joint writing career, the contrasting spheres of action for them were house and plaza, and a kind of "illicit" eroticism behind closed doors right at the center of the oligarchic hearth, the resting place of the patriarch, a benevolent tyrant, it later became a conflict of the nation-state. If, earlier, the tension was between eroticism and obedience, a dilemma of choosing one of two men, then in their later narrative the tension was between the state and the state-armed opposition. In the diary and in the novel, Woman was the space where sensual attraction and security opposed each other, and where self-determination was an impertinence. Is it, perhaps, in the nature of the narrative protocol of those two genres to confine women within the areas of sexuality, both in the form of sensuality and in the form of economic (moral) security? Is it in the codes of testimonial literature to trace different limits, to uncover other circuits for Woman? Here, it seems, woman must break free of the inner confines of home and walk toward the plaza, where she dies giving orders.

I want to propose that *They Won't Take Me Alive* is a metaphor for women as well as for the New Man, written by an international couple as the pattern of a new mode of coupling. In a certain manner, however, this new narrative does not abandon all the previous narrative strands. It wrestles with questions coming from the former oligarchic horizon, such as the concepts of home and coupling. Yet, security and honor are kept on a different shelf. Analogy and simile between former and latter are no longer possible. In other words, the Salvadoran woman in struggle transforms the husband into a lover, into a transitory and temporal relation, clandestine not within the bounds of the oligarchic home but within the larger space of the state. Men and love, as character and plot of Romantic narratives, become lover in love, lover because he unconditionally loves. The pressure inflicted on women as wives in the prison-house of monogamy is transferred from the family to the state and from the house to the nation. The power of the father/husband is reconstituted as the repressive state apparatus.

The masses on the plaza and the masses as combatants are juxtaposed in Eugenia's essence. Eugenia and the masses are, in their vulnerability and death, one and the same. In dying, Eugenia occupies their subject position. But the masses in *Ashes of Izalco* and the masses in *They Won't Take Me Alive: Salvadorean Woman in Struggle for National Liberation* are not the masses either. In the former the masses are Amerindians; in the latter, they are the organized army of the people, a National Liberation Front. A word on how the cultural story of the subaltern subverts official accounts of history is relevant; Alegría/Flakoll's testimonial constructs Eugenia as a subaltern, enclosing her in ever narrower circuits, enveloping her in the web of political commitment, making her a fugitive, like the Amerindians, in the public spaces of the State, therefore, Woman = *ethnie*.

The oligarchic mansions have vanished. Seignorial ethics are also gone. Very humble abodes and circumscriptions, the collective narrow spaces of the poor, have come to replace old seignorial houses, old seignorial visions and sensibilities. The problems and questions concerning the Salvadoran oligarchy have been pushed to the edge and emerge only as Army (positivistic success), displaying its brutish face (positivistic failure). As Ranajit Guha argues in his definition of the subaltern, the problems of the petty bourgeoisie are compatible with the problems of the people.[5] Hence, the politics of a common front. Although the informants on Eugenia's life insist that only the people can liberate themselves, Eugenia's problems are located side by side with the problems of the teacher, the seamstress, the petty street merchant.

Nevertheless, as in *Ashes of Izalco*, the narrative of the constitution of the subaltern gendered subject is woven postmortem. Eugenia dies at the hands of the repressive state apparatus. The voices of friends and family reconstruct her for us. Eugenia, like the "little man" in the insurgent narratives of Ramírez, traverses the text swiftly. And in her constitution, she weaves together the convergence of the popular revolutionary organizations. The social and political histories of the popular organizations—FECCAS, FAPU, ANDES, FUS, FMLN-FDR, BPR[6]—and the personal, conjugal, maternal life of the protagonist are one and the same. This is the sign of the first triumph of women in the text, a sign of her empowerment. The same is not true in male texts. In male texts, struggle is a male condition and does not concern itself with houses/home but with mountain, city, and *Montaña*. In those testimonials, Woman is an image, a *figura*; in this she is not invoked, she is not a parenthesis, a dash adjoining *Montaña* and home/hearth, the resting place of male heroism, an expression, a script, but rather an unequivocal center.

These confluences are not evident if the reading follows the script of politico-military narratives, which nevertheless retain their own allure. Only if the reading considers immersing itself in the Romantic plot and love, the Romanticism and eroticism of the love story, can the overlapping of the two worlds uncover its seams. The very sparse description of surroundings, the lack of lyricism and metaphors, the prioritization of action over reflection, are rhetorical devices forcing us to come to terms with the swift and accelerated pace of Eugenia crossing the stage, plotting Eugenia more visibly and immediately as an insurgent military woman. The construction of suspense, stressing orders, could make the reader lose sight of the reflective character of the narrative that constitutes women as a subject. Reflection is the thread taking her from home to garrison, from paternal obedience to organizational obedience—first, *eclesia* and, subsequently, politics. Woman disengages herself from the family to engage herself with the state, and in so doing, she also defends her rights to a fulfilling coupling, to an emotional relationship, a move that signals her femininity. A string of equally weighed words is proof: the banana for the daughter, bullets and machine guns, a Kotex for a friend, her diapers and clothing, menstruation.

In the convergence of these "little" details, the firm hand of a woman writer is evident, as much as the male hand is evident in keeping the borders of concepts of the masculine and the feminine moving always in close contact and dialogue with the concept "men" as maleness decentered. Javier, Eugenia's *compañero*, is naturally the sketched figure around which the foregrounded characters are grouped, but, in this sketch, one can note observations on sharing responsibilities, home, "little" chores. In revising macrotopics, those of the master narratives defining the generational discussion at large—social classes, electoral struggle, popular prolonged war, oligarchies, the Foco Theory, mass politics, vanguards—the difficulties of the *compañera*, her disbelief in her own capacity for leadership, are also incorporated. Thus, in the same way that geography plots the history of these "little" towns and hamlets into the national history of El Salvador for national and international consumption, in the Christian education of middle-class women, and in their struggle with these two distinct ways of being, a man and a woman emerge.

In the trajectory from *Ashes of Izalco* to *They Won't Take Me Alive: Salvadorean Woman in Struggle for National Liberation* lies the idea that Eugenia was constantly looking ahead: "Eugenia was never static, was never the same. She was always developing. Eugenia was always future" (59). In the long road from novel to testimonials, the authors recognize the collective production of textuality as sexuality. They trespass the borders of the seignorial house of the oligarchy as well as the borders of the plaza of the oligarchy to leave a printed register of a moment in the reflexive thinking of the heterosexual couple in reference to patriotic/erotic insurgencies. In the momentary but important seizure of the urban social spaces and in decentering the importance of the house for coupling, we note the triumph of the collective narratives of Claribel Alegría, Salvadoran, and Darwin Flakoll, North American. In their collaborative writing life, there is proof of the possibilities of the erotic/patriotic international common fronts.

CHAPTER FOURTEEN

Solidarity in Affinity

Woman Constitutes Woman

> He spilled many human ears on the table. . . . He swept the ears to the floor
> with his arms and held the last of his wine in the air. Something for your
> poetry, no? he said. Some of the ears on the floor caught this scrap of his
> voice. Some of the ears on the floor were pressed to the ground.
> Carolyn Forché, *The Country Between Us*

> What is important about *testimonio* is that it produces if not the real
> then certainly a sensation of experiencing the real and that this has
> determinate effects on the reader that are different from those
> produced by even the most realistic or "documentary" fiction.
> John Beverley and Hugo Achugas, *La voz del otro*

In a stimulating article entitled "Occidentalism as Counterdiscourse: 'He
Shang' in Post-Mao China," Xiao-Mei Chen examines the Orientalist and
Occidentalist positions within post-Maoist Chinese cultural discourse.[1] In
analyzing the television program *He Shang* (*He*, river; *Shang*, "dying before
one comes of age")—"a survivor's mourning for the martyrs who had sacri-
ficed their lives for their country" (695)—Chen juxtaposes Orientalist Occidentalism's circuit of images with Occidentalist Orientalism's circuit of
images, suggesting a specular vision incessantly reproducing itself. In the
unraveling of that logic of reciprocities, she also confronts a concept of cul-

ture woven through a perpetual debate over the impressions, readings, and exegesis of Western culture.

Her analysis of the mass reception of He Shang is illustrative. On one hand, analysts criticized the program for its historical infidelity, that is, the inaccurate and partial representation of historical facts, and on the other, they failed to explain its overwhelming popular acceptance. Chen suggests that "the critique of He Shang was problematic since it is predicated on a fundamental confusion about genre" (701), and proposes that the intersection of historical inaccuracy with rhetorical accuracy forces the examination of the documentary as a poetic rather than historical text. Grappling, then, with He Shang's popularity as historical representation, Chen argues that it "struck a chord in the national sensibility by glossing over the jump from the factual to the symbolic" (701).

This critical approach is striking, for up to a certain point, it captures John Beverley's dilemma in his examination of testimonial literature, that is, the dynamic between literary discourse and testimonial discourse, which he considers illustrative of the uneven discursive practices of Rigoberta Menchú, but above all in the contrasts between discursive moments like those narrating the death of her brother and mother and the rest of the narrative. The dramatization of death by torture touches the reader profoundly, like literature, that is, in Chen's words, jumping from a narrative of facts to register in the symbolic.

The debate over correct and incorrect representations of historical facts, discursive practices illustrating a given type of Occidentalism in the case of He Shang, appears here as discursive distinctions—literature/testimonial literature—and as hermeneutics of the politico-emotive reception of cultural products.[2] In the specific case of Rigoberta's narration of her brother's death, the debate over proper and improper history extends to comparison of the perception and truth of her story with the perception and truth of a North American anthropologist's collection of testimonial of the same event from other informants, and then to the elucidation of this representational dilemma by cultural critics (Beverley 14). Also at stake is the direct reception of other indigenous subjects, such as Ignacio Bizarro Ujpan, to signal integrationist propositions—which is exactly the case Lauro Flores makes for and in Chicano testimonials.[3]

The examples of the Chinese documentary and of Central American testimonial traverse, then, very similar signifying circuits. The predicament posed by the reading of He Shang afflicts any narratology or (re)presentation crossing not only the vectors of History and literature but many others, as well. In the case of testimonial and *He Shang*, history, politics, literature, and literary and cultural criticism are greatly exercised by the ideological and political practices of subjects and subjectivities within insurgent, patriotic, and/or trade union contexts in revolutionary or revolutionizing nation-states. The variables in the analysis of testimonials necessarily traverse all these fields, much as the variables of market economics pervade every cultural activity, from teaching to the (re)presentation of the Third World and its subjects and subjectivities, as very pertinently pointed out by Carr. Thus, Chen argues that the "rhetorical force of '*He Shang*,' therefore, lies in the intricate interplay between history, poetry, and politics, having to do, for the most part, with the symbolic rather than with the factual. To single out any one of these three dimensions for critique is to miss the better part of the picture" (702). It is in this same tenor that we must understand Spivak's warning on double displacements that "serve imperialist subject-constitution, mingling epistemic violence [Orientalisms or Occidentalisms for Said and Chen] with physical violence and torture [neo-liberal positivisms or literary brotherhoods in our case] with the advancement of learning and civilization."[4]

The web of variables determining the interplay of sensibilities—First World/Third World—brings testimonial literature, and even information from a witness converted into "literature," to converge with what in the Chinese example is "a successful combination of both popular-cultural media and 'elite,' 'scholarly' [transnational] discourse" (Chen 702). That is, as in the example of *He Shang*, its massive popularity is related "to the popularity of a particular work among the ordinary people" (702)—East/West, center/periphery.

Chen's critical discourse extends to other epistemological terrains such as the nation, the national, and nationality, which, in our field as in hers, are not neutral arenas, but neural points, particularly if they are applied to those testimonials gathered in places in which the revolution did not win power, and where, therefore, the task of gathering information from above, demonizing the enemies, did not take place.[5] Thus, in situations such as Menchú's—Venezuela/France/Guatemala—and Maria [Marenn]'s—El Salvador/United States/Central Europe—nuanced by a diversity of political, social, and ideological circumstances ordering national/party mediations in a highly definitive transnational environment, the constitution of the subjectivity of the female subaltern could still be analyzed in terms of solidarity and the commitment of the (woman) writer.

Through narrative fragments one can show epistemological slippages moving from what is properly ideological to the biological, to the body itself, and from there to the psyche, later to project themselves fully into the dimension of international solidarity. This is a trajectory that cannot exist in the case of Chen's analysis because of the circumstances created by "official nationalism" and because of the Chinese ideological circuit at the moment of the cultural product she analyzes. Nonetheless, it is useful to my argument to point out that Chen utilizes a cultural product to illustrate how the representation of a given type of "reactionary/conservative" Occidentalism is used against an equally conservative status quo, against which reactionary Occidentalism serves as resistance, as negation of negation. What is negative in a system is here illustrated through other cultural accomplishments, which have been, in turn, (re)presented by that same system as negativities.

Testimonials seek identical aims. They constitute the production of a cultural item to (re)present a reality circumscribed by the perimeter of the official fatherland, and counter that reality with the constitution of an internal subjectivity that illustrates, in its own body, the contradictions of systemic negotiations. In the case of the fatherland, the external is invoked (the interplay of states *qua* states); in testimonial's constitution of an internal subjectivity, the internal is called upon to produce, through rhetorical apparatuses, a symbolic reality in one and a truth or "reality effect" in the other, both instrumentalized to index an ideological struggle.

Nother/Mother

This is perhaps the title that would do some justice to Lea Marenn's *Salvador's Children: A Song for Survival*. Marenn's text, Elizabeth Burgos Debray's *I, . . . Rigoberta Menchú, An Indian Woman in Guatemala*, and Margaret Randall's *Sandino's Daughters: Testimonies of Nicaraguan Women in Struggle* constitute a group of narratives on Central America in which three non-Central American women begin to take part in the politics of cultural representation, collecting women's experiences from the region.[6]

It is not my intention here to reiterate arguments and analyses readily available in the volumes on testimonial edited by John Beverley and Hugo Achugar, and by René Jara and Hernán Vidal.[7] I simply wish to refer to the instances of women's solidarity obvious in the constitution of subjectivities and nationalities, glossing the discussion of whether these solidarities were constituted from above, below, or the side. These three politically sympathetic collections mark a dissatisfaction with the previous processes of cultural representation, despite Carr's forceful and urgent argument, highlighting the elements of gender and ethnicity. Burgos Debray accepts that "in Latin America, those of us who are culturally white denounce with ease—and with reason—American imperialism, but we were never concerned, save few exceptions, to denounce internal colonialism" (28). She reminds us that this indigenous woman

> wanted to make [her] understand, and to make the world understand that she also was in the possession of culture, and of a millenarian culture, and that her struggle was to overcome misery . . . but also that her culture was recognized and accepted as any other. (28)

Critics have already called our attention to the intersubjectivity of testimonial voices. Franco, for example, has warned that sexual gendering is also a producer of difference (Franco 115); Yúdice considers the testimonial "a creation of solidarity, of an identity which is forming in and through the struggle" (Yúdice 212); and Carr points to "the importation of these written texts into the spheres of the elite [where] the subject thus occupies a consistently slipping place within the discourse of the empowered and their institutions, both labor and management" (Carr 377).[8]

Every critical reader of testimonials, I think, notes the absence of the great epistemic macros in these narratives of encounter between writer and witness. In the play on words Nother/Mother, for instance, the presence of a *petit récit,* on the contrary, could be illustrated, just one of the possible misunderstandings occurring at the moment of confrontation between a young Salvadoran child from the peasantry and her adoptive mother, a professor of literature. The linguistic misapprehension represented in this phonemic play indexes not only idiomatic lacks—the mother speaks no Spanish, the child no English—but also the ideological untranslatable or emotive resistance—Kristeva's body—and the epistemological misencounters in the encounters of two women, very different in origin, who join their lives through an emotion translated into solidarity—which also, in Chen, accounts for the success of *He Shang.* Their respective corresponding needs, to be a mother and have nother/mother, lend themselves to simultaneous mutual fulfillment. That is why Nother/Mother serves, too, underlining the mother/daughter relationship, the important processes of the recomposition of the concept of family unfolding in these three texts.

Already in Randall's testimonial—thanks to which some of the initial moments of the organization of women in Cuba, Santo Domingo, and Nicaragua are preserved—the chapters are marked by the relationship mother/

daughter, which signals an absence or the lack of commitment of the father toward the daughter in matrilocal societies, and its corollary, solidarity among women, very similar to that which Guha foregrounds in "Chandra's Death."[9] This affinity among women, nuanced by the engendering of difference Franco points to, is, nevertheless, the other side of Che's dynamics of friendship with(in) the guerrilla troop, which I could also call solidarity in affinity.[10] However, nothing akin to that model of man is established in these women's narratives by women. What is evidenced instead is a definition of family—biological and nonbiological—in which women take care of and assist women, and in which the participation of men in the struggle is regarded by women in the same way Lupe, Argueta's peasant woman, regards her relationship with her husband. Women overlook gender disputes, focusing instead on bodily experiences—of both men and women—as pain during the resistance.

In retaining the concept of maternity, translated now into insurgent solidarity, and in instrumentalizing the epistemes of family, translated into democratic desires—which Masiello and Franco have pointed out in the cases of the Mothers of the Plaza de Mayo and Alaide Foppa, respectively—these women make it clear they are not interested in plotting gender difference but rather in emphasizing the collectivity of men and women within social situations.[11] As in the case of Occidentalism, to which the authors of the Chinese documentary appeal, and which certainly seems a recycling of what official Occidentalism calls reactionaryism, keeping the *sema mater* Nother/Mother as a nucleus of meaning in these testimonials also instrumentalizes the conservative concept of motherhood, in order to disregard gender divisions and relegate all sense of otherness to the repressive army. In exchanging phonemes (N/M) or genres (literature/testimonial literature, rhetoric/history), a de- or counter-nationalization is proposed, and in it, the conservative moment is less relevant than the nerve touched in narrating the subject from positions of anger in affinity, the anger of the mother during the torture of the son, for example, or of the daughter during the torture of the mother. In this sense, these narratives, written in a journalistic prose, a style not always rhetorically interpellating, locate themselves in a dimension very different from that of literature, from the narratives of other women writers—Oreamuno, Guardia, Belli—and come closer to Alegría/Flakoll, mainly *They Won't Take Me Alive: Salvadorean Woman in Struggle for National Liberation,* and for different reasons, to Naranjo in *Diario de una multitud.*

In the three testimonials we are exploring, patriotism is understood as insurgency, a position against the army and the state power it represents. Patriotism is here somewhat different from what it is in the novels. The novels primarily address a social and intellectual sector—sorority or sisterhood—privileging, in literature, the relation between men and women, erotics plotted in the construction of nationality. Conversely, what the testimonials in question point out, as in Alegría/Flakoll, is the constitution of the subject Woman—peasant, indigenous, militant—from the point of view of narratives of resistance. Erotics, sexual and loving coupling, don't seem to be part of this conceptual horizon. What emerges instead is an extensive concept of family as solidarity. Consequently, these testimonials are narratives more of patriotism than of eroticism, and they are more militant and organizational than familial.

Among the differences between "literature" and "*testimonio*" marked by these testimonials are those of the proximity to the popular subject, a certain respect for the voice of the informant, the "erosion of monological discourse, central, european, white, male, heterosexual, lettered" already pointed out by literary criticism.[12] In the work of Burgos Debray as much as in that of Lea Marenn, language and/or reflections on language are evident; in Debray, this is because Rigoberta's style denotes ethnicity and political commitment. In the Spanish edition of *Rigoberta* we cannot possibly ignore her "indigenisms," her "Indian speech," her inflections, vocabulary, syntax, use of nouns, reiterated reflexives, unfamiliarity with verbs of action, diminutives, and so on, in which her ethnic-political identity is coded. Rigoberta's identity is constituted through words, just as are the identities of Argueta's characters and Marenn's Salvadoran children. As striking as Beverley's distinction between literature/testimonial literature in his discussion of Rigoberta may be, as with idiomatic misunderstandings between mother/daughter registered in Marenn's testimonial, the problem is no more the lack of linguistic precision (Yúdice), than it is the lack of historical precision in the Chinese example (Chen). What matters is the symbolic jump producing what Beverley calls the "reality effect," or "truth-effect," that is, the direct appeal to the reader's/audience's sensibility, producing in both cases the yes of solidarity.

A comparative study of Asturias's imaginary indigenous ideolect in *Men of Maize*, and that of Rigoberta—even considering a highly selective editing—reveals sharp distinctions. The same can be argued for Marenn's dramatic experience between mother and daughter, where the mother's lack of a Spanish vocabulary will create acute tensions between storytelling and story gathering, manifested once more in the transcription of the child's ideolect into English—for example, *mens, womens,* the Spanish words in the English text, the use of drawings to illustrate situations. All of these cases are instances of what I call the nontranslatables illustrated in my discussion of Argueta. These instances recall the implicit interactions between informants and writers, totally absent in Asturias. The language of the speaker as much as the language of the listener, to the degree that it claims to be an encounter and a transcription thereof, lends the narrative a sense of authenticity totally lacking in literature. It is perhaps in this moment, where the mediation between writer, sender, and reader disappears, that Beverley specifically locates his "truth-effect."

The narrative subject is also presented through her silences and caesurae. It is very important to notice that (as well as when and how) Rigoberta affirms and reiterates her silences, for in her silences is located what it means to protect her culture and her people, although sometimes she reveals those secrets, for example, how to set traps at the entrance of the house to ambush the army.[13] These voids are not epistemological, but instances of translation and safety zones—that which is not Western. Moreover, the noticeable deference in the compilation of testimonials also constitutes instances of solidarity and complicity, protected spaces signaled in the grammatical cases the compiler does not want to correct, because to correct means to alter, and, in the case of the lack of vocabulary, to register a misunderstanding which is just the opposite, the will to understand against all idiomatic odds, a bridge to cross the distance between nother/mother. In the work of Randall, as in the other two testimonials, editing is not undertaken rigorously. Idiomatic expressions, repetitions, and untranslatable words are kept. In the voices of the informants not only are each of the included sectors' idiomatic expressions preserved, but their particular areas of meaning are also maintained, and, in several testimonial instances, the vast array of people's voices offers "the benefit of multi-vocal interventions from a shared cultural context in order to establish parameters of difference" that Carr and Zimmerman demand (Carr 377, Zimmerman 233).

If this plurality of voices does not preclude from the interpretive terrain "the danger of reading the subject as a full, transparent other operating on the basis of a shared lost origin [or political and historical position]" (Carr 377), and neither does it necessarily include the indigenous Other as indigenous (Ignacio Bizarro), it must, nevertheless, be recorded. It is equally important to record the fact that, in the three narratives under consideration, the conservative ideologies of maternity and maternal feelings persists. Maternity establishes the link between informant and writer; it is the medium creating solidarity between mothers and daughters with which Randall expresses her solidarity. It explains Rigoberta's mother's feelings for her son, and what the woman later to become mother to the Salvadoran child feels when at the very end of the book she pleads with Cándida, the child's biological mother, to "give María another push with [her] leg / as she swings with her baby dolls into the wind" (Marenn 217).

Nevertheless, women's testimonials by women (re)present instances of the constitution of the subaltern feminine subject of insurgence. In all of them, the climax is situated in the literature, which establishes identities between the narratives, and among the narrative subjects themselves. Objections regarding the transparency of the subject, the unnecessary representation of all by one (individual or ethnicity) as a transcendental signifier, arise from this point. But what this criticism ignores is that the unified policies of terror—such as those of the repressive Central American armies—tend to produce identical effects in the minds of subjects, united in and by their common repressive experience.

The first condition for the production of testimonials is the acknowledged necessity of filling a void. In this sense testimonials are like a catalogue; they compile anecdotes and constitute themselves into listings, instances documenting that women did in fact participate. They are in charge of inscribing the feminine subject as rebel, patriotic, committed, of stating that woman constitutes patriotism and contributes to nationality, that woman is, therefore, citizen. This type of feminine testimonial also argues for women's courage, documents her strength, and presents counterarguments against the alleged weakness of her gender and the feeble and brittle character of her consciousness. It presents another episteme (Yúdice), the affirmation of courage and the constitution of a counter-axiological scheme. Beyond that, it affirms a rebellion against the established norms, showing absences, like the absence of male commitment, of the lack of solidarity between father and daughter, as well as the political strength of maternity, documenting at the same time that political struggles cross the body of international feminist consciousness. That is, there is a transnational reconstitution of woman in struggle as mother, daughter, militant, or all of the above, and a reconsideration of marriage and the relation among women.

In this sense the narrative does assume, in its reading and writing, the transparency of language. The writer/transcriber presumes an acritical solidarity, a suspended judgment; she does not concern herself with it or dismiss it. Hers is a cataloguing prose, not only in the listings of names—the possibility of making a list is already exceptional—but also in the listings of professions and trades—teachers, nurses, spies, couriers, proselytizers—which concurs, very much, with the assignation of trades and offices to women registered by the masculine narratives, several of which, as Yúdice contends, were imposed from above (210). Despite this, one of the discernible themes of the testimonials written by women on women is the expression of hope and the vote of confidence in the highly questionable equation between national and sexual liberation. Distinguished militant women mark, as one of the instances of women's liberation, that the militant acknowledges the authority of women as army officers, and that women have distinguished themselves even more in the political arena than in the military. The top priority, however, is the vindication of woman's body, primarily in areas related to sexuality—maternity or rape—and for that reason, women's chief area of participation during insurgency is noncombative, and her chief punishment is torture, rape.

Besides a change in epistemes, these books, then, support a gathering of data that collects, in many instances from below or from the side—site of the solidarity of the writers Argueta, Alegría/Flakoll, Randall, Burgos Debray, Marenn. They record the instances, the difficulties and obstacles, of women's participation, and commentary on the reasons women did not participate in this or that action. In this sense, testimonials are also argumentation and self-defense before the tribunal and judgment of history by the Westernized "official nation." In this respect, the census serves to illustrate a methodology, not only a representation or a representational moment, but the politics and techniques of representation (Yúdice). Masculine epistemologies, ideologies, and hegemonic practices are also counterrepresented.

There are, however, three controversial discursive instances I find relevant to this analysis: the relation militancy/army (inside and outside of male methodologies), the playing with elective affinities and the conservation of attitudes, and the persistence of feminine maternal postures and ideolectical parallelism, signposts of the intercultural abyss women intend to cross.

Militancy/Army

Militancy is the formation of an army; it is also the second moment of an army and the representation of an alternate concept of power. The behavior that both concepts of army demand within the context of everyday life is, in some instances, very similar. The emphasis on discipline, for instance, is identical. The imperative to underline human strength and resistance, secrecy above all, is also the same. The formation of the army, or the army in formation, follows this conditioning. The narratives by Che as well as those of Cabezas underline physical resistance, the "pushing one's self" that constitutes itself in moral resistance, and the conditions and attributes of the New Man. In feminine narratives and epistemes there is a coincidence of values. The testimonials by Charlotte Baltodano Egner, Commandant Dora María Tellez, and Salvadoran Commandants gathered by Alegría/Flakoll emphasize physical/moral resistance and discipline, that is, manliness in Woman.[14]

Furthermore, in every one of these instances, the ethos crosses the body. Charlotte resists the blows and rape. Dora María exemplifies the moral courage of the individual because she can carry fifty pounds and, in carrying them, she faints, and in fainting she gains the respect of the troop. Commandant María Eugenia feels offended when her comrades-in-arms, seeing her bleeding feet, offer to help her carry the weapons, because she, as a militant woman, must endure and resist. Discursively, Woman begins acquiring aspects similar to those of the New Man: "a belligerent attitude and a strong, rugged, enduring personality" (Randall 45), an attitude different in the different stages of the struggle—women's liberation = national liberation; an "identity" between the specific women's task and those of the revolution—liberation = insurgency; and "full participation in all fields" (70), which attempts to give "not a new man to the world but a new world to man" (83), and in which, as Dora says, there is "a new woman equal to the new man" (88).

However, in spite of this struggle to reach semantic parity, women's narratives about women are traversed by an axial principle not crossing the military discourse of the New Man. Maternity and children are not part of the revolutionary axiology except as an aside—"the resting place of the warrior." In these circumstances, the persistence of woman's maternal postures constitutes a dilemma. Woman takes hold of fortitude, the persistence of the ideologies of maternity, and constitutes herself as mother of all suffering humanity, a Woman/pillar as much at the ideological level as at the emotive and economic level. Leticia Herrera tells, with apparent disregard, what it means for her to deliver and then leave her kids with her parents and not to see them again for two years. But as we saw earlier, Commandant María Eugenia develops a complete hermeneutics of the family in which the children of militants begin as militants from an early age. This observation, apparently without consequence, also intervenes in the politics of representation, to the degree that children are also included as non-citizens and that they become, if not protagonists, at least actors, a conscious presence in the everyday life of the other army. It is the representation of this new army that will constitute some of the principal aspects of the collection of data that women's narratives on women undertake. Children are present as witnesses of the military story compiled by women, mediately or in their immediacy.

In this way, children's testimonials are, perhaps, and at a different level, an instance of the phenomenon of conversion (Canclini), not only of a cultural moment but of the interference between two types of armies whose disciplinary aspects are similar but whose goals are located, at least discursively, in different positions.[15] It is the women's and children's testimonials gathered by women that establish the measure of that difference, in emphasizing solidarities beyond distinctions of gender for a new type of familial affinity that, granted, begins at the level of the biological family but does not remain bound by its limits. This is playing with elective affinities and the conservation of attitudes.

The denunciation and rejection of the disarticulation of the body crosses the narratives of insurrection, in which the families and the concepts of family are recycled as enclaves against the hegemony of masculine epistemes. These epistemes are retained from the authoritarian hegemonies, which the army and the principle of the army establish over the body of entire populations, named and unnamed peasant families, ethnic groups, or women. I have selected three epistemological instances illustrating this relationship through the anxiety of consciousness and the conversion of feelings into rage, impotence, or psychic withdrawal, which marks the limits of liminal moments.

First Instance: From Ideology to Biology

> They tied up, they tied up his testicles, my brother's organs, back with a thread and he was ordered to run. Then, that was not allowed, my brother could not endure the enormous pain and he yelled, asking for help. (Burgos Debray 279)

The force with which the noun *balls* is enunciated in male testimonials, and the shyness in enunciating the word *testicles,* marks one of the differences between perceptions of gender at insurgent moments and the symbolic processes in both. *Balls* was, for the male testimonials, the localization of value, site of manliness, barricade, trench, while in this sentence it simply signals, for women, biology: it comes down from the symbolic to the facts in an inverse direction to that traced by Chen. The word also registers humiliation, dreadful distress—not castration or de-masculinization, but an instance of torture that will later come to constitute an example. Then the scene of torture will be reenacted before the population, where the entire community will become audience, and the mountains, auditorium—an instance of punishment as spectacle (Foucault), or discipline as demobilization (Guha).[16] The instrumentalization of pain treats the body as biology, the public display of the same as schooling. Rigoberta carefully details every moment of pain. She does not privilege one part of the body over the other. Tying up the testicles is as painful as cutting out "the fatty part of the face" (280) or as cutting out "the skin of the head" (280) or "parts of the soles of the feet" (283).

The communal body is present during the punishment of the body in their own body. The place, hour, day, month is registered (Chajul, 8:00 A.M., September 24); children, elders, stances, relationships, *Kaibiles* (the worst of the military thugs), everything is minutely detailed. From the biological body then to the social body; and in the social body, narrative discourse stresses communal, ethnic, and consanguine relationships, above all, the presence of children—We.

Second Instance: From Biology to Psychology

The soldiers found there the woman and the little girl in the *tienda*. . . .
The *soldados* took them all in front of the *pared* right next to the *tienda*—you know, a wall is a *pared*. First they raped the women and the girls; then they shot all the people standing there. But here it is too far down for the paper, so I'll leave off the *pared* and the *tienda*.
María, were you there? Did you see the people killed?
No answer.
Did your parents go there and see what happened? Did somebody tell them about it?
No Answer. (Marenn 127)

There were many killings there, many. That was the first time I saw so many dead bodies. I was scared all the time. They were in the mornings lying on the road or beside the road, and near the houses. I think that's when I stopped being happy and stopped talking so much. . . . We were all of us scared and more quiet. (Marenn 136)

Children are eyewitnesses and then they give their testimonial, in their autism, in their aphasias, and in silence. There is a difference between the linguistic hiatus and the silencing produced in personal life by the idea of

punishment and demobilization. After having undergone punishment, silence is the correct response. María does not answer. María does not speak.
The silence Rigoberta speaks of to protect her secrets—the secrets of a culture they don't want anyone to know and they want everyone to know at the
same time—is abundant in the testimonial by Lea Marenn in which the girl
speaks, very eloquently, through fragments and drawings. She is a Salvadoran child, very different from Adolfina, Lupe's granddaughter in Argueta's
narrative, who is, perhaps, more fictionalized than this girl, María, who does
not speak much. The terror suffered by Central American children, which
these three women narrate, could silence them. Forever? Terror silenced
languages, spaces, opinions. It intimidated. In another fragment by Marenn,
the child refuses to enjoy camping. Terror has extended itself over a terrain,
over a geography, over a landscape, nationality, language. Mountain, in this
case, is not the site of gestation for the new nation but a forbidden place, the
place where terror was enacted, where biology penetrated psychology and
psychology expressed itself as aphasia, autism, and silence. To differ from
Yúdice and Foley, in this case, there is "an absence of a felt resolution," for,
remembering the case of the Jews, the confrontation is with tropical fascism
(Yúdice 214).

Third Instance: From Psychology to Solidarity

They tortured him like you wouldn't believe: they strung him up and put a
crown of electric wires on his head, they gave him electric shocks with a cattle
prod over and over, they sliced off his heels and made him walk barefoot
carrying a pack. And in spite of the fact he knew everything . . . he died like a
man. . . . Bernardino is a man and we admire him. (Randall 124)[17]

The moment is narrated by a peasant woman, Amada Pineda, who defines herself as a peasant. "I am a peasant woman. I was born . . . raised . . .
married in the hills" (81). Besides the identifying characteristics, Amada's inventory of data includes the following: she was "raped seventeen times" by
army men; she has always been poor. One of her children, a girl, "died of
measles, another of pneumonia . . . we had to go into hiding. My husband
fled in one direction and I and the kids ran in the other. My baby died in a
rainstorm" (Randall 81).

The informant peasant woman speaks in the name of the family and the
communal collectivity: "The repression had cracked down on us [the com-
munity] and one of my children was dead—what could I do but fight back?"
(84). The life of the woman, her biography, is a sociobiography; it includes

the unincluded—children, elders, the community, We. In the testimonial literature of insurgency, only women include the disenfranchised—which is the majority: the people, masses, bases, troops. Her narrative is, therefore, a more inclusive and democratic one, in which the condition of women is narrated as the link between the condition of the peasant as worker and the condition of the people.

The semes of her speech are related fundamentally to poverty and repression. The cultures she represents are, therefore, those of poverty—as ethnicity or social sector—and those of the army. Both are novel, first, because coming from them, in their own ideolect, they sensitize the field by introducing new variables of analysis, and, second, because in narrativizing the army, they establish the difference between army and army, power and power, projecting themselves toward the utopian spaces where reconversion is possible. Chen no longer situates herself within the confrontation of armies, returning instead to the confrontation army/people, on the other side of the revolutionary experiment.

A powerful focus of Pineda's testimonial is the torture and death of Bernardino Díaz Ochoa, a peasant leader. Torture illustrates values: courage and lack of courage, moral strength and criminality, virtue and venality, emphasizing the symbiosis between pain and manliness, and between pain and communal respect. The narrative aims to notify and make public, to negotiate concepts of the abusive interpersonal relations in which one institution terrorizes large collective units of the population, rather than to privilege the unity of the couple and coupling. In this manner compilation and enunciation are sectorial and national; the people giving their testimony are spokesperson for a social group, and their words are directed against one national institution, the army. In its sectorial character they tend to unify behavior. If the army distinguishes, it distinguishes between men and women to make men examples. And in the popular sampling, there are more men than women tortured. In the case of Pineda there were "seven men, and only I as a woman," and the officer says, "Look, I don't like to hit women, because I am the son of a woman" (126).[18] In the case of Rigoberta's brother there is only one woman. Testimonials need to speak about torture, about how they bury people in ants, how they keep them hanging for days, and how the bodies of the tortured burst.

I wonder if it is necessary to end this book by invoking the name of Foucault to validate, with his theoretical vocabulary and study of institutions of punishment, the experience and realities of ethnic societies and cultures, or whether Chen's testimonial and her analysis of post-Maoist China is sufficient. I also make mine Beverley's dilemma and ask if an "innocent, solitary reading of testimonial is preferable to a deconstruction of its 'metaphysics of presences'—seen as accomplices of neo-colonial mechanisms of representation and/or frankly in the interest of the First World intellectual" (17). As he says, it all depends.

Notes

Introduction

1. In Cuba today some people are paid in dollars. This currency gives them access to the special stores the government created for diplomats. In this context *diplo-people* means those who have special privileges that were formerly reserved only for Party leaders—*dirigentes*.

2. Lizandro Chávez Alfaro. *Los monos de San Telmo*. San José: EDUCA, 1971.

3. John Beverley and Hugo Achugar, eds. "La voz del otro: Testimonio, subalternidad y verdad narrativa." *Revista de Crítica Literaria Latinoamericana,* Año 18, No. 36, Lima, Perú: 2do. Semestre, 1992.

4. Margaret Randall. *Gathering Rage: The Failure of 20th Century Revolutions to Develop a Feminist Agenda.* New York: Monthly Review Press, 1993.

5. In Jamaica, "higglers" is the name given to people who go to Miami and return with items for sale. It is the name given to members of this "informal economic sector."

6. For a bibliography on the subject I refer the reader to Carlos Vilas, *The Sandinista Revolution: National Liberation and Social Transformation in Central America.* New York: Monthly Review Press, 1986. See also Bryan Meeks, *Caribbean Revolutions and Revolutionary Theory: An Assessment of Cuba, Nicaragua and Grenada.* London and Basingstoke: Macmillan, 1993. These two books give a fairly comprehensive and intelligent account of beginnings and endings.

7. John Beverley and Marc Zimmerman. *Literature and Politics in the Central American Revolutions.* Austin: University of Texas Press, 1991.

8. Among the numerous studies on the subject, the most outstanding are Daniel Bell, Jean-François Lyotard, and Jacques Attali.

9. George Yúdice, Juan Flores, Jean Franco, eds. *On Edge: The Crisis of Contemporary Latin American Culture.* Minneapolis: University of Minnesota Press, 1992.

10. George Yúdice, Juan Flores, Jean Franco, eds. *Cultural Studies Series.* Minneapolis: University of Minnesota Press, forthcoming.

Excursus

1. Taylor Branch. "Back-Stage, January 20, 1993." *Life*. January 1993.

2. Jean-François Lyotard. *Political Writings*. Minneapolis: University of Minnesota Press, 1993.

3. Daniel Ortega was the president of Nicaragua under the Sandinista administration. Joaquín Villalobos is a member of the National Directorate of the Farabundo Martí National Liberation Front. Juan José Dalton is Roque Dalton's only surviving son.

4. *El País*. May 22, 1993, p. 60.

5. E. J. Hobsbawm. *Nations and Nationalism since 1780: Programme, Myth, Reality*. Cambridge: Cambridge University Press, 1990. Benedict Anderson. *Imagined Communities: Reflections on the Origin and Spread of Nationalism*. London: Verso, 1983.

6. Partha Chatterjee. *Nation and Its Fragments: Colonial and Postcolonial Histories*. Princeton: Princeton University Press, 1993. See also his *Nationalist Thought and the Colonial World*. Minneapolis: University of Minnesota Press, 1993.

7. Edelberto Torres Rivas. *Crisis del poder en Centroamérica*. San José: EDUCA, 1981.

One. The Place of Gender as a Sign of Denationalization

1. Michel Foucault. *The History of Sexuality*. New York: Random House, 1980.

2. Sergio Ramírez. *Castigo Divino*. Managua: Editorial Nueva Nicaragua, 1989. Tomás Borge. *La paciente impaciencia*. Managua: Editorial Vanguardia, 1989. Translated as *The Patient Impatience, From Boyhood to Guerilla: A Personal Narrative of Nicaragua's Struggle for Liberation* by Russell Bartley, Darwin Flakoll, and Sylvia Yoneda. Willimantic, Conn.: Curbstone Press, 1992.

3. Quoted in Marshall Blonsky, ed., *On Signs*. Baltimore: The Johns Hopkins University Press, 1985, p. 416.

4. Julia Kristeva. "The Speaking Subject." In Marshall Blonsky, ed., *On Signs*, pp. 210–20.

5. Cora Kaplan. "The Thorn Birds: Fiction, Fantasy, Femininity." In Victor Burgin, James Donald, and Cora Kaplan, eds., *Formations of Fantasy*. New York: Methuen, 1986.

6. Josué Harari, ed. *Textual Strategies: Perspectives in Post-Structuralist Criticism*. Ithaca: Cornell University Press, 1979.

7. Michel Foucault. *The Order of Things: An Archeology of the Human Sciences*. New York: Vintage, 1973.

Two. Vanishing Bodies, Woman/Nation

1. Doris Sommer. "Irresistible Romance: Foundational Fictions of Latin America." In Homi K. Bhabha, ed., *Nation and Narration*. London: Routledge, 1990, pp. 71–98.

2. Jean Franco. "Killing Priests, Nuns, Women, Children." In Marshall Blonsky, ed., *On Signs*. Baltimore: The Johns Hopkins University Press, 1985.

3. See Kemy Oyarzún. "Edipo, autogestión y producción textual: Notas sobre crítica literaria feminista." In Hernán Vidal, ed., *Cultural and Historical Grounding for Hispanic and Lusobrazilian Feminist Literary Criticism*. Minneapolis, Minn.: Institute for the Study of Ideologies and Literature, 1989. See also Nelly Richard. *Masculino/Femenino: Prácticas de la diferencia y cultura democrática*. Chile: Francisco Zegers Editor, 1989.

4. Gloria Guardia. *El último juego*. San José: EDUCA, 1977.

5. Michael Riffaterre. *Semiotics of Poetry*. Bloomington: Indiana University Press, 1978, p. 23.

6. Roman Jakobson. "Metonymic and Metaphoric Aphasia." In Krystyna Pomorska and Stephen Rudy, eds., with Brent Vine, *Verbal Art, Verbal Sign, Verbal Time*. Minneapolis: University of Minnesota Press, 1985.

7. Michel de Certeau. *Heterologies: Discourse on the Other*. Trans. Brian Massumi. Minneapolis: University of Minnesota Press, 1986.

8. Julia Kristeva. Excerpt from "Revolution in Poetic Language." In Toril Moi, ed., *The Kristeva Reader*. New York: Columbia University Press, 1986.

9. Francine Rose Masiello. "Texto, ley, transgresión: especulación sobre la novela (feminista) de vanguardia." *Revista Iberoamericana* (July-Dec. 1985): 807–22; also her "Cuerpo/presencia: mujer y estado social en la narrativa Argentina durante el proceso militar." *Nuevo Texto Crítico* 2:(4) 1989, 155–71.

10. Gayatri Spivak. "Deconstructing Historiography." In Ranajit Guha and Gayatri Spivak, eds., *Selected Subaltern Studies*. Oxford: Oxford University Press, 1988.

11. Jean Franco. "Beyond Ethnocentrism: Gender, Power, and the Third-World Intelligentsia." In Lawrence Grossberg and Cary Nelson, eds., *Marxism and the Interpretation of Culture*. Urbana: University of Illinois Press, 1988, pp. 503–15.

12. Michel Foucault. *Discipline and Punish: The Birth of the Prison*. Trans. Alan Sheridan. London: Allen Lane, 1977.

13. José de Jesús Martínez. *Mi general Torrijos*. Buenos Aires: Editorial Contrapunto, 1987.

Three. Problems in the Constitution of the New Individual/Collective Subject as Masculine and Feminine

1. Susan Kirkpatrick. *Las Románticas: Women Writers and Subjectivity in Spain, 1835–1850*. Berkeley, Los Angeles, London: University of California Press, 1989.

2. In her *Gynesis: Configurations of Woman and Modernity* (Ithaca and London: Cornell University Press, 1985), Alice Jardine compiles a list of dichotomies defining borders associated with masculinity and femininity (p. 72):

Male	Female
Mind	Body
Culture	Nature
Techne	Physis
Intelligible	Sensible
Activity	Passivity
Sun	Moon
Day	Night
Father	Mother
Intellect	Sentiment
Logos	Pathos
Form	Matter
Same	Other

These dichotomies form part of the system of differences between the masculine and the feminine. Jardine, as much as MacKinnon and de Lauretis, among others, argues against the conception of gender as difference. In order for these writers to make their point, they probe the logic of masculine epistemes. In turning masculine logic against itself, feminist theoreticians make room for the entrance of the epistemes belonging to the *domus*, thus "domesticating" them.

3. Doris Sommer. "Irresistible Romance: Foundational Fictions of Latin America." In Homi K. Bhabha, ed., *Nation and Narration*. London: Routledge, 1990, pp. 71–98.

4. Omar Cabezas. *La montaña es algo más que una immensa estepa verde*. Mexico: Siglo Veintiuno Editores, 1982. Translated as *Fire from the Mountain* by Kathleen Weaver. New York: Crown, 1985.

5. Gioconda Belli. *The Inhabited Woman*. Trans. Kathleen March. Willimantic, Conn.: Curbstone Press, 1994.

6. Cf. Terry Eagleton. *The Rape of Clarissa*. Minneapolis: University of Minnesota Press, 1982.

7. Tomás Borge. *The Patient Impatience, From Boyhood to Guerilla: A Personal Narrative of Nicaragua's Struggle for Liberation.* Trans. Russell Bartley, Darwin Flakoll, and Sylvia Yoneda. Willimantic, Conn.: Curbstone Press, 1992.

8. Cf. Fredric Jameson. *The Political Unconscious: Narrative as a Socially Symbolic Act.* Ithaca: Cornell University Press, 1981.

9. Agnes Barr Bushell. *Days of the Dead.* Salem, Ore.: John Brown Books, 1995.

10. Cf. Georg Lukács. *Studies in European Realism.* New York: Grosset & Dunlap, 1964; *Realism in Our Time.* Trans. J. and N. Mander. New York: Harper, 1964. See also Fredric Jameson. "Reflections in Conclusion," in his *Aesthetics and Politics.* London: New Left Books, 1977, pp. 196–213.

11. Borge. *The Patient Impatience.* Willimantic, Conn.: Curbstone Press, 1992.

12. Cf. Hélène Cixous. *La Jeune née.* Paris: 10/18, 1975.

13. Cf. Karl Marx. *Early Writings.* Trans. Rodney Livingstone and Gregor Benton. London: Penguin/NLB, 1975.

14. Cf. Georg Lukács. *History and Class Consciousness.* Trans. Rodney Livingstone. Cambridge, Mass.: MIT Press, 1971.

Four. Constituting the Narrative "I" as Difference

1. Regis Debray. *Che's Guerrilla War.* Trans. Rosemary Sheed. Baltimore: Penguin, 1975. Chapter epigraph is from pages 11–12. The internal reference is to his *A Critique of Arms.* Trans. Rosemary Sheed. New York: Penguin, 1977. This particular quote is taken from the Spanish edition. All other quotes are from the Sheed translation.

2. Ernesto Guevara. *Guerrilla Warfare.* Trans. J. P. Morray. New York: Random House, 1969.

3. Omar Cabezas. *Fire from the Mountain: The Making of a Sandinista.* Trans. Kathleen Weaver. New York: Crown, 1985.

4. Teresa de Lauretis. *Technologies of Gender: Essays on Theory, Film and Fiction.* Bloomington and Indianapolis: Indiana University Press, 1987.

Five. Constituting the Individual Subject "I" as Difference

1. Fidel Castro. "¡Hasta la victoria siempre! En Ernesto Che Guevara." In *La guerra de guerillas.* Havana: Ciencias Sociales, 1972. Chapter epigraph is from page 12. All the translations in this chapter are ours, taken directly from the Spanish texts.

2. Ernesto Che Guevara. *El diario del Che en Bolivia.* Havana: Instituto del Libro, 1968. Translated as *The Diary of Che Guevara: Bolivia, November 7, 1966–October 7, 1967.* Ed. Robert Sheer. New York: Bantam Books, 1968.

3. Regis Debray. *Che's Guerrilla War.* Trans. Rosemary Sheed. Baltimore: Penguin, 1975.

4. Julia Kristeva. "Stabat Mater." In Susan Suleiman, ed., *The Female Body in Western Culture: Contemporary Perspectives.* Cambridge and London: Harvard University Press, 1986, pp. 99–118.

5. Juan Almeida Bosque. *Desembarco.* Havana: Ciencias Sociales, 1982.

6. *Güegüense* is the title of a Nicaraguan drama from the colonial period portraying the mestizo as false, cunning, deceptive. It is used in Nicaragua to signal a social profile marked by those traits. *The Güegüense: A Comedy Ballet in the Nahuatl–Spanish Dialect of Nicaragua.* Ed. D. G. Brinton. Philadelphia: AMS Press, 1883.

7. Alejandro Bendaña. *Testimonios de la Resistencia: Una tragedia campesina.* Managua: Editoria de Arte, 1991.

Six. Constructing People/Masses as Subaltern: "Little Man"/New Man

1. Sergio Ramírez. *Confesión de amor.* Managua: Ediciones Nicarao, 1991. All translations, with the exception of Asturias, are ours. Chapter epigraph is from page 119.

2. Roque Dalton. *Pobrecito poeta que era yo*. San José: EDUCA, 1984. All translations ours.

3. Cf. Miguel Angel Asturias. *Hombres de Maíz*. San José: EDUCA, 1984. Translated as *Men of Maize* by Gerald Martin. New York: Delacorte Press/Seymour Lawrence, 1975.

4. "*Socio*"—hence *Sociolismo*—is a Cuban term for partnerships established to circumvent the anomalies bureaucratic governments exert for nonmembers of the Party elite.

5. See Alejandro Bendaña. *Testimonios de la Resistencia: Una tragedia campesina*. Managua: Editoria de Arte, 1991.

6. See chapter 7 on Dalton's *Pobrecito poeta*, and chapter 13 on testimonial literature.

7. Ranajit Guha and Gayatri Spivak, eds. *Selected Subaltern Studies*. Oxford: Oxford University Press, 1988. Michel Foucault. *Discipline and Punish: The Birth of the Prison*. Trans. Alan Sheridan. London: Allen Lane, 1977.

8. Carmen Naranjo. *Diario de una multitud*. San José. EDUCA, 1984.

Seven. Politico-Military/Poetic Narratives: Who?

1. Roque Dalton. *Pobrecito poeta que era yo*. San José: EDUCA, 1984. All translations ours. Chapter epigraph is from page 398.

2. Partha Chatterjee. *The Nation and Its Fragments: Colonial and Postcolonial Histories*. Princeton: Princeton University Press, 1993.

3. See Gayatri Spivak. "Subaltern Studies: Deconstructing Historiography." In Ranajit Guha and Gayatri Spivak, eds., *Selected Subaltern Studies*. Oxford: Oxford University Press, 1988, pp. 3–32.

4. Jean Franco. "Apuntes sobre la crítica feminista y literatura hispanoamericana." *Hispamérica* 15(45): 1986, 31–43.

5. Ernesto Che Guevara. *El diario del Che en Bolivia*. Havana: Instituto del Libro, 1968. Translated as *The Diary of Che Guevara: Bolivia, November 7, 1966–October 7, 1967*. Ed. Robert Sheer. New York: Bantam Books, 1968.

6. Mario Roberto Morales. *El esplendor de la Pirámide*. San José: EDUCA, 1986.

7. Sergio Ramírez. *Confesión de amor*. Managua: Ediciones Nicarao, 1991.

Eight. The Masculine "I" as Other

1. Mario Roberto Morales. *El esplendor de la Pirámide*. San José: EDUCA, 1986. All translations ours.

2. Page DuBois. *Sowing the Body: Psychoanalysis and Ancient Representations of Women*. Chicago: University of Chicago Press, 1988.

3. Jacques Lacan, *Écrits: A Selection*. Trans. Alan Sheridan. New York and London: W. W. Norton, 1977.

Nine. The Body as Excess

1. Yolanda Oreamuno. *La ruta de su evasión*. San José: EDUCA, 1984. All translations ours.

2. Teresa de Lauretis. "Gramsci Notwithstanding, or, The Left Hand of History." In Teresa de Lauretis, *Technologies of Gender: Essays on Theory, Film, and Fiction*. Bloomington and Indianapolis: Indiana University Press, 1987, pp. 84–94.

3. Cf. Jacques Derrida. *Of Grammatology*. Trans. Gayatri Spivak. Baltimore and London: Johns Hopkins University Press, 1982.

4. Cf. Alice Jardine. "Death Sentences: Writing Couples and Ideology." In Susan Rubin Suleiman, ed. *The Female Body in Western Culture: Contemporary Perspectives*. Cambridge and London: Harvard University Press, 1986, pp. 84–98.

Ten. Implosions: Narcissus Becomes a "Signifying Monkey"

1. Henry Louis Gates, Jr. *The Signifying Monkey: A Theory of Afro-American Literary Criticism*. New York: Oxford University Press, 1988.

2. Carmen Naranjo. *Diario de una multitud.* San José: EDUCA, 1984; *Ondina.* San José: EDUCA, 1985; *Sobrepunto.* San José: EDUCA, 1985; *Otro rumbo para la rumba.* San José: EDUCA, 1989. All translations ours.

3. Jean Baudrillard. *Simulations.* Trans. Paul Foss, Paul Patton, and Philip Beitchman. New York: Columbia University Press, 1983.

4. Clarice Lispector. *The Hour of the Star.* Trans. Giovanni Pontiero. Manchester: Carcanet, 1986.

5. David Forgacs, ed. *An Antonio Gramsci Reader: Selected Writings 1916–1935.* New York: Schocken Books, 1988.

6. Ranajit Guha. "Chandra's Death." In *Subaltern Studies V.* Ed. Ranajit Guha. New Delhi: Oxford University Press, 1988, pp. 135–65.

7. Gino Germani. *Política y sociedad en una época de transición: La sociedad tradicional a la sociedad de masas.* Buenos Aires: Paidos, 1971.

Eleven. Them

1. Ranajit Guha. "Chandra's Death." In *Subaltern Studies V.* Ed. Ranajit Guha. New Delhi: Oxford University Press, 1988, pp. 135–65.

2. Manlio Argueta. *One Day of Life.* Trans. Bill Brow. New York: Aventura/Vintage/Random House, 1983. Brow's translation has been modified wherever nuances lost are important. Brow also eschews the vocabulary of English-speaking peoples of color in his translation.

Twelve. "There Is Nothing like a Man Astride . . . in War, or in Love"

1. Miguel Angel Asturias. *Men of Maize.* Trans. Gerald Martin. New York: Delacorte Press/Seymour Lawrence, 1975. This chapter's title is taken from page 105.

2. Fredric Jameson. *The Ideologies of Theory: Essays 1971-1986.* Minneapolis: University of Minnesota Press, 1988.

3. Martin Lienhard. *La voz y su huella: Escritura y conflicto étnico-social en América Latina (1492–1988).* Havana: Casa de las Américas, 1990. This book won the Casa de las Américas award for best essay in 1989. The members of the jury were Afranio Coutinho, Claudia Kaiser-Lenoir, Francoise Pérus, Mónica Walter, and Ambrosio Fornet.

4. Irlemar Chiampi. *A poetica do realismo maravilhoso: Los pasos perdidos.* Roberto González Echeverría. *Alejo Carpentier, The Pilgrim at Home.* Ithaca: Cornell University Press, 1977. Emir Rodríguez Monegal. *El boom de la novela latinoamericana.* Caracas: Tiempo Nuevo, 1972. Klaus Müller-Bergh. *Alejo Carpentier, estudio biográfico-crítico.* Long Island City, N.Y.: Las Américas, 1972.

5. Roland Barthes. "L'Effet de réel." *Communications* 11 (1968): 88.

6. José Coronel Urtecho. *Prosa.* San José: EDUCA, 1972.

7. José Lezama Lima. *Paradiso.* Trans. Gregory Rabassa. New York: Farrar, Straus and Giroux, 1974.

Thirteen. Case B: Of Testimonial and Diaries

1. Ranajit Guha and Gayatri Chakravorty Spivak, eds. *Selected Subaltern Studies.* Oxford: Oxford University Press, 1988.

2. Claribel Alegría and Darwin J. Flakoll. *They Won't Take Me Alive: Salvadorean Woman in Struggle for National Liberation.* London: Women's Press, 1983.

3. Robert Carr. "Re-presentando el testimonio: Notas sobre el cruce divisorio Primer Mundo/Tercer Mundo." In *Revista de crítica literaria latinoamericana.* Año XVIII–No. 36, 1992, pp. 73–94. Dinesh D'Souza, "*I, Rigoberta Menchú*: A Modern Study in Cultural Hypocrisy." In *The Federalist Paper,* October 21, 1991, pp. 2, 7.

4. See Sally Quinn. "Who Killed Feminism? Hypocritical Movement Leaders Betray Their Own Cause." *Washington Post,* Sunday, January 19, 1992, C1.

5. Ranajit Guha. "On Some Aspects of the Historiography of Colonial India." In *Selected Subaltern Studies.* New York, Oxford: Oxford University Press, 1988, pp. 37–44.

6. FECCAS, FAPU, ANDES, FUS, FMLN-FDR, BPR stand for, in order, Federación Estudiantil Centroamericana, Asociación Nacional de Maestros, Frente Unitario, Frente Farabundo Martí para la Liberación Nacional, Frente Democrático Revolucionario, Bloque Popular Revolucionario, Frente de Acción Popular Unificado.

Fourteen. Solidarity in Affinity

1. Xiao-Mei Chen. "Occidentalisms as Counterdiscourse: 'He Shang' in Post-Mao China." *Critical Inquiry* 18 (Summer 1992): 686–712.

2. Robert Carr. "Re(-)presentando el testimonio: Notas sobre el cruce divisorio primer mundo/tercer mundo." In John Beverley and Hugo Achugar, eds., *Revista,* pp. 73–94. John Beverley. "Testimonio." In John Beverley and Hugo Achugar, eds., *Revista,* pp. 7–20.

3. Marc Zimmerman. "El *otro* de Rigoberta: Los testimonios de Ignacio Bizarro Ujpan y la resistencia indígena en Guatemala." In John Beverley and Hugo Achugar, eds., *Revista de crítica literaria latinoamerica,* Año 18, No. 36, Lima, Perú: 2do. Semestre, 1992, 229–243.

4. Gayatri Spivak. "Can the Subaltern Speak?" In Lawrence Grossberg and Cary Nelson, eds. *Marxism and the Interpretation of Culture.* Urbana: University of Illinois Press, 1988, pp. 271–313, quote on p. 295.

5. George Yúdice. "Testimonio y concientización." In John Beverley and Hugo Achugar, eds., *Revista,* 207–28.

6. Lea Marenn. *Salvador's Children: A Song for Survival.* Columbus: Ohio State University Press, 1993. Elizabeth Burgos Debray. *I, . . . Rigoberta Menchú, an Indian Woman in Guatemala.* Trans. Ann Wright. New York, London: Verso, 1984. Margaret Randall, *Todas estamos despiertas: Testimonios de la mujer nicaragüense de hoy.* Mexico: Siglo Vientiuno Editores, 1980; *. . . y también digo mujer. Testimonios de la mujer nicaragüense hoy.* Santo Domingo: Populares Feministas, 1984. The Randall volumes have been edited and translated as, respectively, *Sandino's Daughters: Testimonies of Nicaraguan Women in Struggle,* ed. and trans. Lynda Yanz, Vancouver/Toronto, Canada: New Star Books, 1981; and *Sandino's Daughters Revisited: Feminism in Nicaragua,* New Brunswick, N.J.: Rutgers University Press, 1994.

7. John Beverley and Hugo Achugar, eds. "La voz del otro: Testimonio, subalternidad y verdad narrativa." In *Revista de crítica literaria latinoamericana,* Año 18, No. 36, Lima, Perú: 2do. Semestre, 1992. René Jara and Hernán Vidal, eds. *Testimonio y literatura.* Minneapolis: Institute for the Study of Ideologies and Literature, 1986.

8. Jean Franco. "Si me permiten hablar: La lucha el poder interpretativo." In John Beverley and Hugo Achugar, eds., *Revista,* pp. 109–16.

9 Margaret Randall. *Part of the Solution/Portrait of a Revolutionary.* New York: New Directions, 1973.

10. See chapter 4.

11. Writing about Alaide Foppa, Franco states: "I wrote [this article on killing priests, nuns, women, children] thinking of an old friend of mine, Alaide Foppa, who in 1954 provided sanctuary for those of us left behind in Guatemala and trying to get out after the Castillo Armas coup. I have a vivid memory of her reciting a poem about her five children 'like the five fingers of her hand.' Today there are only three children left. During the 1960s and 1970s, Alaide Foppa became the driving force behind the feminist movement in Mexico. She was used to going back home once a year to Guatemala to visit her mother. In 1980 she did not come back. A Guatemalan newspaper reported that her whereabouts, and that of her chauffeur, were 'unknown.' To this day Alaide 'continues disappeared' in the words of the newspaper, like many other men, women, priests, nuns and children in Latin America who no longer occupy space but who have a place" (Blonsky 420).

12. Hugo Achugar. "Historias paralelas-historias ejemplares: La historia y la voz del otro." In John Beverley and Hugo Achugar, eds., *Revista*, 49–71.

13. Doris Sommer. "Rigoberta's Secrets." *Latin American Perspectives*, 18(3): 1991, 32–50.

14. Charlotte Baltodano Egner. *Entre el fuego y las sombras.* Managua: Centro de Investigación de la Realidad de Américalatina (CIRA), 1989.

15. Néstor García Canclini. "Cultural Reconversion." Trans. Holly Staver. In George Yúdice, Jean Franco, and Juan Flores, eds., *On Edge: The Crisis of Contemporary Latin American Culture.* Minneapolis: University of Minnesota Press, 1992.

16. Michel Foucault. *Discipline and Punish: The Birth of the Prison.* New York: Vintage, 1979. Ranajit Guha. *Elementary Aspects of Peasant Insurgency in Colonial India.* New Delhi: Oxford University Press, 1983.

17. Translated from the Spanish text. For the edited English version, see Randall 1981, p. 84. Unless otherwise noted, all translations are from the English version of the text.

18. Translated from the Spanish edition.

Index

L'Abbaye, Yonville, 8
Achugar, Hugo, 171, 185n, 191n, 192n
Adolfina, 133, 135, 137, 139, 181
Agency, 33, 58, 109, 117
Alegría, Ciro, 66
Alegría, Claribel, xi, 44, 167
Alegría, Claribel/Flakoll, Darwin, xviii,
     97–98, 116, 125, 158, 160–62, 164–65,
     173–74, 177–78
Alienation, 42, 59, 116, 124
Allende, Salvador, xxi
Almeida Bosque, Juan, 188n
Althusser, Louis, 79
Alxit (queen), 153
Amerindians, 6, 58, 65–66, 110–11, 141,
     144–46, 150–51, 153, 165
Ana María (*comandante*), 161
Anderson, Benedict, 186n
Andes, 166, 191n
Anticommunism, 82, 86
Argentina, 29, 52, 57, 61, 187n
Argueta, Manlio, xvii, 60, 116, 123, 133–36,
     138–40, 150, 173–75, 177, 181, 190n
Arias, Arturo, xvii, 80, 116, 153
Arms, 72, 159, 162, 168, 188n, 191n

Army, 52, 54, 58, 60, 66–67, 71–73, 133–34,
     138, 164–65, 173–79, 181–82
Arosamena, Justo, 25
Ashes of Izalco, 158, 160, 162, 165–67
Asturias, Miguel Angel, 64–65, 116, 133, 136,
     139, 141–47, 149–53, 174–75, 189n,
     190n
Attali, Jacques, 185n
Aurora, 105, 111–14
Aymara, 43, 58
Azul, 6

Balboa, Ferdinand, 29
Balls, 44, 89, 179
Baltodano Egner, Charlotte, 178, 192n
Balzac, Honoré, 84
Barr, Bushell Agnes, xi, 34, 188n
Barrios de Chamorro, Violeta, 72
Barthes, Roland, 18, 146, 151–52, 190n
Batman, 80, 83–84
Battle, 59, 95, 122–23
Baudelaire, Charles-Pierre, 142
Baudrillard, Jean, 115, 117, 120, 126, 190n
Beatles, 97, 100
Beauvoir, Simone de, 111–13

Belli, Gioconda, xi, 32, 47, 187n
Bendaña, Alejandro, 188–89n
Bengali poetry, 131
Beverley, John, xv, xix, 168–69, 171, 174–75, 183, 185–86n, 191–92n
Bhabha, Homi, 186n
Bizarro, Ignacio, 175
Blonsky, Marshall, 186n, 191n
Bloomingdale's, 124–27
Bolívar, Simón, 31, 57–58
Bolivia, 42–43, 50–52, 57, 59–61, 188n
Borge, Tomás, xi, xvii, 3–11, 14–17, 28, 31–33, 36, 44, 47, 79, 85, 88, 106, 111, 186n, 188n
Borges, Jorge Luis, 80, 115–16, 118–20, 126
Bosch, Hieronymus, 88
Bourgeoisie, 26, 34, 70–71, 85, 132, 149
Bovary, Charles, 7–8
Bovary, Emma, 6–10, 111
Braulio, 54, 58
Bravo, Soledad, 100
Brecht, Bertoldt, 65, 77–78, 81, 83
Buendía, Aureliano, 19
Burgos Debray, Elizabeth, 171–72, 174, 177, 179, 191n

Cabezas, Omar, 5, 31–32, 44–47, 54, 79, 85, 96, 103, 137, 178, 187n
Campesinado, 51, 58, 61, 69, 70–73
Campesino, 58–59, 61–63, 65–70, 73–74, 81, 123–24, 139
Camus, Albert, 80, 83
Capitalism, 31, 44, 58, 69, 81
Cardenal, Ernesto, xi, 132–33
Cardoza y Aragón, Luis, 149
Carpentier, Alejo, 150, 190n
Carr, Robert, xii, 161, 170, 172, 175, 190–91n
Carter, Jimmy (president), xxv, 25
Castañeda, Oliviero, 10, 12, 15–16, 18
Castigo Divino, 4, 10, 12, 15–16, 18, 186n
Castro, Fidel, xxi, 8–9, 33, 49–50, 57, 61, 124, 137, 188n
Catín, Nachito, 123, 151–52
Cemí, José Eugenio, 151
Cérémonie des adieux, 111
Certeau, Michel de, 12–14, 23, 27, 47, 86, 88, 186n
Chalatenango, Chalate, 135
"Chandra's Death," 131–36, 139, 173, 190n

Chatterjee, Partha, xxiv, 78, 186n, 189n
Chávez Alfaro, Lizandro, xi, xiv, 150, 185n
Chen, Xiao-Mei, 168–72, 174, 180, 182, 191n
Chiampi, Irlemar, 146, 190n
China, 168–74, 182, 191n
CIA, 85–86, 88
Cixous, Hélène, 37, 188n
Clark, Michael, xx
Class, 42, 58–60, 70, 72, 75, 80, 135, 138, 149, 152, 159, 167, 188n
Clinton, Bill (president), xxiii, xxv
Coloma, Fidel, xi
Colón, Cristóbal, 25
Colonialism, 72, 172
Combat, 51, 55–56, 60, 66, 141, 159
Combatant, 19, 50, 53, 57, 165
Commandant, 5–6, 161–62, 178
Communism, 57, 80–81, 85–86, 124, 135, 139
Compañera, 137, 167
Compañero, 50, 158, 164, 167
Comrade, 5, 9, 32–33, 55, 83, 97, 102, 124, 136, 159, 178
Consciousness, 38, 48, 59, 65, 69, 78–79, 87, 137–38, 144, 152, 158, 176, 179, 188n
Contras, 3, 17–18
Contreras (the), 11
Copula, 9, 27, 66–67, 75, 87, 95, 106, 152
Coronel Urtecho, José, xi, xii, 150, 190
Counterrevolution, 59, 68
Couples, 111, 162–63, 165, 167, 182, 189n
Creole, 74, 149, 151
Criollo, 146, 149, 151
Cruz, Artemio, 27, 100
Cuba, 52, 57, 60–61, 68–69, 79, 82, 100, 172, 185n, 189n
Culler, Jonathan, 142, 144

Dalton, Juan José, xxiv, 186n
Dalton, Roque, xxiv, 15, 64–66, 68–69, 77–83, 86–89, 116, 139, 150–51, 186n, 189n
El Danto, 137
Darío, Rubén, 6
Days of the Dead, 34, 188n
Debray, Regis, 41–43, 50–55, 59–60, 188n
De–eroticization, 4, 10, 13, 31, 111, 135
De Lauretis, Teresa, 48, 106, 108, 187–89n

Deleuze, Gilles, 117
Democracy, 31, 34–35, 37, 47, 55, 60, 63–67,
    72–73, 90, 121–22, 135, 146, 173, 182
Denationalization, 3, 18, 29, 57, 86, 89,
    115–16, 121–22
Derrida, Jacques, 107, 189n
Desire, 30–31, 33, 35, 41, 50–53, 55, 89, 94,
    97, 99–100, 105–10, 112, 114, 131–33,
    137, 146–47, 173
Diary of a Multitude, 71, 116–17, 119–21,
    125–26, 173, 189–90n
Díaz Ochoa, Bernardino, 181–82
Dickens, Charles, 74, 138
Discipline, 44–46, 53, 55–57, 77, 79, 112, 143,
    160, 162, 177–78, 180, 187n, 189n,
    192n
Dissidence, 67, 69
Domesticity, 53–55, 96
Domus, 111, 187n
Don Carmen, 11
Don Casualidón, 151
Don Vasco, 105–7
D'Souza, Dinesh, 161, 190
Dystopia, 37–38

Eagleton, Terry, 33, 187n
Elena, 105, 108–11
Empowerment, 29, 33, 99, 101, 136–40, 160,
    166
Endurance, 32, 45, 48
Engels, Friedrich, 84
Eros, 20, 28, 30–31, 147
Erotica, 5–8, 13, 94–95, 98, 103, 110–11, 125
Eroticism, 6–7, 9, 13, 18, 25–26, 28, 36, 73,
    88–89, 114, 134, 153, 164, 166, 174
Eroticization, 7, 9, 13, 31, 111, 135
Erotics, 21, 174
Esplendor de la Pirámide, 189n
Esquipulas, xxv
Ethnicity, 65, 70, 110–11, 122, 172, 174, 176,
    182
Ethnie, 66, 165
Eugenia Maria, 158–61, 163, 165–67, 178
Eugenio, 32

Faggot, 45–46, 89, 138
FAPU, 166, 191n
FECCAS, 166, 191n
Feminism, 20, 32, 96–97, 102, 104, 190–91n
Flakoll, Darwin, xi, 158, 167, 186n, 188n

Flaubert, Gustave, 142
Flores, Lauro, 169
FLMN, 166, 186n, 191n
Fonseca Amador, Carlos, 5, 9, 34, 36
Foppa, Alaide, 173, 191n
Forgacs, David, 118, 190n
Fornet, Ambrosio, 190n
Foucault, Michel, 4, 11–12, 15–17, 25, 115,
    118, 132, 180, 182, 186–87n, 189n, 192n
Franco, Jean, xix, 4, 19, 23, 25, 29, 33, 42–43,
    86, 172–73, 185n, 186n, 187n, 189n,
    191n
Freud, Sigmund, 14, 23, 27
FSLN, 34, 36
Fuck, 8, 20, 98, 100–101, 107, 125
Fuentes, Carlos, 27
Fuentes, Guadalupe (Lupe), 133–34, 136,
    138–39, 173, 181
FUS, 166, 191n

Gabriel, 105, 108–10, 112–14
Gaitán, Jorge Eliecer, 62
García Canclini, Nestor, 179, 192n
Garrido, Tito (Roberto Augusto), 20–27
Gaspar Ilóm, 65–66, 141, 145–48, 150–52
Genette, Jean, 145
Germani, Gino, 125, 190n
Girón, María Elena, 161
Glasnost, 4, 78
Globality, 31, 125, 127
Godoy, Colonel, 141, 147, 150, 153
Gogol, Nikolay, 6
González Echeverria, Roberto, 190n
Gorki, Maxim, 6
Government, 10, 18–19, 22, 28, 34, 36, 60,
    62–63, 66–68, 71, 73–75, 80, 82–83, 89,
    123, 125, 185n, 189n
Goyo Yic, 141, 146, 148, 152–53
Gramsci, Antonio, 108, 111, 118, 190n
Grenada, 185n
Group of Twelve, 71
Guajiro, 151
Guaraní, 43, 59
Guardia, Gloria, xviii, 20–21, 23, 27–28, 31,
    87, 125, 173, 186n
Guattari, Félix, 117
Güegüense, 59, 74, 188n
Guevara, Ernesto (Che), xvi–xvii, 8–10,
    31–34, 42–47, 49–57, 59–61, 63, 65–67,
    69–77, 79–80, 82–83, 85–86, 88–89,

95–97, 103–4, 116, 124, 137, 160, 173, 178, 188–89
Guha, Ranajit, 86, 125, 131–35, 139, 166, 173, 180, 187n, 189n, 190n, 191n, 192n
Gynesis, 187n

Haendel, Schaffick, 79
Harari, Josué, 16, 186n
Havana, 52, 61, 188n, 190n
Hernández, Helio, 140
Heroine, 161–62
He Shang, 168–70, 172, 191n
Herrera, Leticia, 178
Heterosexual, 7, 18, 19, 25, 28, 31, 34, 99, 106–8, 162, 167, 174
Hikmet, Nazim, 81
Hobsbawm, Eric, 186n
Hom(m)osexual, 34
Hom(m)osexuality, 7, 32, 34, 104
Home, 4, 10, 13, 23, 33, 54, 70, 81, 95–96, 100, 102, 110, 121, 126, 163, 165–67, 190–91n
Homelessness, 99, 125–26
Homosexuality, 33–34, 87, 89, 138
Homosociality, 7, 19, 33–34
Hour of the Star, The, 118
Huasipungo, 145

Imperialism, xx, 52, 86, 170, 172
Incest, 112, 114
India, 132, 191–92n
Indians, xvii, 6–7, 59–60, 70, 74, 95, 116, 136, 143, 150–51, 171, 174, 191n
Internationalism, vii, 43, 53

Jakobson, Roman, 21, 186n
Jamaica, xx, 93, 95, 185n
Jameson, Fredric, 34–35, 44, 142, 144–46, 188n, 190n
Jara, René, 171, 191n
Jardine, Alice, 37, 98, 111–13, 187n, 189n
Jed, Stephanie, 15
Judas Iscariot, 112
La Jeune née, 188n

Kafka, Franz, 80, 83–84
Kagemusha, 15
Kaiser-Lenoir, Claudia, 190n
Kaplan, Cora, 9, 186n
Kirkpatrick, Susan, 30–31, 34, 187n
Kolko, Gabriel, 155

Korea (North), xxv
Kristeva, Julia, 9–10, 23, 54, 172, 187–88n
Kurosawa, Akira, 15–16

Lacan, Jacques, 50, 100, 152
Ladino, xvii, 59, 74, 143, 146, 149–52
León (Nicaragua), 10
Letona, Mercedes, 161
Lezama Lima, José, 150, 190n
Lienhard, Martin, 142–43, 145–46, 190n
Lispector, Clarice, 118, 190n
"Little man," 62, 64–66, 73, 78, 85, 103, 116, 166
López, María Milagros, xix
Loro, 55, 58, 61
Los perros no ladraron, 116
Ludmer, Josefina, xvi, 31
Lukács, Georg, 38, 77–78, 84, 188n
Lyotard, Jean-François, xxiv, 32–33, 42, 98, 185n, 186n

Machado, Antonio, 134
Machista, 80, 94–95
Macho, 96, 98, 139, 153
Machojón, 141, 146, 148, 150, 152
MacKinnon, Catharine, xvi, 187n
Magic realism, 142–46, 149, 151, 153
Maquiladoras, xviii
Marenn, Lea, 170–71, 174, 176–77, 180–81, 191n
Mariamor, 27
Mariana, 20–22, 24–26
Marin, Louis, 15–16
Martí, José, 61
Martínez, José de Jesus, 12, 28, 74, 89, 134, 137, 187n
Martínez Peláez, Severo, 74
Marx, Karl, 38, 94, 188n
Marxism, xx, 187n, 191n
Masiello, Francine, 23, 29, 33, 173, 187n
Matagalpa, 5–8, 36
Maya, 139, 142–49, 151
Meeks, Bryan, 185
Men of Maize, 141–43, 146–47, 149, 174, 189n, 190n
Menchú, Rigoberta, 64, 161, 169–71, 174–76, 180–82, 190n, 191n
Mestiza, 110–11
Mestizaje, 74, 135, 149
Mestizo, 149, 152, 188n

Mexico, 93, 95, 100, 143, 187n, 191n
Mi general Torrijos, 28, 187
Migration, xviii
Milanés, Pablo, xx
Minnelli, Liza, 100
Modernism, xx, 142, 144–46, 150
Modernist, 145–46, 150
Modernity, xx, 63, 69, 136, 153
Moi, Toril, 187n
Montaña, 69, 166, 187n
Montenegro, Sofía, v, xii
Morales, Mario Roberto, xii, xvii, 64, 80, 87–88, 93, 95–104, 108, 116, 189n
Mountain, ix, 4, 5, 32, 45–47, 51, 54, 58–59, 61, 68, 72–73, 80–81, 85, 87, 96–99, 101–2, 160, 166, 180–81, 187n
Mowoe, Isaac, xii

Nachito Catín 123, 151–52
NAFTA, xxv
Ñancahuazú, 50
Naranjo, Carmen, xviii, 71, 99, 107, 115–21, 124–27, 173, 189–90n
Narcissus, x, 115
Nelson, Willie, 100
Neoliberalism, viii, xx, xxiv, 4, 170
Neopositivism, 151
New Man, 32–35, 42, 45–48, 51, 55, 62–64, 66–68, 79, 81, 86–87, 94–96, 98, 102, 165, 178
Nicaraguan Institute of Agrarian Reform, 63
Nicarao, 188n
Nicho, 146
Nother/Mother, x, 171–73, 175
Nunca hubo alguna vez, 119

Occidentalism, 168–71, 173, 191n
Of Grammatology, 189n
Ohio State University, xii, xx
Oligarchy, xv, 70, 160, 165, 167
One Day of Life, 123, 139, 190n
Oquist, Paul, 89
Oreamuno, Yolanda, xviii, 99, 101, 105–10, 112, 114, 125, 173, 189n
Orgasm, 12, 14, 26, 94, 153
Orientalism, 168, 170
Ortega, Daniel, v, xxi, xxiv, 186n
Otro rumbo para la rumba, 119, 190n
Oyarzún, Kemy, 186n

La paciente impaciencia, 186n
Palacios, Nadia, 161
Panama, 19, 21–29
Paradiso, 150
Parra, Violeta, 97, 100
Pascal, Blaise, 15
Patient Impatience, The, 4–5, 8, 186n, 188n
Patriarch, 164
Patriarchy, xvi, 46, 55, 106–7, 110, 114
Patriotica, 8, 13, 94, 97–98, 125
Patriotics, xvii
Patriotism, ix, 9, 25–26, 28, 36, 89, 98, 102, 138, 173–74, 176
Payeras, Roberto, 44, 64, 85
Perestroika, 69
Periphery, xxv
Pérus, Françoise, 190n
Phallocentrism, 72, 76
Phallus, 73, 89, 95, 100
Pineda, Amada, 181–82
Pirámide (Pir, Pira), 93, 97, 102, 189n
Pobrecito poeta que era yo, 69, 77, 83, 189n
Politico-military, 77–78, 158–59, 166
Popol Vuh, 74, 133, 149
Positivism, 122, 144–46, 150–51, 153, 160, 170
Post-Maoism, 168, 191n
Postmodernism, xx, xxi, 27, 136, 144
Post–perestroika, xix
Prison, 11, 81, 85, 88, 102–3
Program, 62–63, 168–69, 186n
Progress, 69, 142, 147, 149–52, 159, 164
Proletariat, 43, 57, 71
Proto-state, 71–74
Puebla, Carlos, 100
Pussy, xvii, xx, 34, 87, 90, 94, 103
Pyramid, 93–97, 99–101, 104

Rabassa, Gregory, 190n
Rama, Angel, 6
Ramírez, Emilio, 140
Ramírez, Sergio, 4, 10–12, 14, 16–17, 31, 44, 59, 62–65, 67–68, 70–71, 73, 75, 78–80, 89, 103, 106, 116, 133, 138–40, 150–51, 166, 186n, 188n, 189n
Randall, Margaret, xviii, 98, 171–72, 175–78, 181, 185n, 191n, 192n
Rape of Clarissa, The, 187n
Real-effect, 120
Realism, 6, 27, 100–101, 127, 142–46, 149–50, 161, 182, 188n, 190n

Rearguard, 54, 58, 89
Rebel, 67, 69, 176
Rebellion, 45, 176
Region, 4, 42–43, 52–53, 60, 81, 171
Relationship, 95, 98–100, 105–6, 109–11,
　　133, 150, 163, 166, 172–73, 179–80
Repression, 25, 181–82
Reproducing, 149, 168
Reproduction, 15, 17–18, 69, 71, 73, 139
Republic, xvii, 6, 15, 29, 31, 86, 122
Resistance, xxv, 171–74, 177–78, 188–89n
Richard, Nelly, 186n
Riffaterre, Michael, 21, 186n
Rivera, Francisco ("El Zorro"), 5
Roa, Raul, 50
Rodríguez Monegal, Emir, 146, 190n
Romance, 7–8, 19, 186n
Románticas, 30, 187n
Romanticism, xvii, 30–31, 33–35, 38, 109, 114,
　　160, 166
Romelia, 133, 135–37
Rubio Marcos, 55–58, 60, 79

Said, Edward, 170
Salarrué, 77–78, 133, 149–50
Sánchez, Juana, 119–21
Sandinistas, xix, 3, 5, 16–18, 36, 62, 185n,
　　186n
Sandino, Augusto César, xiv, 71, 171, 191n
Sartre, Jean-Paul, 111–12
Schucht sisters, 106
Seed, Patricia, xix
Sex, 10–11, 33–34, 72–73, 86–88, 90, 147, 163
Sexuality, xx, 12–13, 37, 46–47, 73, 87–90,
　　94, 99, 107, 131–32, 153, 160, 165, 167,
　　177, 186n
Showalter, Elaine, 87
Sicambro, 151
Sobrepunto, 124–25, 190n
Socialism, xiii, xviii, xix, 67, 69, 79
Sociolismo, 67, 83, 189n
Socios, 83, 189n
Socius, xviii, 119–20, 126–27
Solidarity, x, xii, 7, 103, 168, 170–77, 179, 181
Sommer, Doris, xix, 19, 23, 28, 31, 36, 175,
　　186n, 192n
Somoza, 70
Sovereignty, xxv, 79, 86, 159
Spivak, Gayatri Chakravorty, 3, 24, 86–87,
　　157–58, 170, 187n, 189–91n

Stabat Mater (Dolorosa), 52, 138, 160,
　　188n
Subaltern, xviii, xx, xxiii, xxv, 19, 62–63, 65,
　　68, 70, 74, 86–87, 90, 118, 120, 129, 131,
　　134–36, 139, 151, 157–58, 165–66, 170,
　　176, 185n, 187n, 189n, 190n, 191n
Summerhill, Stephen, xii
Superman, 80, 84

Tania, 33, 58, 61
Tata Higinio, 64–66, 139, 151
Tecún/Tecuna(s), (Maria), 141, 147–48,
　　152–53
Tecún Umán, 153
Tellez, Dora María, 178
Tello, 44–46
Testicles, 88, 179–80
Testimonial, xviii, 32, 34–37, 44, 47, 53, 59
They Won't Take Me Alive, 158, 160, 165, 167,
　　173, 190n
Tiempo de Fulgor, 123
Torlonia, 129
Torres Rivas, Edelberto, 63, 186n
Torrijos, General, 28, 137, 187n
Torrijos/Carter Canal Treaties, xxv, 25

Urraca, 20–28
Urrutia, Elena, xii

Vaca Manuela, 141, 146, 150, 153
Vagina, xx, 22, 28, 72, 87, 103, 147
Vanguard, xiv–xv, xvii, xix, xxiii, 36, 43,
　　46–47, 52, 57–60, 64, 66, 68, 70, 75, 78,
　　80, 89, 167, 186–87n
Velázquez, Diego Rodríguez de Silva, 17
Ventura, 32, 137
Vidal, Hernán, 171, 186n, 191n
Vietnam, 69
Vilas, Carlos, xii, 185n
Villalobos, Joaquín, xxiv, 186n
Violation, 14, 24, 28, 34, 46, 67
Virgin, 5, 25–26, 54

War, xvi, xx, xxiii–xxv, 44, 50–51, 68–70, 72,
　　74, 139, 141, 147, 152–53, 164, 167,
　　188n
Warfare, 2, 34, 42, 52, 56, 158, 160, 188n
Warrior, xvii, 42–44, 141, 178
Weapon, xxiii, 32, 56, 73, 147, 160
Whore, 25–26, 87

Winnetou, 6–10, 36
(Wo)man, 35, 91, 99, 108–11, 155

Yevtuschenko, Yevgeni, 82
Yoneda, Sylvia, 186n, 188n
Yúdice, George, xx, 172, 174, 176–77, 181,
    185n, 191n

Zacher, Christian, xii
Zamora, Daisy, xii
Zapoa, 3, 4
Zavaleta Mercado, René, 60
Zimmerman, Marc, xii, xix, 175, 185n, 191n
Zola, Émile, 6

Ileana Rodríguez, associate professor at The Ohio State University, was born in Nicaragua. She attended the National University of Mexico for three years and then came to the United States to study at the University of California, San Diego, where she got her B.A. and Ph.D. in Spanish literature. She has taught at the University of Minnesota and the National University of Managua, and has held seminars at El Colegio de Mexico. She has been awarded a Rockefeller Fellowship, a Fulbright Fellowship, and an American Council of Learned Societies grant-in-aid. She has published extensively on Caribbean and Central American literatures, and worked at the Ministry of Culture under Ernesto Cardenal during the Sandinista administration. Her most recent book is *House/Garden/Nation: Space, Gender, and Ethnicity in Postcolonial Latin American Literatures by Women.*